COLLINS COMPUTER SCIENCE 8

PADMAJA SUBHASH

Collins

8

COLLINS COMPUTER SCIENCE

BASED ON WINDOWS 10 & MS OFFICE 2013

Series Editor
PADMAJA SUBHASH

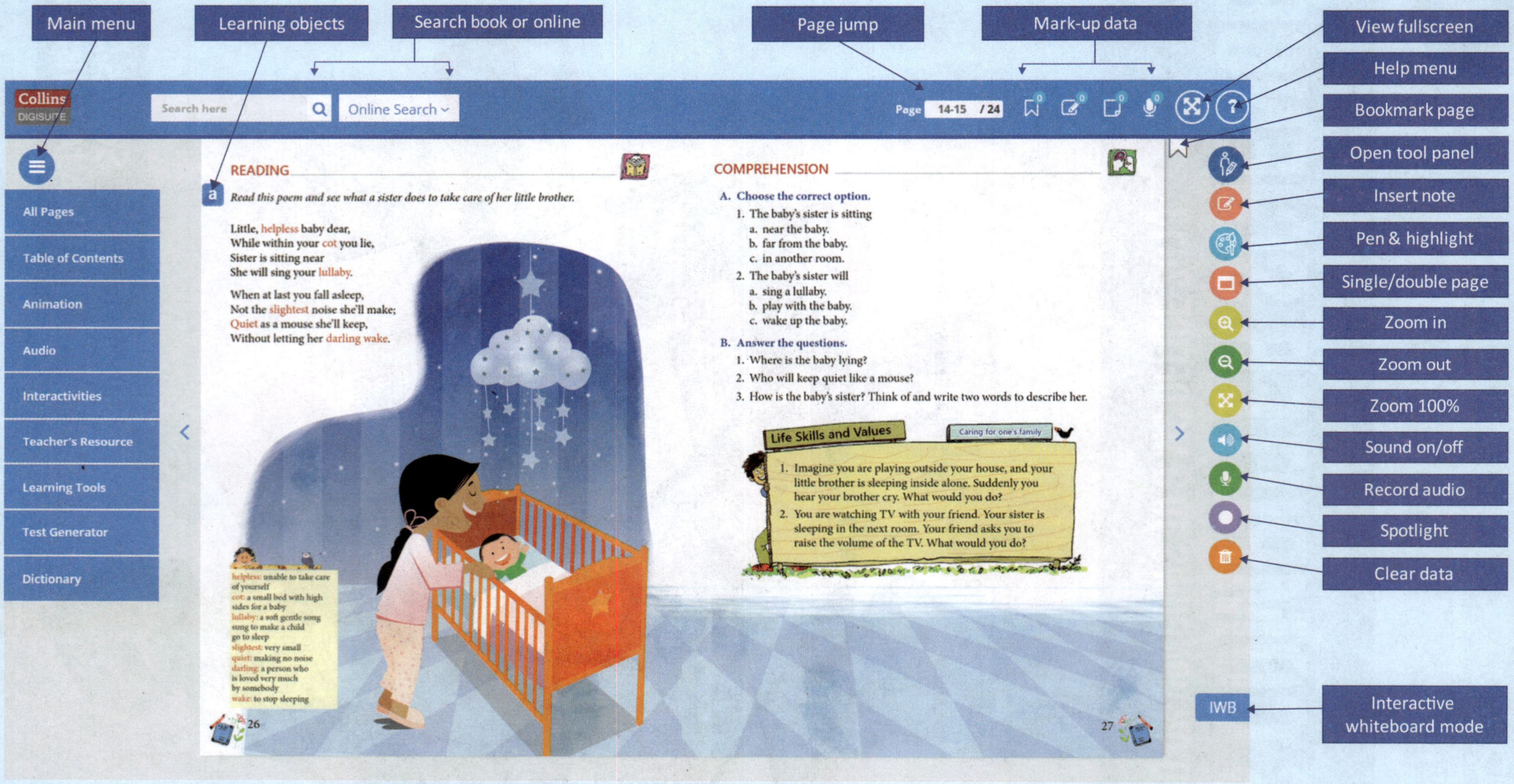

Student + Teacher			Teacher-only	
a animations	**ia** activities	**g** games	**lp** lesson plans	**tn** teacher's notes
ilt instructor-led tutorials	**w** worksheets	**v** videos	**w** worksheets	**ak** answer keys
	audio			

PREFACE

Collins Computer Science, a series of eight books for Classes 1 to 8, is an interesting amalgamation of the latest technologies powered with interesting and innovative teaching methodologies. This combination ensures that learning outcomes at all the pedagogical levels conforms to the requirements of **National Curriculum Framework** and complies with the syllabus requirements of various boards.

The aim of this series is to create awareness among students about the latest in technological field and at the same time provide them with a strong foundation of the concepts to apply knowledge in real-life scenarios.

The course is based on **Windows 10** and **MS Office 2013** with updates on Open Office and Windows 8. This course also has the **National Cyber Olympiad** paper for students to practice. The concepts are presented in a straight forward manner and the understanding is tested at different levels.

The focus is to introduce computers for primary classes in a simple and lucid manner and extend the course to cover topics like animation, programming, logic building, web-designing in a detailed manner mentioning the steps and supporting it with self-explanatory screenshots. Care has been taken to keep the content updated as on the date of developing the content.

Apart from the basic software applications and operating system like MS Office and Windows, we have introduced the following topics like:

- Scratch Programming
- App Inventor
- Java
- Web 2.0 Education tools
- HTML 5
- Microsoft Visual Studio Code
- Cloud Computing

For creative software applications, we have covered open source software applications like Synfig Studio, OpenShot Video Editor and GIMP so that students can download them easily.

We have covered topics like tablets, electronic readers, smart gadgets, e-commerce and payment gateways so that students stay tuned to the developments in digital arena. Last but not the least, we have given a holistic approach to make the students aware about taking Computers as a career.

The course books are complemented by a comprehensive digital resource, Collins DigiSuite. We also have a detailed Teachers' Manuals for the teachers with suggestive period plan, lesson plan, answers to course book questions, test papers and worksheets with answers. These digital learning and teaching aids strengthen the course offerings empowering the teachers and students in the right way.

We would like to thank all the teachers who have reviewed the series and have ensured that all the pedagogical requirements are met keeping in mind the digital exposure that the student should get. We welcome constructive feedback and suggestions to improve these books further in subsequent editions.

Authors

Key Features

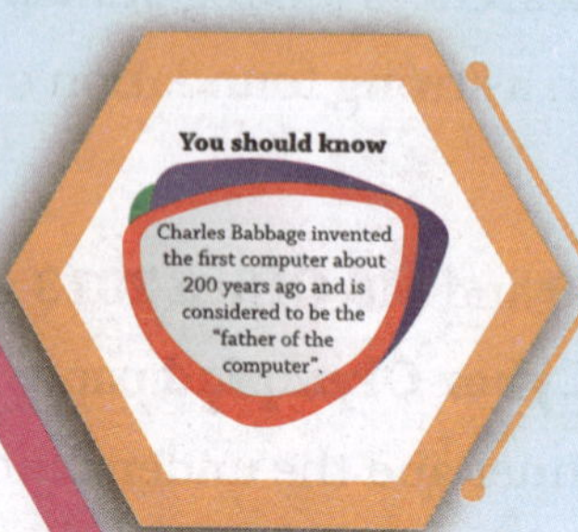

You should know

This feature includes interesting facts about the topic.

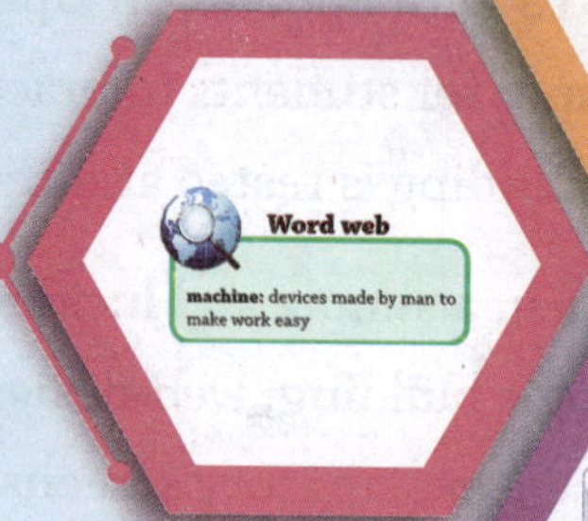

Word web

This feature lists the meanings of all the difficult words.

Recall

This feature lists the procedural difference between MS Office 2013 and MS Office 2010.

Digital geek

This feature mentions additional technical information about the topic.

Concepts learnt

This feature recapitulates all the important points covered in the chapter.

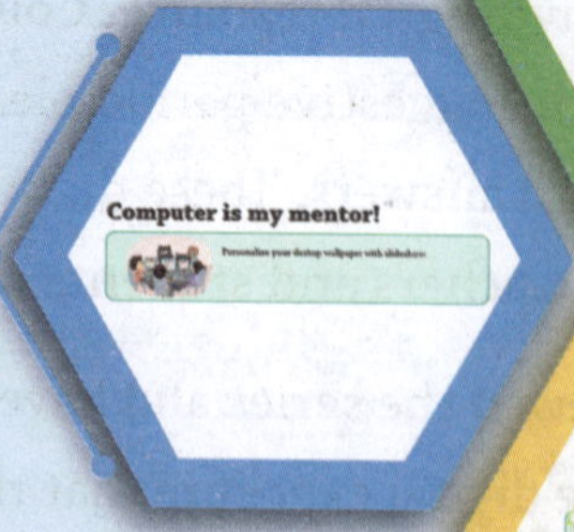

Computer is my mentor!

This feature is given to test the practical application of the concept.

Net search

This feature lists the important websites that students can refer to extra information.

Key Features

Hands-on practice
This feature provides solution to hands-on practice questions given after important concepts.

Exercise
This feature is given to reinforce understanding of the concepts covered in each chapter.

Teacher's notes
This feature contains interesting topic-related notes that teacher can take up in class and demonstrate to students.

Worksheets
This feature facilitates the students and teachers with additional questions.

Revision worksheets
This feature adds on to the variety of questions that can be framed for various topics.

National Cyber Olympiad
This features gives the actual Olympiad paper for practice and exposure.

Mastering keyboard
This feature highlights all the keyboard shortcuts for the menu commands.

Contents

1 Number System

Learning log

- The computer number system
- Types of number system—Decimal, Binary, Octal and Hexadecimal
- Conversion of decimal numbers into binary, octal and hexadecimal numbers

Introduction

The distance between the Sun and the Earth is 1,4960,0000,000 metres and the distance between the Sun and Mars is 2,27,900,000,000 metres. Convert metres into kilometres. (Hint: 1 kilometre = 1000 metres)

____

____

____

In the above example, we saw that 1000 is a multiple of 10, three times by itself. An **exponent** is a number that represents the number of times it is multiplied by itself. Larger numbers are converted into exponents for our convenience and ease.

A kilometre is equal to 1000 metres, a kilogram is equal to 1000 grams, and so on. This can be expressed in multiples of 10 as 1000 = 10 × 10 × 10. This can also be written as,

$$1000 = 10^3$$

Where 10^3 is called the **exponential form** of 1000. The notation 10^3 represents the product of 10 × 10 × 10. This number is read as 10 raised to the power of 3. Any other number can also be represented using base as 10.

For example: $43861 = 4 \times 10000 + 3 \times 1000 + 8 \times 100 + 6 \times 10 + 1$

$$43861 = 4 \times 10^4 + 3 \times 10^3 + 8 \times 10^2 + 6 \times 10^1 + 1$$

Number System

A mathematical notation for representing numbers using digits or symbols is called as number system. The number system we use in our day-to-day life is called decimal **number system** or base ten system. There is evidence to show that early Egyptians were using the decimal number system about five thousand years ago. Romans used letters to represent the numbers, which is a different type of number system. Before the invention of calculating devices like calculators, abacus and computers, ten digits or fingers were used for counting. Even today, many of us use our fingers to count.

You should know

Quantum computers are used in artificial intelligence. These computers do not use the binary number system.

In the computer system architecture, every value that we are saving or getting into or from computer memory has a defined number system.

Computer architecture supports the following number systems.

- Binary number system
- Octal number system
- Decimal number system
- Hexadecimal (hex) number system

Word web

number system: a system that denotes numbers as digits or symbols

binary number system: a number system that uses two digits, namely 0 and 1 only

Converting numbers from decimal to octal and vice versa

Conversion of decimal to octal number system: The base of the octal number system is 8. A decimal number is converted into an octal number by dividing it by its base number 8 until the remainder is zero or the quotient is smaller than the octal base-8.

For example: $(177)_{10}$ = 177 /8= 22 remainder 1

22/8 = 2 remainder 6

2/8 = The quotient is smaller than the octal base-8 and hence the number is taken as remainder 2

The remainders are written in the reverse order from bottom to top as 261 $(177)_{10} = (261)_8$

Conversion of octal to decimal number system: The numbers are expressed as the sum of the base-8 raised to its bits.

For example: $(432)_8 = (4 \text{ x } 8^2) + (3 \text{ x } 8^1) + (2 \text{ x } 8^0)$

$(432)_8 = (4 \text{ x}64) + (3 \text{ x } 8) + (2 \text{ x } 1)$

$(432)_8 = 256 + 24 + 2$

$(432)_8 = (282)_{10}$

Converting numbers from decimal to hexadecimal number system

Conversion of decimal to hexadecimal number system: The base of the hexadecimal number system is 16. One hex bit is equal to four bits. A hexadecimal number is expressed as the power of 16. A decimal number is converted into a hexadecimal number by dividing it by its base number 16 until the remainder is zero or the quotient is smaller than the hexadecimal base-16.

For example: $(3768)_{10}$ = 3768 /16=235 remainder 8

235/16 = 14 remainder 11 (B)

14/16 = The quotient is smaller than the hexadecimal base-16 and hence the number is taken as remainder 14 (E)

The remainders are written in the reverse order from bottom to top as EB8 $(177)_{10} = (\text{EB8})_{16}$

Conversion of hexadecimal to decimal number system: The numbers are expressed as the sum of the base-16 raised to its bits.

For example: $(F3C)_{16} = (F \times 16^2) + (3 \times 16^1) + (C \times 16^0)$

$(F3C)_{16} = (15 \times 256) + (3 \times 16) + (12 \times 1)$

$(F3C)_{16} = 3840 + 48 + 12$

$(F3C)_{16} = (3900)_{10}$

Decimal number system

The number system with a base of 10 is called **decimal number system**. In this system, any number can be expressed as a decimal number between 1.0 and 10.0 including 1.0 multiplied by a power of 10. A decimal number being expressed is also called its **standard form**.

For example, 56789 can be expressed as 5.6789×10^4.

The base-10 number system has 10 digits or symbols from 0 to 9. Using decimal notations, a number can be written as a string of symbols. Each number in the number string represents one of the ten digits and can be expressed either as a decimal number or in an exponential form.

For example:

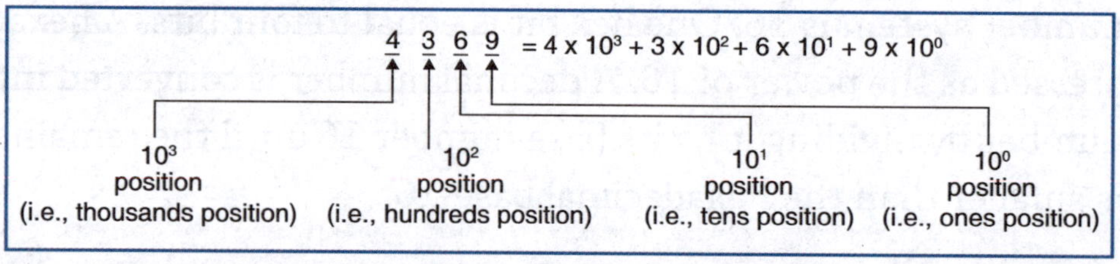

Some of the other commonly used base is 12. It is used for representing a dozen and base-60 for representing minutes in a degree and seconds in a clock. The decimal number system is extensively used as it is easy to count using 10 fingers.

Binary number system

A number system that uses only two digits, namely 0 and 1 is called **binary number system**. In other words, it is a number system with a base of 2. Computers use binary number system consisting of 0s and 1s to represent data. The symbols 0 and 1 of the binary number system are also called as binary digits or bits. For example, 11011 is a five-bit number.

In base-2 system, after counting two digits 0 and 1, they form one group of two bits. For example, a binary number is pronounced as each digit. For example, the binary number 101 is spoken as "one zero one"; this way it doesn't get confused with the decimal number. This is helpful where multiple bases are used to represent the same number. For example, $4_{10} = 100_2$

Fig. 1.1: Binary numbers used by computers

A binary number can also be written as a string of symbols of 0 and 1. To indicate the position of the digit, each digit is multiplied by the power of 2. (Fig. 1.2)

For example:

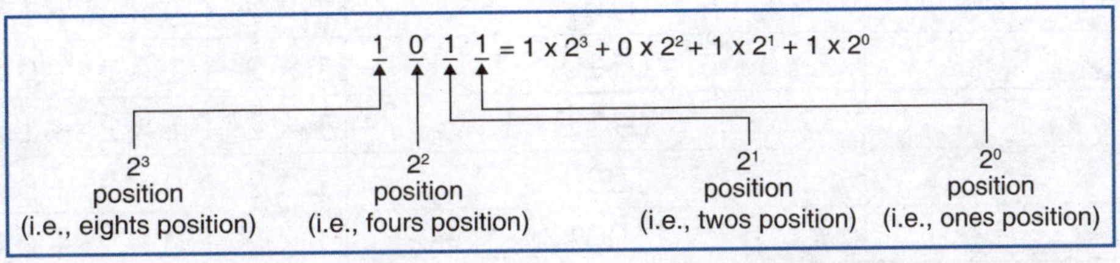

Fig. 1.2: Binary number as a string of 0s and 1s

A string of eight bits such as 11001100 is called as a byte.

Converting numbers from decimal to binary and vice versa

The sum of powers of base-2 of a binary number represents a decimal number. In other words, a binary number can be converted into a decimal number by the sum of power of base-2 of its bits.

For example: $1011 = 1 \times 2^3 + 0 \times 2^2 + 1 \times 2^1 + 1 \times 2^0$

$= 1 \times 8 + 0 \times 4 + 1 \times 2 + 1 \times 1$

$= 8 + 0 + 2 + 1$

$= 11_{10}$

Alternatively, this conversion can be simplified by writing the position value below the binary digit as follows:

The binary number 10111 can be converted into decimal as shown below:

1	**0**	**1**	**1**	**1**
16	**8**	**4**	**2**	**1**

Adding the position values, 16 + 0 +4 +2 +1= 23

And thus, $10111_2 = 23_{10}$

Similarly, a decimal number can be converted into a binary number as discussed earlier.

Decimal number (Base 10)	Binary number (Base 2)	Binary expansion of the number
0	0000	0×2^0
1	0001	1×2^0
2	0010	$1 \times 2^1 + 0 \times 2^0$
3	0011	$1 \times 2^1 + 1 \times 2^0$
4	0100	$1 \times 2^2 + 0 \times 2^1 + 0 \times 2^0$
5	0101	$1 \times 2^2 + 0 \times 2^1 + 1 \times 2^0$
6	0110	$1 \times 2^2 + 1 \times 2^1 + 0 \times 2^0$
7	0111	$1 \times 2^2 + 1 \times 2^1 + 1 \times 2^0$
8	1000	$1 \times 2^3 + 0 \times 2^2 + 0 \times 21 + 0 \times 2^0$
9	1001	$1 \times 2^3 + 0 \times 2^2 + 0 \times 2^1 + 1 \times 2^0$
10	1010	$1 \times 2^3 + 0 \times 2^2 + 1 \times 2 + 0 \times 2^0$

There are positive and negative numbers in a decimal number system. In binary system, the negative numbers are the two's complement notations. To find a two's complement notation of a number, each bit is reversed (its complement) and then 1 is added to it.

For example, the two's complement of 100100 is 011011 + 1 = 011100.

Hands-on practice

Convert the given binary numbers to decimal numbers.

1. 0101
2. 00010000
3. 00010011

Octal number system

In this type of number system, the base is 8. The digits of the octal number system are 0, 1, 2, 3, 4, 5, 6 and 7. Like the other bases, we know the equivalent of 8 in octal is $(10)_8 = 1 \times 8 + 0$ and thus,

Decimal number (Base 10)	Octal number (Base-8)	Octal expansion of the number
$(0)_{10}$	$(0)_8$	0
$(1)_{10}$	$(1)_8$	1
$(2)_{10}$	$(2)_8$	2
$(3)_{10}$	$(3)_8$	3
$(4)_{10}$	$(4)_8$	4
$(5)_{10}$	$(5)_8$	5
$(6)_{10}$	$(6)_8$	6
$(7)_{10}$	$(7)_8$	7
$(8)_{10}$	$(10)_8$	$1 \times 8 + 0$
$(9)_{10}$	$(11)_8$	$1 \times 8 + 1$
$(10)_{10}$	$(12)_8$	$1 \times 8 + 2$

Hexadecimal number system

In this type of number system, the base is 16. The digits from 0 to 9 are written like the octal system. Digits 10 to 15 are represented by alphabetical letters either in lowercase or uppercase as 'a, b, c, d, e and f' or 'A, B, C, D, E and F'. The equivalent of 16 in hexadecimal number system is written as $(10)_{16}$.

Decimal number (Base 10)	Hexadecimal number (Base 16)	Hexadecimal expansion of the number
$(0)_{10}$	$(0)_{16}$	0×16^0
$(2)_{10}$	$(2)_{16}$	2×16^0
$(10)_{10}$	$(A)_{16}$	10×16^0
$(15)_{10}$	$(F)_{16}$	15×16^0
$(16)_{10}$	$(10)_{16}$	$1 \times 16^1 + 0 \times 16^0$
$(17)_{10}$	$(11)_{16}$	$1 \times 16^1 + 1 \times 16^0$
$(18)_{10}$	$(12)_{16}$	$1 \times 16^1 + 2 \times 16^0$
$(19)_{10}$	$(13)_{16}$	$1 \times 16^1 + 3 \times 16^0$
$(20)_{10}$	$(14)_{16}$	$1 \times 16^1 + 4 \times 16^0$
$(26)_{10}$	$(1A)_{16}$	$1 \times 16^1 + 10 \times 16^0$
$(165)_{10}$	$(A5)_{16}$	$10 \times 16^1 + 5 \times 16^0$

netsearch

For additional information, visit:
https://cie-wc.edu/binary-numbers-7-12-2011.pdf
https://www-edlab.cs.umass.edu/cs230/weeks/w02/binary-overview.pdf

Teacher's note

Demonstrate the conversion of decimal number system into binary, octal and hexadecimal number system. Guide students to use a scientific calculator to do the same calculation. Discuss their observation.

Concepts learnt

1. Number system is a notation for representing numbers using digits and symbols.
2. Base 10 number system is called as decimal number system.
3. A standard form of a decimal number is expressed as a multiple of 1.0 with the power of 10.
4. Computers use binary number system consisting of 0's and 1's to represent data.
5. The number system with base 2 is also called binary number system.
6. Negative integers are represented by 2's complements of the binary number.
7. Octal number system uses 8 as its base.
8. Hexadecimal number system uses 16 as its base. Alphabetical letters from A to F are used to denote digits from 10 to 15.

Exercise

A **Fill in the blanks.**

1. The number 10^3 is called as the ________________ (exponential/binary) form of 1000.
2. The ________________ (octal/decimal) number system is used in our day-to-day life.
3. The digit $(10)_8$ represents the digit ________________ (8/10) in the octal number system.
4. A number system with a base of 16 is called ______________ (hexadecimal/octal) number system.
5. The digit $(1A)_{16}$ represents the digit ________________ (26/16) in the hexadecimal number system.

B **Write T for True or F for False.**

1. Negative numbers cannot be expressed only in base-10 number system. ☐
2. Digits and symbols are used to represent integers in number system. ☐
3. Computers use octal number system. ☐
4. Octal number system has 8 digits. ☐
5. Alphabets are used to denote digits in hexadecimal number system. ☐

C **Choose the correct option.**

1. Which of the following is a decimal number?
   (a) $(1)_{10}$ (b) $(1)_8$
   (c) $(0001)_2$ (d) $(1)_{16}$
2. Which of the following indicates a byte of data?
   (a) 1100 (b) 110011
   (c) 10010011 (d) 00011
3. Which of the following is the position of the underlined digit of the given binary number 1**1**10?
   (a) 2^0 (b) 2^1
   (c) 2^2 (d) 2^3

4. Which of the following is equal to 11_{10}?
   (a) 1000 (b) 1011
   (c) 1001 (d) 0001
5. Which of the following is equal to 10_{10}?
   (a) 12_8 (b) 10_8
   (c) 1000_2 (d) 0010_2

D Answer these following questions briefly.

1. What is the use of 2's complement notation of a binary number?
2. Convert the decimal number 62 into a binary number. Write the binary expansion of the number.
3. Convert the decimal number 258 into its binary equivalent number.
4. What is the hexadecimal equivalent of $(26)_{10}$?
5. Represent the decimal number 164958 in its standard form.

E Application-based questions.

1. Sunita asked the shopkeeper to pack 12 dozen of bananas. Which base is she referring to? How many bananas is she buying altogether?
2. Radha wants to convert decimals into degree. Suggest the suitable multiple to do the conversion.
3. Diya wants to convert the decimal number -156 into its binary equivalent. How can she achieve this?

Computer is my mentor!

Guide students to convert a set of decimal numbers into binary, octal and hexadecimal numbers, and represent them in a tabular form.

2 Queries, Forms and Reports in MS Access 2013

Learning log

- Create simple queries by using a wizard
- Create queries manually
- Summarise the data by using queries
- Update records by using queries
- Create forms by using a wizard
- Create reports by using a wizard
- Preview and print reports

Introduction

Consider the tables Student List (Table. 2.1) and Student Attendance (Table. 2.2) given below.

Student List

ID	First Nam	Last Nar	Roll N	Date of Birtl	Mother's N	Father's N	Contact N	Address	Fee	Remarks
1	Aruna	kumari	0001	1/16/2009	Pushpalatha	Sainathan	(809) 572-428	F3 Fortuna se	$960.00	Good
2	Lakshmi	K	0002	3/4/2012	Indira	Murthy	(912) 546-821	Teacher's col	$720.00	Good
3	Nachiketh	H G	0003	1/16/2015	Aruna	Guru	(961) 134-965	Bangalore	$480.00	Good
4	Tejas	K	0004	4/7/2015	Lakshmi	Shankar	(987) 531-264	T.Dasarahalli	$720.00	Average
5	Shashank	K	0005	4/1/2008	Lakshmi	Shankar	(947) 861-323	T.Dasarahalli	$1,200.00	Good
8	Nithyashree	H M	0006	6/12/1990	Roopa	Ravi	(964) 572-158	Padmanabhc	$22,000.00	Good
9	Jagadeesh	B	0007	10/25/1985	Radha	Venkatesh	(987) 451-362	Marathalli, Bc	$18,000.00	Good
(New)									$0.00	

Table. 2.1: Student List

Suppose we want to perform the following tasks.

- View the details of all the students who are absent on a particular day or view all male students' records.

Student Attendance

ID	Student	Attendanc	Status
1	0001	4/2/2018	P
2	0002	4/2/2018	A
3	0003	4/2/2018	P
4	0004	4/2/2018	P
5	0005	4/2/2018	A
6	0006	4/2/2018	A
7	0007	4/2/2018	A
(New)			

Table. 2.2: Student Attendance

- Find the total fee collected from all the students or the average school fee, etc.
- To update the records, say to increase the fee by 20 per cent.

Queries in MS Access help us to perform all the above tasks. Let us learn about them in detail in the following sections.

You should know

Databases in Access are composed of four main objects—tables, queries, forms and reports.

Queries

A **query** is a statement of question about the data stored in the tables or it can be a request to perform an action on the data. It describes the conditions that must be satisfied for records to be matched in one or more tables. When we run the query, the matching records appear in a new datasheet.

Types of queries

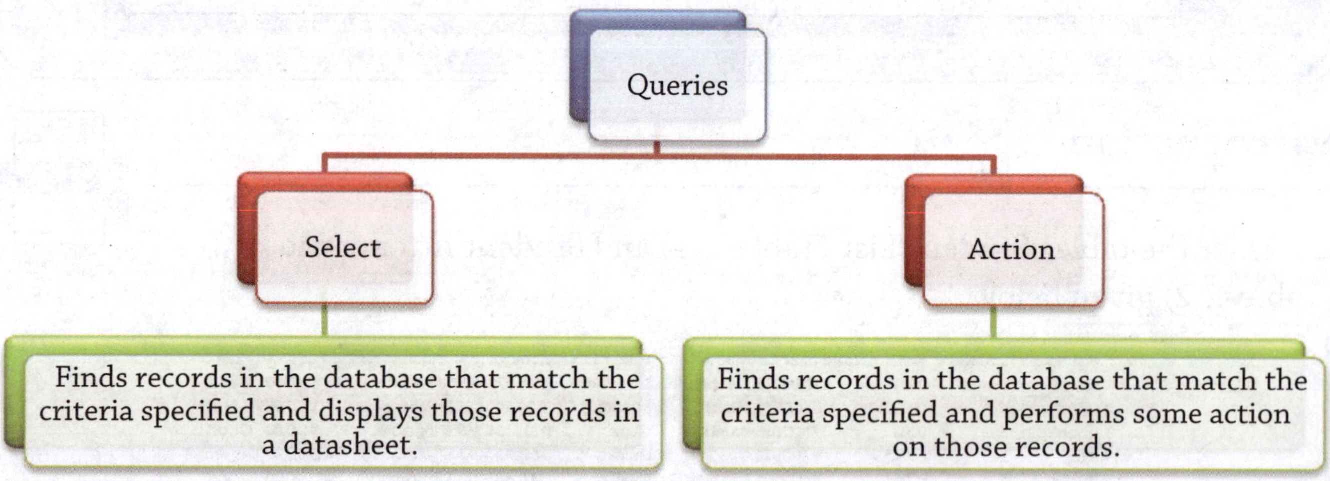

Mastering keyboard

Working with wizards

- **Alt + N:** Moves to the next page of the wizard
- **Alt + B:** Moves to the previous page of the wizard
- **Alt + F:** Completes the wizard

Creating queries

Queries can either be created using a wizard or can be written manually too.

(a) By using a wizard

MS Access 2013 helps us in creating the queries easily using the wizard. There are four wizards available in Access 2013 as shown below.

Simple	Find Duplicates	Find Unmatched	Crosstab
• Sets up a query to retrieve data from one or more fields or tables and displays the results in a datasheet. • Example: We can extract the contact numbers of all the students.	• Sets up a query to locate records that have the same information in one or more fields that are specified. • Example: We can retrieve the names of all the students who have registered for more than one course.	• Sets up a query to locate records in one table that don't have related records in another table. • Example: We can retrieve the names of all the students who have not participated in any sports.	• Sets up a query to calculate. • Example: We can calculate the sum, average, etc.

To create a query using the wizard, follow the steps given below:

1. Click on CREATE tab → Queries group → Query Wizard button as in Fig. 2.1. New Query dialog box appears.

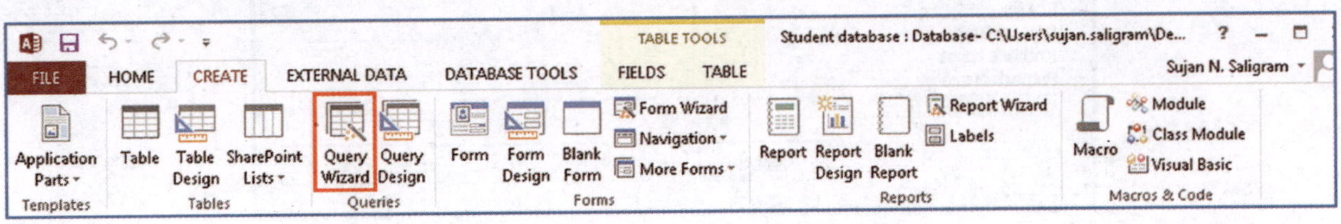

Fig. 2.1: Create tab: Query Wizard

2. Select Simple Query Wizard which creates a select query from the fields that we pick up and click on OK (Fig. 2.2). Simple Query Wizard appears.

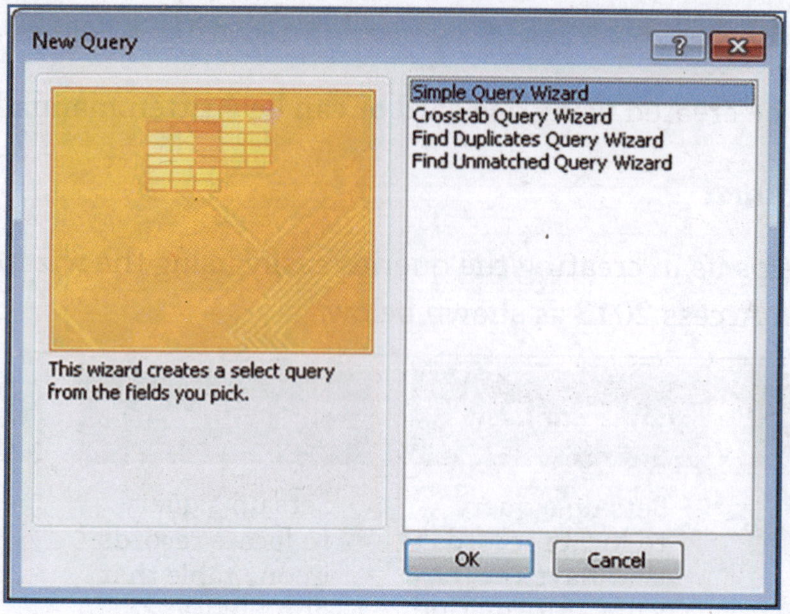

Fig. 2.2: New query dialog box

3. Select the table to be displayed from the Tables/Queries drop-down list as shown in Fig. 2.3. On selecting the table, available fields are displayed in Available Fields List.

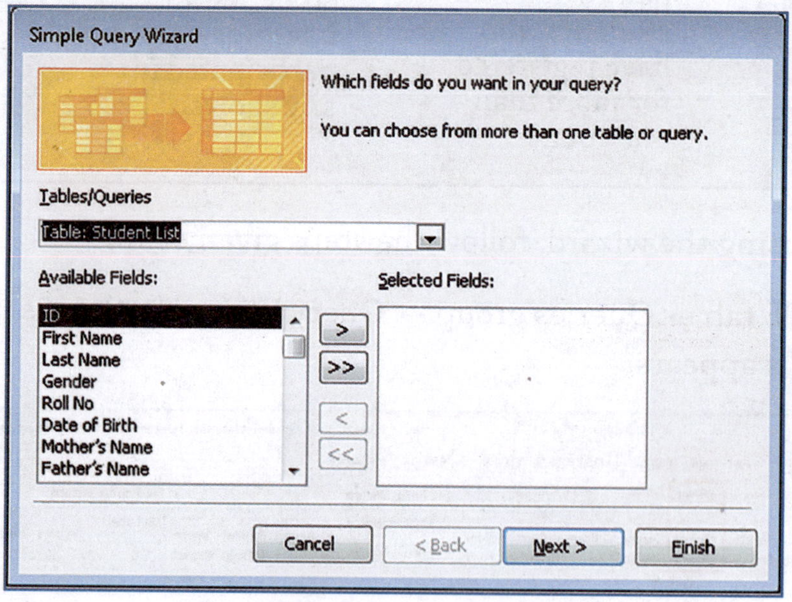

Fig. 2.3: Simple Query Wizard

4. Select the field that you want to display and click on the button '>' to move it to the Selected Fields window. If you want to display all the fields, click on the button '>>'. After selecting the fields, click on Next.

   Note: We can select fields from more than one table. In Fig. 2.4, we have selected fields from the two tables—Student List and Student Attendance.

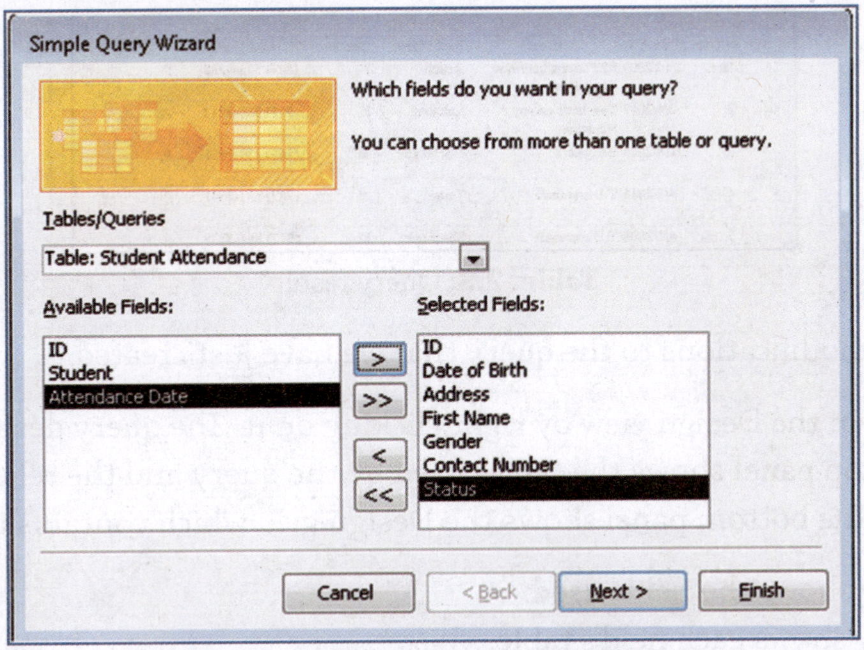

Fig. 2.4: Selecting fields from multiple tables

5. Enter the title for the query in the first text box as shown in Fig. 2.5. With the option Open the query to view information being selected, click on Finish.

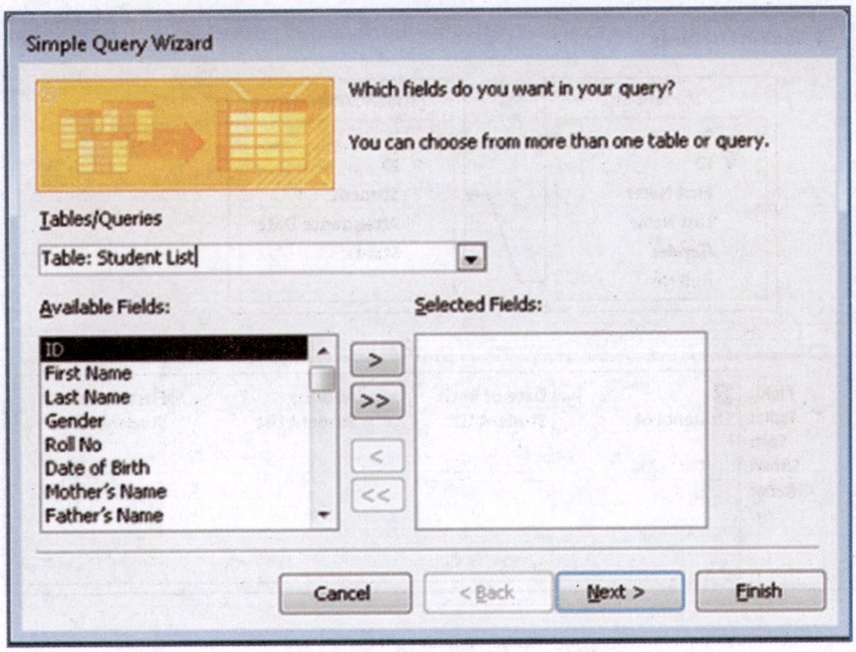

Fig. 2.5: Setting query title

6. It displays the results in a datasheet view. Observe that all the fields that we have selected from both the tables are displayed in Table 2.3.

Student List Query

ID	Date of Birth	Address	First Name	Gender	Contact Number	Status
1	1/16/2009	F3 Fortuna serenity, Bangalore	Aruna	F	(809) 572-4288	P
2	3/4/2012	Teacher's colony Hindupur	Lakshmi	F	(912) 546-8213	A
3	1/16/2015	Bangalore	Nachiketh	M	(961) 134-9651	P
4	4/7/2015	T.Dasarahalli	Tejas	M	(987) 531-2641	P
5	4/1/2008	T.Dasarahalli	Shashank	M	(947) 861-3235	A

Table. 2.3: Query result

Let us do some modifications to the query that we have just created.

Open the query in the Design view by right clicking on it. The query designer is shown in Fig. 2.6. The top panel shows the tables used by the query and the relationship between them. The bottom panel shows the Design grid which contains the following:

- The Field row shows the fields used.
- The Table row shows each field's table.
- The selected check boxes in the Show row indicate the fields to display in the result.
- Criteria row can contain criteria that determine which records will be displayed.
- The or row sets up an alternate criteria.

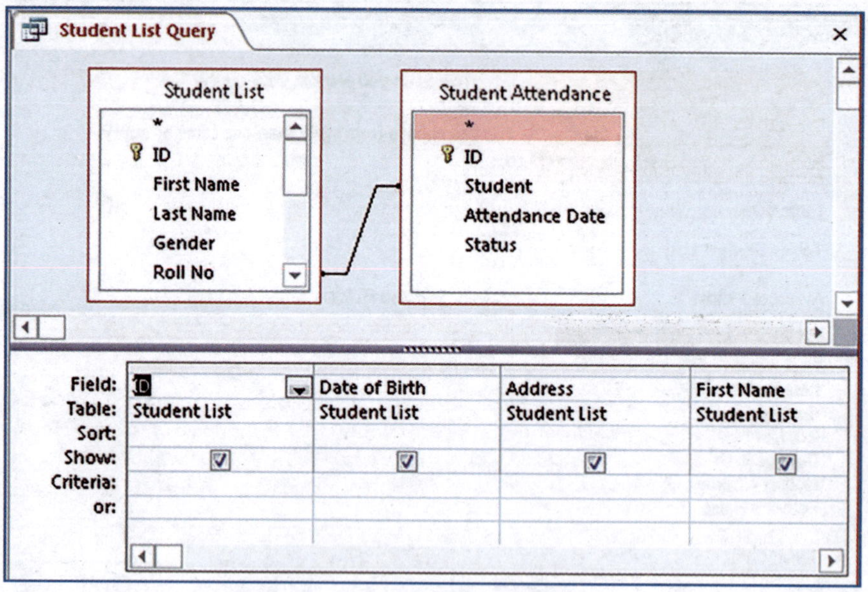

Fig. 2.6: Query Designer

- Let us do the following modifications to our query. If we do not want certain fields to be displayed in the results datasheet, uncheck that field in the Show row. For example, let us uncheck the Address field.

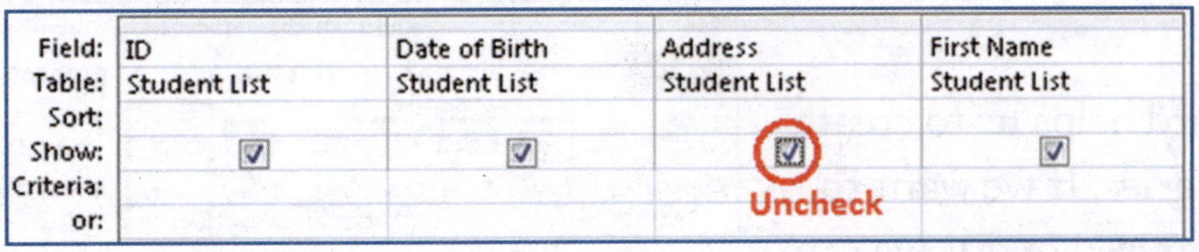

- Let us add a criterion to our query. For example, let us write the criterion to display only the male students' records. To do so, in the **Criteria** row under the field Gender, write = "M".

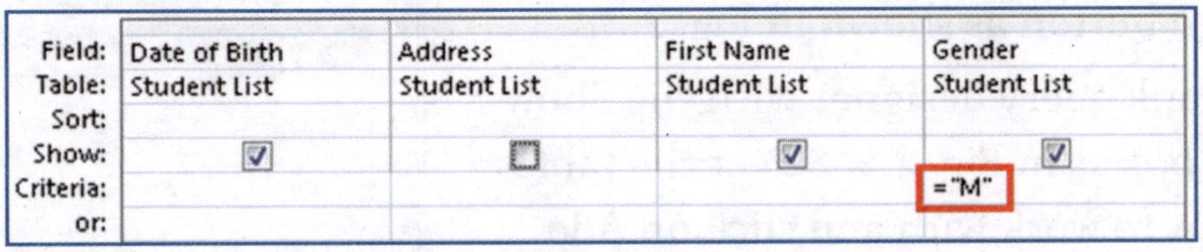

- Let us sort the records according to the Date of Birth of the student. To do so, in the Sort row, click under the field Date of Birth and select Ascending.

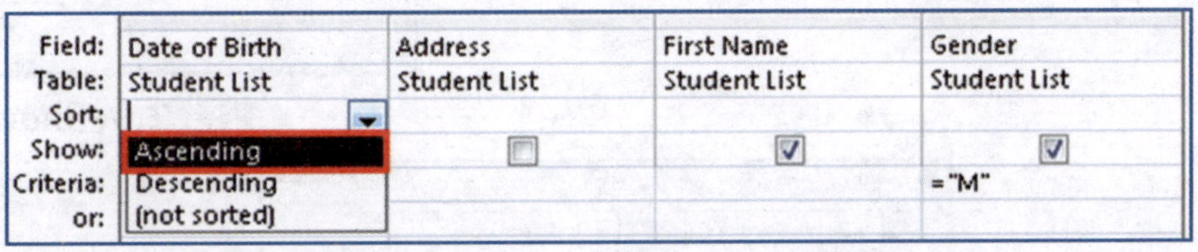

- Once we are done with all the changes, click on DESIGN tab → Results group → Run button as in Fig. 2.7.

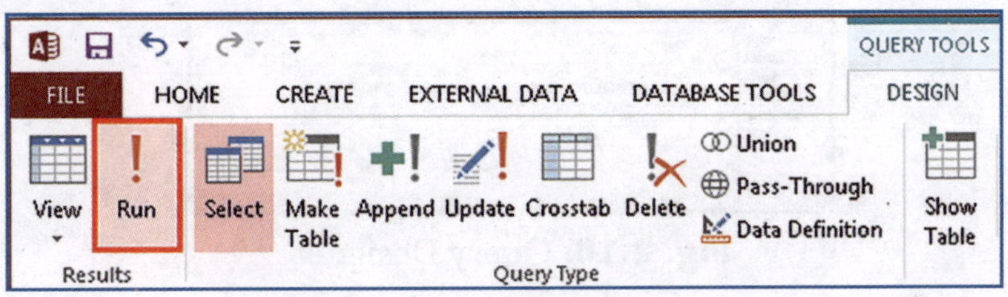

Fig. 2.7: Query Tools: DESIGN tab

- It runs the query with the updated changes and displays the results as shown below.

Student List Query

ID	Date of Birth	First Name	Gender	Contact Number	Status
5	4/1/2008	Shashank	M	(947) 861-3235	A
3	1/16/2015	Nachiketh	M	(961) 134-9651	P
4	4/7/2015	Tejas	M	(987) 531-2641	P

Table. 2.4: Updated results

Observe that only the male students' records are displayed, which are sorted according to their date of birth. Also, the address field is hidden.

(b) Manually

The Query Wizard helps us to create the common queries. If we want to create any customised query, we can create it manually using Query Design.

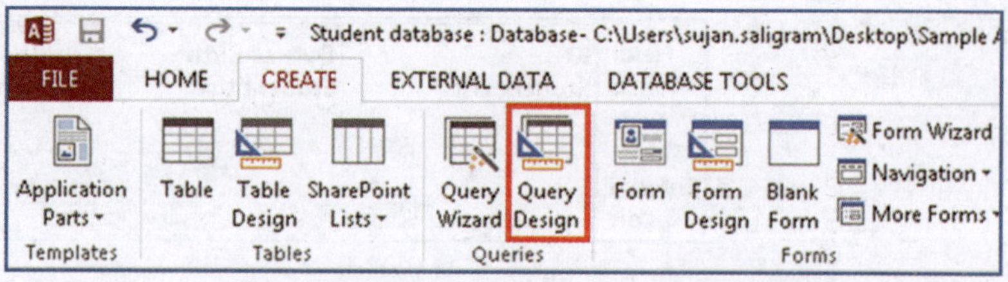

Fig. 2.8: Create tab: Query Design

- Click on CREATE tab → Queries group → Query Design button as shown in Fig. 2.8.
- It opens a blank query designer with the Show Table dialog box as in Fig. 2.9. Select the tables that you want to work with and click on Add.
- You can see the preview of the tables getting added to the top panel. Click on Close to display the query designer as shown in Fig. 2.10.

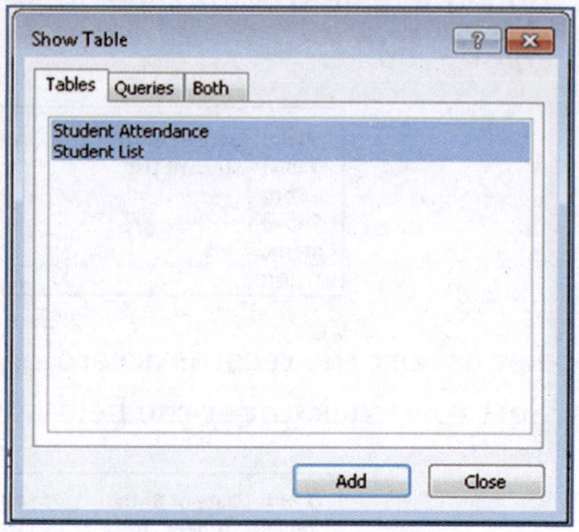

Fig. 2.9: Show Table

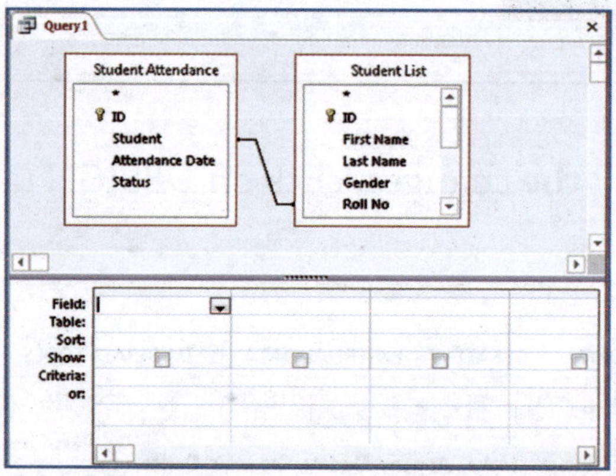

Fig. 2.10: Query Designer

- Select the fields that you want to add to the query from the table (Fig. 2.11).

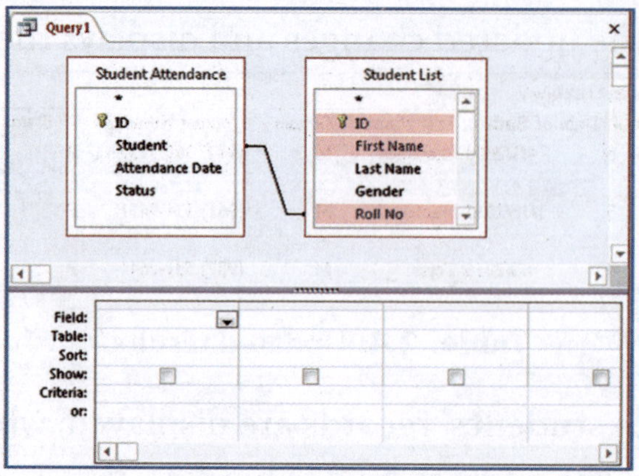

Fig. 2.11: Query Designer: Selecting fields from different tables

Note: If you want to select all the fields double click on the title of the table.

- Drag and drop the selected fields to the field row. Observe that the selected fields appear in columns and the table row is automatically updated as shown in Fig. 2.12. Repeat the same with the other table also.

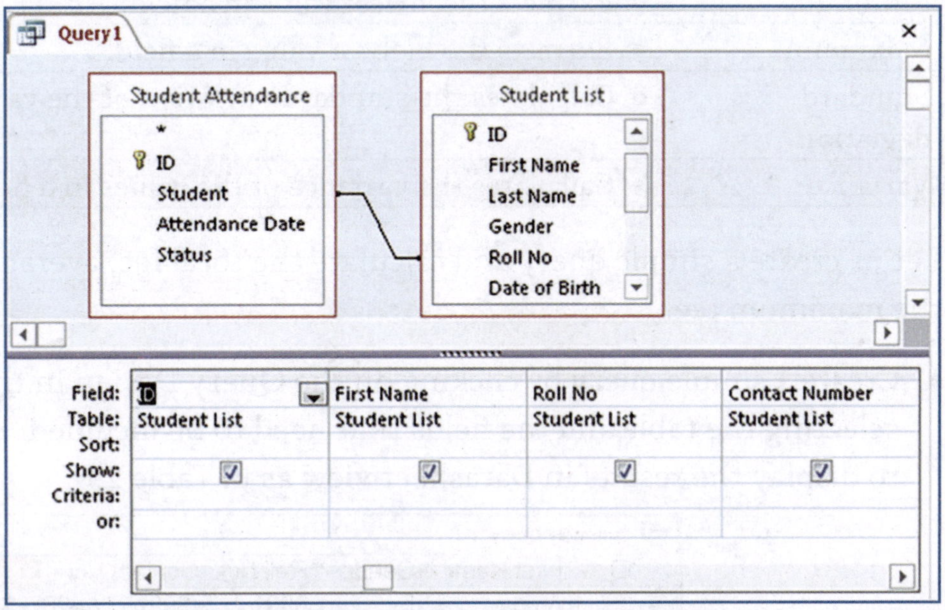

Fig. 2.12: Query Designer: Adding fields

Let us display only those records of the students who are present and sort them as per their Roll No and hide the ID field.

Follow the steps as described on the previous page to perform these tasks. The results are displayed as shown in Table 2.5.

Query1

First Name	Roll No	Contact Number	Attendance Date	Status
Aruna	0001	(809) 572-4288	4/2/2018	P
Nachiketh	0003	(961) 134-9651	4/2/2018	P
Tejas	0004	(987) 531-2641	4/2/2018	P

Table. 2.5: Query results

Save the query by clicking on the Save button in the quick access tool bar and entering the desired name for the query as in Fig. 2.13.

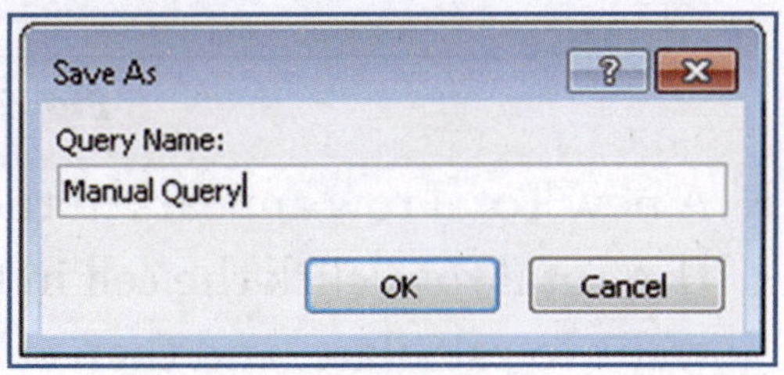

Fig. 2.13: Saving the Query

Till now, we have written the select query which typically locates all the records that meet some criteria. Let us now write a query that performs some calculations based on the data. Some of the common aggregate functions which are used are given below:

Sum	• Calculates the total of the values in a field.
Count	• Counts the number of values in a field.

Average	• Calculates the average of the values in a field.
Minimum	• Extracts the lowest value in a field.
Maximum	• Extracts the highest value in a field.
Standard deviation	• Calculates the standard deviation of the values in a field.
Variance	• Calculates the variance of the values in a field.

Let us create a simple query and calculate the total fee, average fee, minimum fee and the maximum fee.

- Create a simple query by clicking on the Query Design in the CREATE tab and selecting the table and the fields that need to be included. Run the query and save it to display the results in Datasheet view as in Table 2.6.

Summary Query

ID	First Nam	Gende	Roll N	Contact Nu	Fee
1	Aruna	F	0001	(809) 572-428	$20,000.00
2	Lakshmi	F	0002	(912) 546-821	$15,000.00
3	Nachiketh	M	0003	(961) 134-965	$10,000.00
4	Tejas	M	0004	(987) 531-264	$15,000.00
5	Shashank	M	0005	(947) 861-323	$25,000.00
* (New)					$0.00

Table. 2.6: Query result

- Click on HOME tab → Records group → Totals button as in Fig. 2.15.

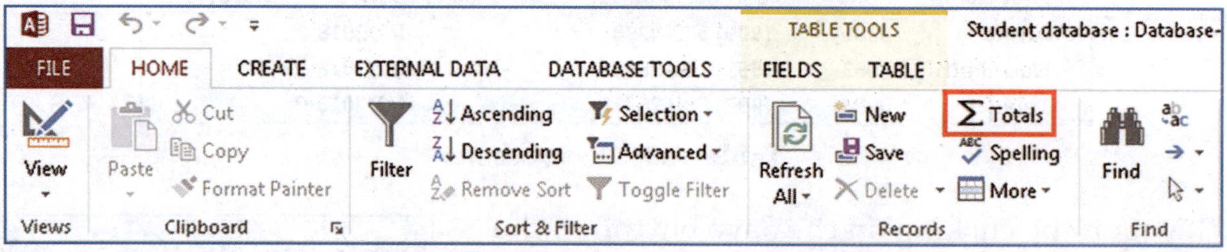

Fig. 2.14: HOME tab: Records group

- A new Total row appears in the datasheet. In the Total row, click the cell in the field that you want to calculate, and then select any aggregate function from the drop-down list as in Fig. 2.14.

Few sample outputs on selecting different aggregate functions are given in Table 2.7.

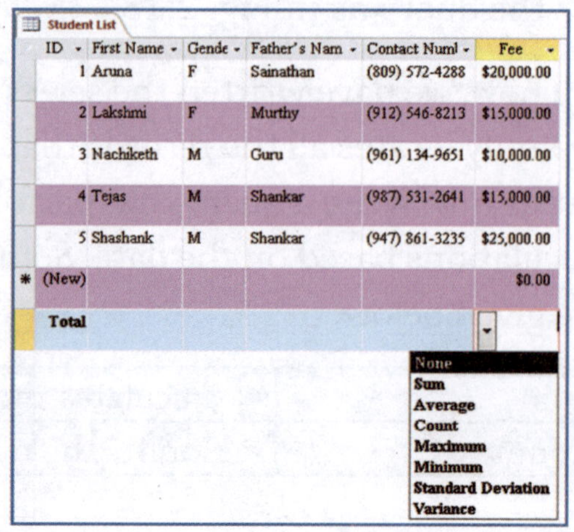

Fig. 2.15: Selecting aggregate function

Summary Query

ID	First Name	Gender	Roll No	Contact Number	Fee
1	Aruna	F	0001	(809) 572-428	$20,000.00
2	Lakshmi	F	0002	(912) 546-821	$15,000.00
3	Nachiketh	M	0003	(961) 134-965	$10,000.00
4	Tejas	M	0004	(987) 531-264	$15,000.00
5	Shashank	M	0005	(947) 861-323	$25,000.00
(New)					$0.00
Total					$85,000.00

Table. 2.7(a): Sum aggregate

Summary Query

ID	First Name	Gender	Roll No	Contact Number	Fee
1	Aruna	F	0001	(809) 572-428	$20,000.00
2	Lakshmi	F	0002	(912) 546-821	$15,000.00
3	Nachiketh	M	0003	(961) 134-965	$10,000.00
4	Tejas	M	0004	(987) 531-264	$15,000.00
5	Shashank	M	0005	(947) 861-323	$25,000.00
(New)					$0.00
Total					$17,000.00

Table. 2.7(b): Average aggregate

Summary Query

ID	First Name	Gender	Roll No	Contact Number	Fee
1	Aruna	F	0001	(809) 572-428	$20,000.00
2	Lakshmi	F	0002	(912) 546-821	$15,000.00
3	Nachiketh	M	0003	(961) 134-965	$10,000.00
4	Tejas	M	0004	(987) 531-264	$15,000.00
5	Shashank	M	0005	(947) 861-323	$25,000.00
(New)					$0.00
Total					$25,000.00

Table. 2.7(c): Maximum aggregate

Summary Query

ID	First Name	Gender	Roll No	Contact Number	Fee
1	Aruna	F	0001	(809) 572-428	$20,000.00
2	Lakshmi	F	0002	(912) 546-821	$15,000.00
3	Nachiketh	M	0003	(961) 134-965	$10,000.00
4	Tejas	M	0004	(987) 531-264	$15,000.00
5	Shashank	M	0005	(947) 861-323	$25,000.00
(New)					$0.00
Total					$10,000.00

Table. 2.7(d): Minimum aggregate

Updating records using queries

Action query helps to manipulate the data stored in the database under certain circumstances. It finds records that match the selection criteria and performs an action on them. There are four types of action queries which are given adjacent.

Let us create an update action query for our student database, which increases the student's fee by 20%.

- **Append** — Adds records from one table to the end of another table.
- **Update** — Makes changes to records in one or more tables.
- **Delete** — Deletes records from one or more tables.
- **Make-table** — Creates a new table from the data in one or more tables.

Note: It is always advisable to create a copy of a table before executing an action query so that there will be a backup in case the query is not successful because once the query is executed, it is not reversible.

- Follow the steps described above and create a simple select query and run it. The results are displayed in the datasheet view as in Table 2.8.

Student List Query1

ID	First Nam	Gende	Roll No	Contact Nu	Fee
1	Aruna	F	0001	(809) 572-428	$20,000.00
2	Lakshmi	F	0002	(912) 546-821	$15,000.00
3	Nachiketh	M	0003	(961) 134-965	$10,000.00
4	Tejas	M	0004	(987) 531-264	$15,000.00
5	Shashank	M	0005	(947) 861-323	$25,000.00
6	Jagadeesh		0007	(987) 451-362	$18,000.00
7	Jagadeesh		0007	(987) 451-362	$18,000.00
* (New)					$0.00

Table. 2.8: Query result

- Switch to the Design view as in Fig. 2.16.

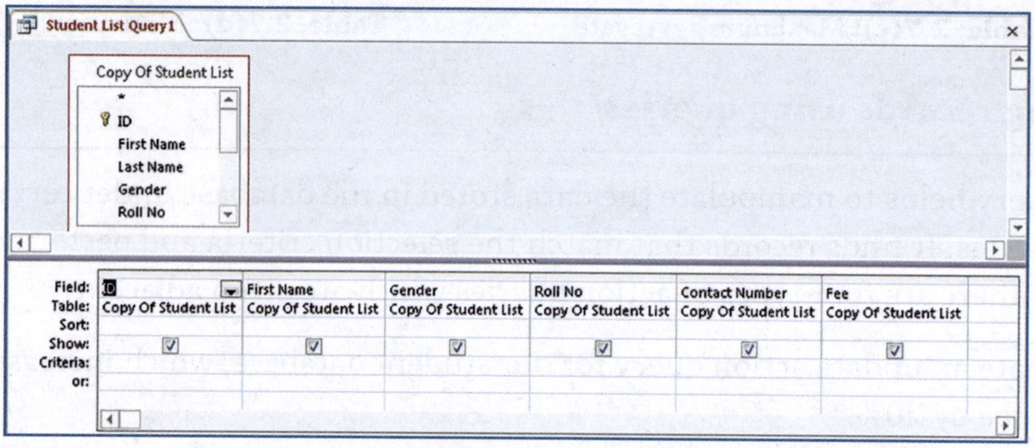

Fig. 2.16: Designing a query

- Click on DESIGN tab → Query Type group → Update button as in Fig. 2.17.

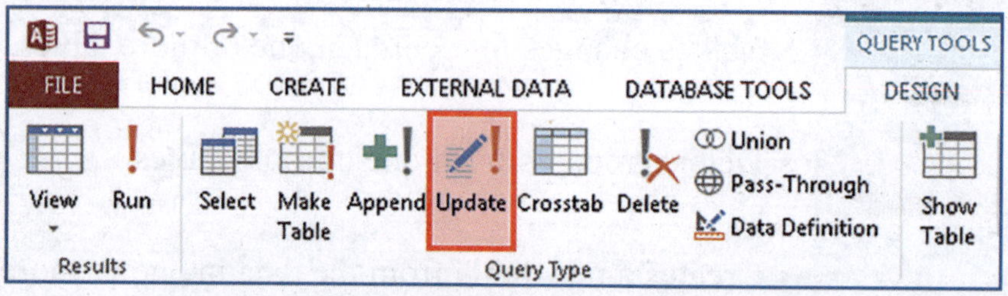

Fig. 2.17: DESIGN tab: Query Type

Observe that in the Design grid, the **Sort** and **Show** rows disappear and an **Update To** row appears.

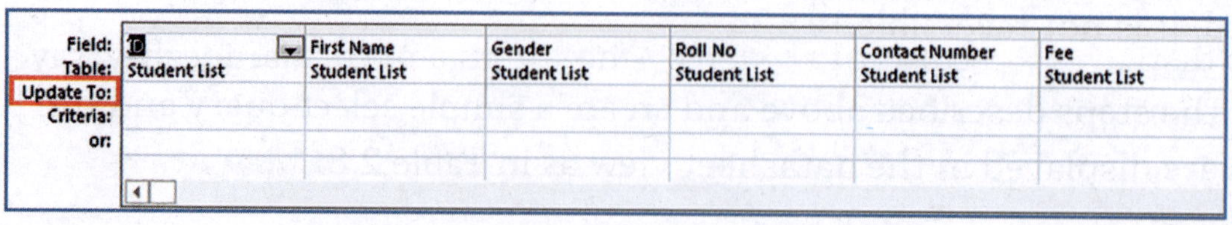

- In the Update To row of the Fee column, enter [Fee] + [Fee]*0.2. Then press the Enter key.

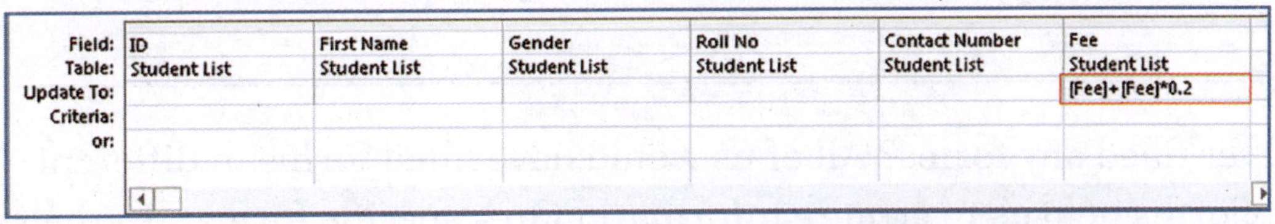

- Before running the query, observe the values in the Fee column and then run the query. It displays a message box asking for the confirmation to update the records. Click on Yes as in Fig. 2.18.

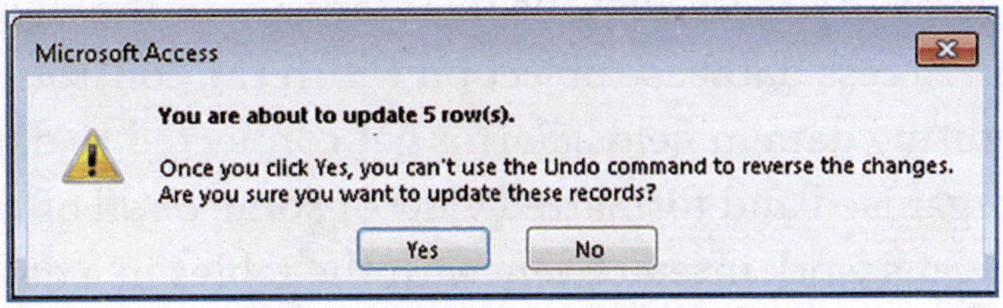

Fig. 2.18: Updating records

- Switch to Datasheet View and observe that the values in the Fee Column have been increased by 20% as in Fig. 2.19 (a) and (b).

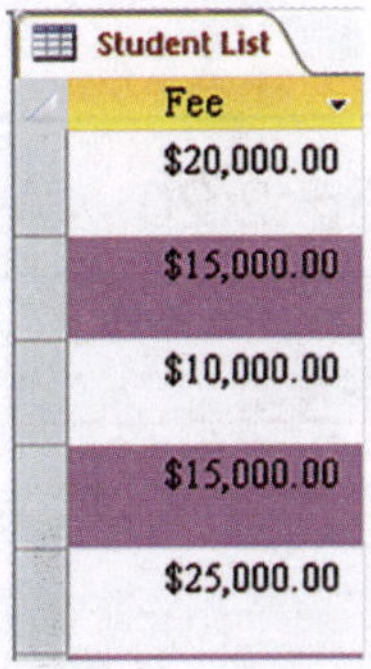

Fig. 2.19 (a): Before running query

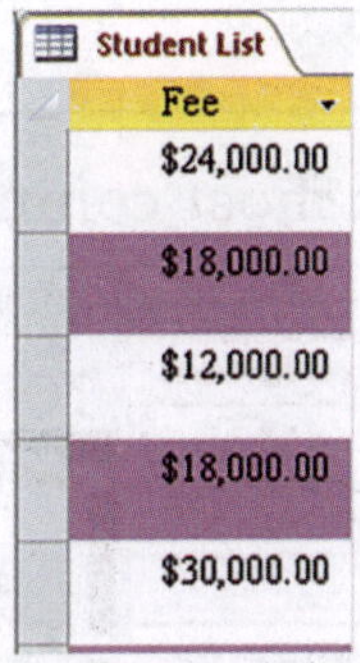

Fig. 2.19 (b): After running query

Hands-on practice

1. Open any existing Access database.
2. Create a table to store the details of all the students of your class. (Think of the fields that you would include like Name, Gender, Location, Phone number, Pin code, Height, Weight, etc.)
3. Create records for all the students.
4. Design queries to perform the following tasks:
   a. To display the records of students who live in a particular locality, say Vijayanagar.
   b. To display only male students' records or female students' records.
   c. To display the records of students whose weight is less than 40 kg.
   d. To display the average weight and height of students in the class.

Forms

Have you ever filled any forms? All of us would have filled forms in different situations. Forms help us to acquire information in a specific format. In the same way, forms in Access allow us to enter data in the right location and right format. A form is an Access database object on which the controls are placed for entering, displaying and editing data in fields. Forms get connected to datasource such as table or query. It is an organised and formatted view of some or all of the fields from one or more tables. Forms work interactively with the tables in a database.

Although tables allow us to enter the data directly under the respective fields, forms make it easier to enter the data for those who are not very familiar with Access.

Form features

A sample form with most common features is given in Fig. 2.20.

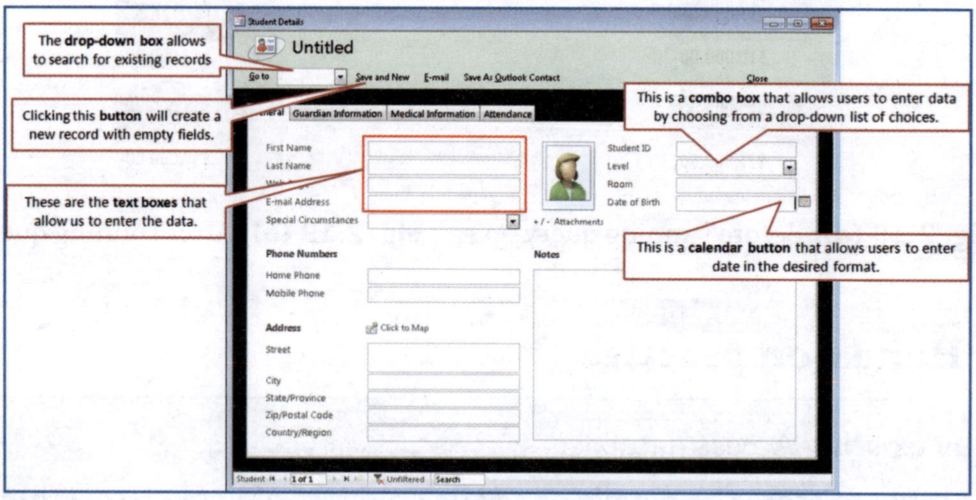

Fig. 2.20: Sample Form

Creating forms using a wizard

- In the Navigation pane, double-click the table for which you want to create the form to open it.
- Click on CREATE tab → Forms group → Form Wizard button as in Fig. 2.21.

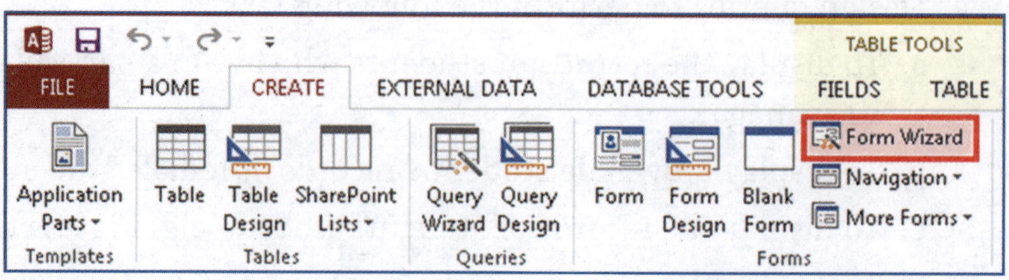

Fig. 2.21: CREATE tab: Form Wizard

- Select the fields that you want to appear in the form and click on > to move them to the Selected Fields and click on Next (Fig. 2.22).
- Select the layout for the form from the available layouts (Columnar, Tabular, Datasheet, Justified) and click on Next (Fig. 2.23).

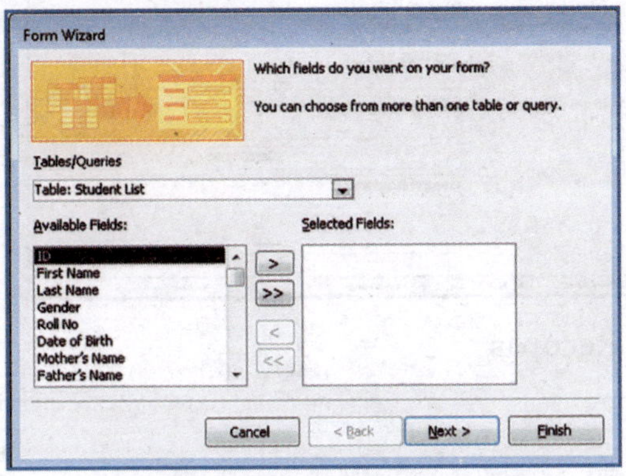

Fig. 2.22: Select fields

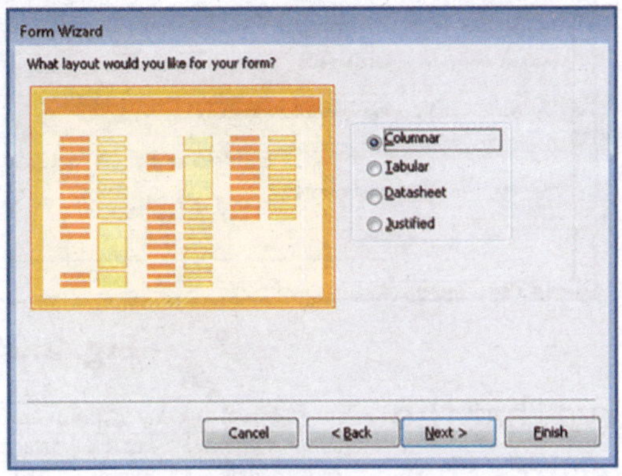

Fig. 2.23: Select Layout

- Write the title for the form and click on Finish (Fig. 2.24).

The Student List Form is created as shown below with the first record of the table being displayed by default as in Fig. 2.25.

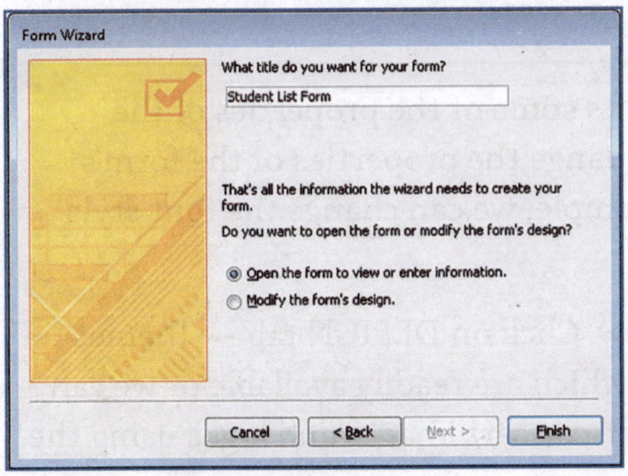

Fig. 2.24: Form Title

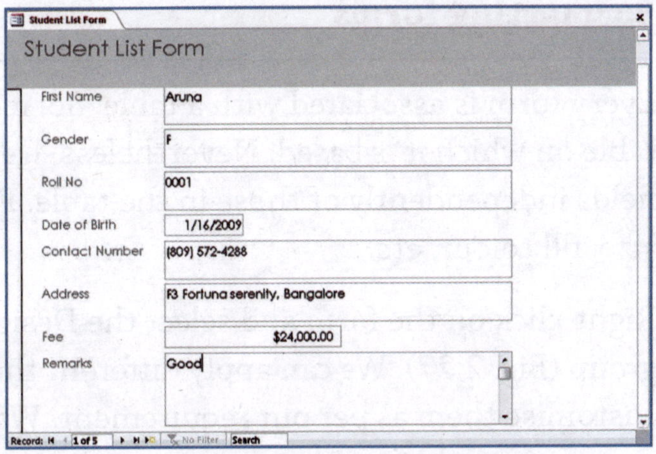

Fig. 2.25: Generated Form

Let us add some new records to the table using the form that is created. Observe that in the existing table, there are 5 records. In the Record Navigation pane, click on the New Record which displays the form with empty fields to enter the new data.

Let us add the following two records. After entering the data for each record, click on Save button (Fig. 2.26).

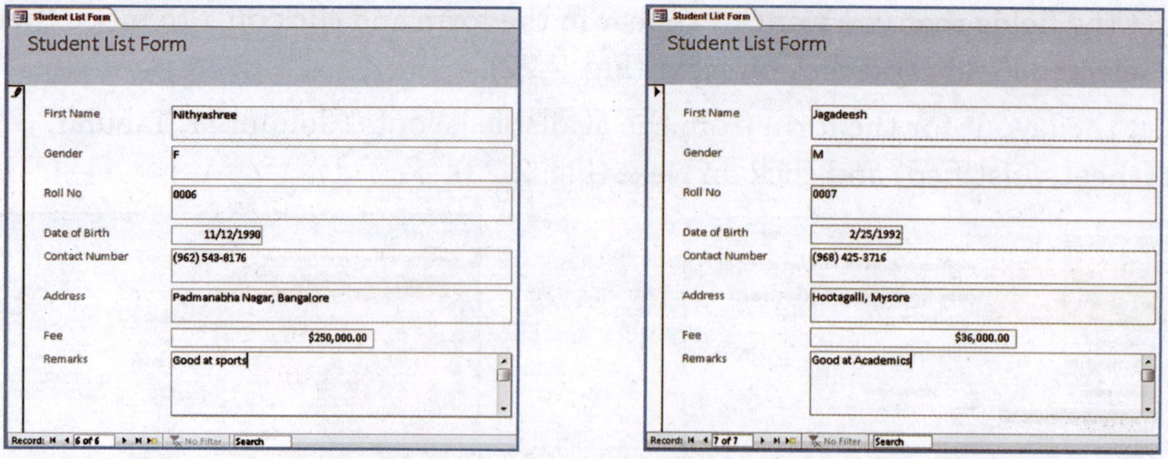

Fig. 2.26: Adding New Records

Observe that the new records that we have added are updated in the Student List table (Table 2.9).

First Name	Last Nami	Roll Nc	Date of Birth	Mother's Na	Father's Nar	Contact Nun	Address	Fee	Remarks
Aruna	kumari	0001	1/16/2009	Pushpalatha	Sainathan	(809) 572-4288	F3 Fortuna sere	$20,000.00	Good
Lakshmi	K	0002	3/4/2012	Indira	Murthy	(912) 546-8213	Teacher's colon	$15,000.00	Good
Nachiketh	H G	0003	1/16/2015	Aruna	Guru	(961) 134-9651	Bangalore	$10,000.00	Good
Tejas	K	0004	4/7/2015	Lakshmi	Shankar	(987) 531-2641	T.Dasarahalli	$15,000.00	Average
Shashank	K	0005	4/1/2008	Lakshmi	Shankar	(947) 861-3235	T.Dasarahalli	$25,000.00	Good
Nithyashree		0006	11/12/1990			(962) 543-8176	Padmanabha N	$25,000.00	Good at sports
Jagadeesh		0007	2/25/1992			(968) 425-3716	Hootagalli, Mys	$36,000.00	Good at Acadei

Table. 2.9: New Records being added

Formatting forms

Every form is associated with a table. So, it inherits some of the properties of the table on which it is based. Nevertheless, we can change the properties of the form's fields independently of those in the table. For example, we can change the font style, size, fill colour, etc.

Right-click on the form and select the Design View. Click on DESIGN tab → Themes group (Fig. 2.27). We can apply different themes which are readily available or we can customise them as per our requirement. We can also insert images and logos using the options available in this tab.

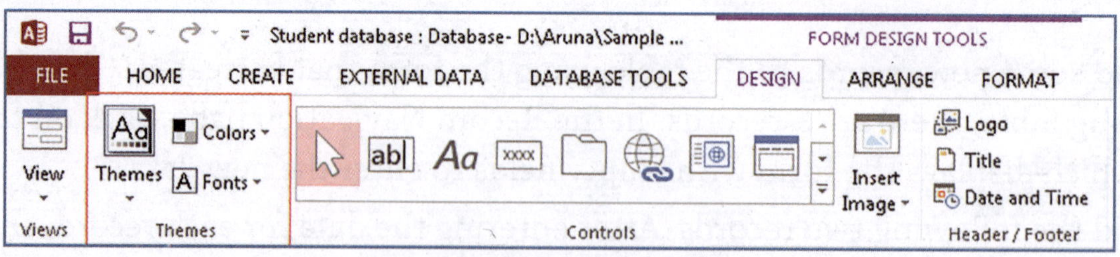

Fig. 2.27: Form: DESIGN tab

Fig. 2.28 shows the formatted version of the previously created form.

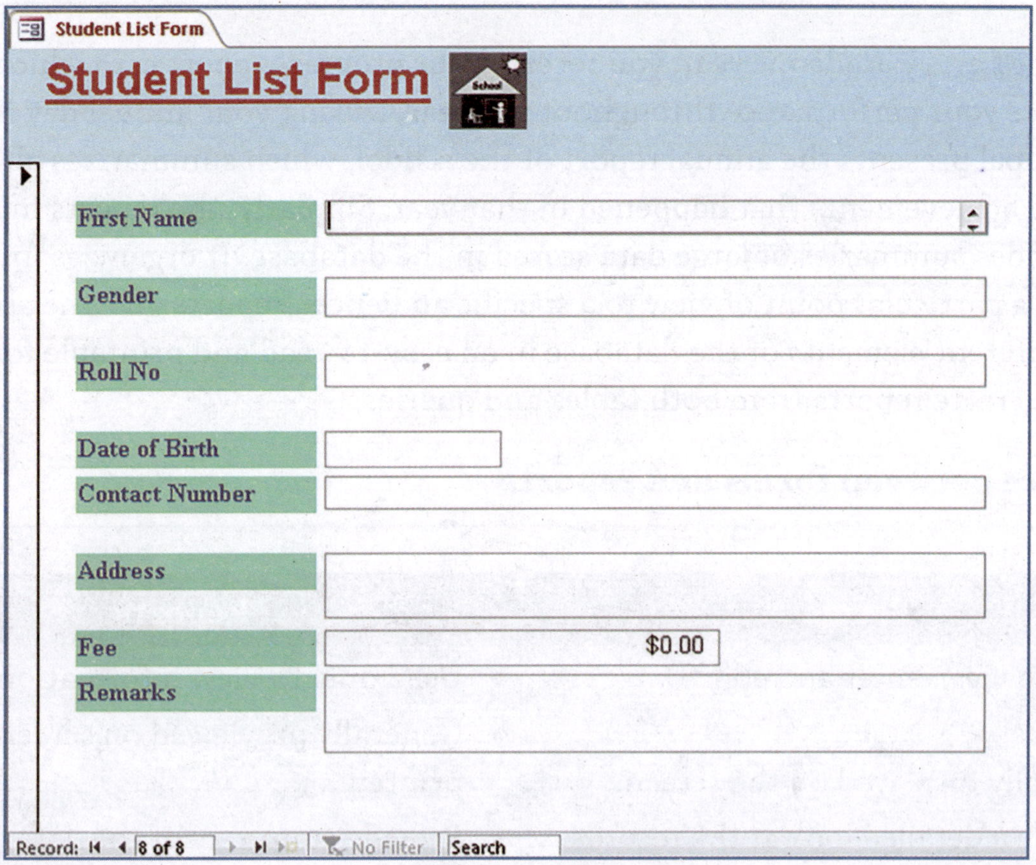

Fig. 2.28: Formatted Form

Hands-on practice

1. Open the database created in the previous exercise.
2. Open the table created for storing student's details.
3. Create a form based on the above table.
4. Choose a new theme and theme fonts.
5. Add a suitable logo to your form.
6. Add few records using the form that is created.

Reports

At the end of every academic year, you receive your progress report card which summarizes your performance throughout the year. During your annual day function, your principal presents the annual report of the school, which summarizes all the events and achievements that happened in that year. Similarly, the reports in Access 2013 provides summaries of large data stored in the database. It organizes information to express a particular point of view to a specific audience. Reports give the ability to present different elements of the database in an easy-to-read and printable format. In Access, we create reports from both tables and queries.

Difference between forms and reports

Forms	Reports
• Used to view, enter and edit information. • Generally displayed on the screen. • Provide a detailed look at the records. • Often used by people who actually work with the database.	• Used only to view information. • Generally previewed on screen and printed. • Provide summary of the data. • Often used by people who do not work with the database but who use the information stored in the database.

Creating reports

Reports can be created by using the report tool or by using a wizard.

(a) By using report tool

- In the Navigation pane, click the table for which you want to create the report.
- Click on Create tab → Reports group → Report button. It creates a report based on all the fields of the selected table and displays it in the Layout view as in Fig. 2.29.

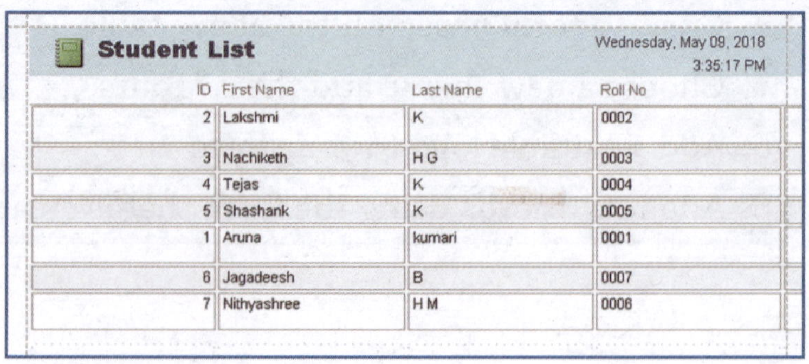

Student List

Wednesday, May 09, 2018
3:35:17 PM

ID	First Name	Last Name	Roll No
2	Lakshmi	K	0002
3	Nachiketh	H G	0003
4	Tejas	K	0004
5	Shashank	K	0005
1	Aruna	kumari	0001
8	Jagadeesh	B	0007
7	Nithyashree	H M	0006

Fig. 2.29: Report

- If you cannot see all the fields in the report, resize the fields by clicking and dragging their edges until all the fields are able to fit in the page as in Fig. 2.30.

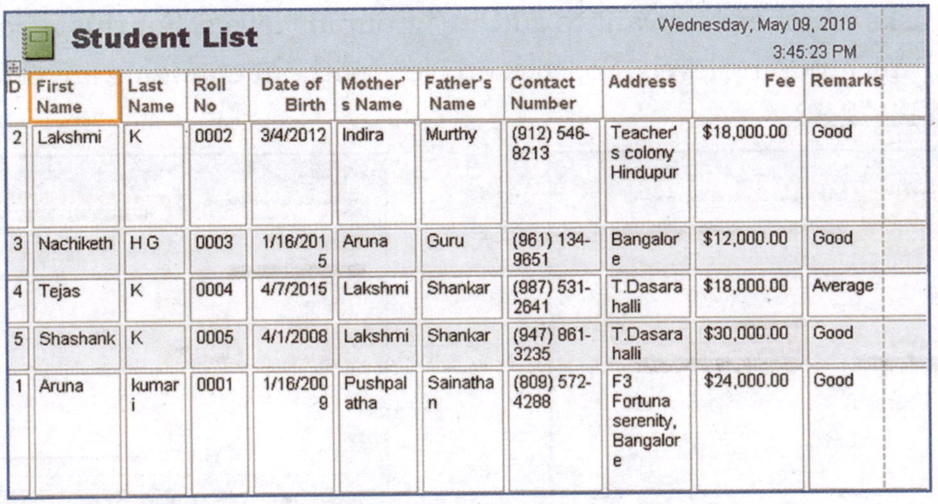

Student List — Wednesday, May 09, 2018 3:45:23 PM

D	First Name	Last Name	Roll No	Date of Birth	Mother's Name	Father's Name	Contact Number	Address	Fee	Remarks
2	Lakshmi	K	0002	3/4/2012	Indira	Murthy	(912) 546-8213	Teacher's colony Hindupur	$18,000.00	Good
3	Nachiketh	H G	0003	1/16/2015	Aruna	Guru	(961) 134-9651	Bangalore	$12,000.00	Good
4	Tejas	K	0004	4/7/2015	Lakshmi	Shankar	(987) 531-2641	T.Dasarahalli	$18,000.00	Average
5	Shashank	K	0005	4/1/2008	Lakshmi	Shankar	(947) 861-3235	T.Dasarahalli	$30,000.00	Good
1	Aruna	kumari	0001	1/16/2009	Pushpalatha	Sainathan	(809) 572-4288	F3 Fortuna serenity, Bangalore	$24,000.00	Good

Fig. 2.30: Resized report

- Save the report by clicking on the Save button in the Quick Access toolbar and provide a name for it.

Reports created in this way are very much similar to the table except that these are appealing. These reports do not summarize the data and we cannot make any meaningful conclusions. Therefore, we use Report Wizard to create meaningful reports.

(b) By using a wizard

Before creating reports, first we need to decide the end result, how the report should look like, what information should be included in the report. Once we decide on this, the Report Wizard guides us through a series of questions and then creates a report based on our answers.

Suppose a school wants to send an absent note to all the parents whose children are absent in the school on a particular day. For this, they need the contact numbers of all the students who were absent. Let us create a report to extract this information from our Student database.

1. Click on Create tab → Reports group → Report Wizard (Fig. 2.31).

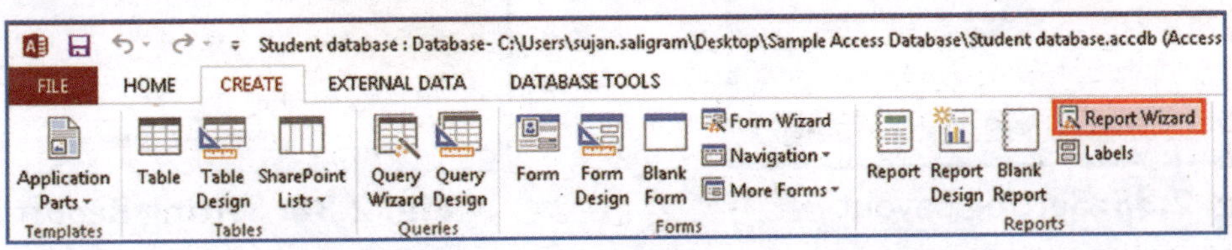

Fig. 2.31: Create tab: Report Wizard

2. Display Tables or Queries, list and select query from which you want to create a report. Select the fields that you want to include in the report and click on Next as in Fig. 2.32.
3. The wizard asks whether you want to add any grouping levels. For this report, we do not need to add any grouping levels. So, click on Next without changing anything in this screen as in Fig. 2.33.

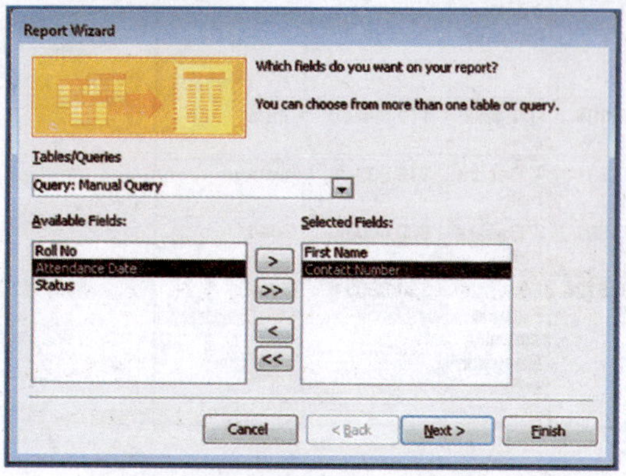

Fig. 2.32: Report Wizard

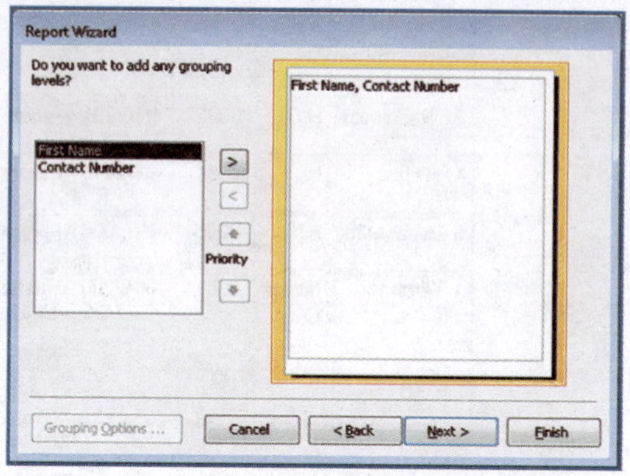

Fig. 2.33: Adding grouping levels

4. The wizard asks whether the data needs to be sorted. Let us sort the data by the First Name. Select the field First Name and Ascending. Click on Next as shown in Fig. 2.34.
5. Select the layout and the orientation. Observe that the option 'Adjust the field width so all fields fit on a page' is automatically checked. Click on Next as in Fig. 2.35.
6. Enter the report name and click on Finish as in Fig. 2.36.

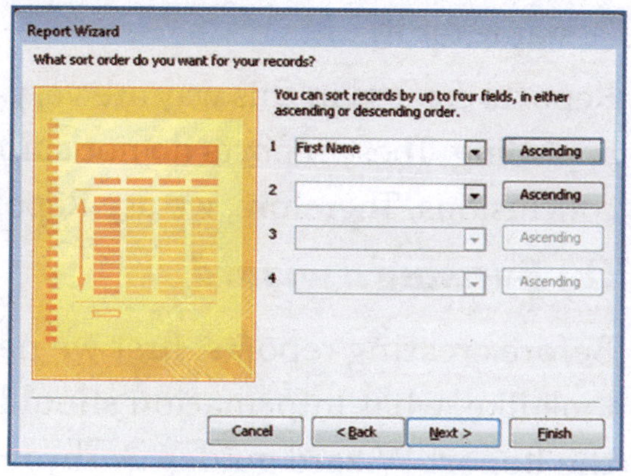

Fig. 2.34: Sorting Data

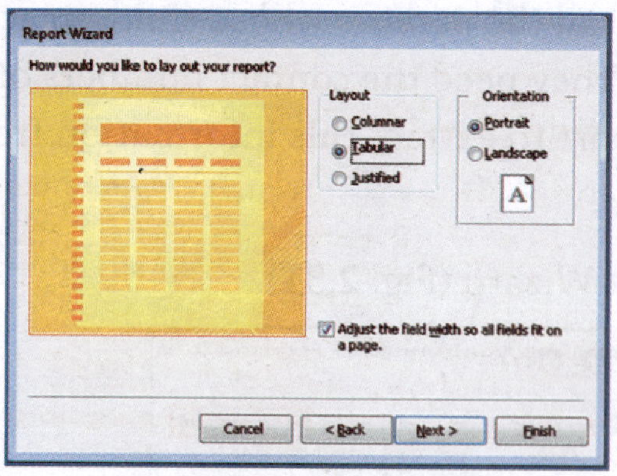

Fig. 2.35: Setting Layout

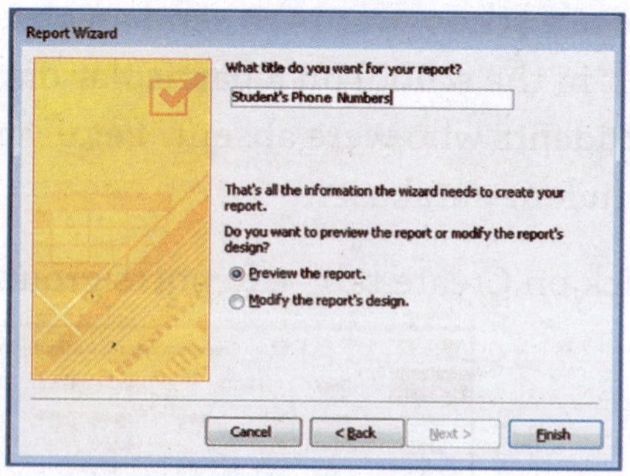

Fig. 2.36: Setting Report Name

7. The report is generated and displayed as shown in Fig. 2.37.

Student's Phone Numbers

First Name	Contact Number
Jagadeesh	(987) 451-3621
Lakshmi	(912) 546-8213
Nithyashree	(964) 572-1583
Shashank	(947) 861-3235

Wednesday, May 09, 2018

Fig. 2.37: Final Report

Formatting reports

Like forms, reports can also be formatted. We can add labels, text boxes, images, and other controls that can be formatted using different commands in the ribbon or by using the Property Sheet pane.

The formatted report of the above generated Student's Phone Numbers report is shown in Fig. 2.38.

Students' Phone Numbers

First Name	Contact Number
Aruna	(809) 572-4288
Nachiketh	(961) 134-9651
Tejas	(987) 531-2641

Tuesday, July 17, 2018 Page 1 of 1

Fig. 2.38: Formatted Report

Mastering keyboard

Press F4 to open and close the Property Sheet pane.

Digital geek

Calculations Using Queries

In addition to the aggregate functions which are readily available, we can do customized calculations using the Expression Builder. For example, if we want to increase the fee by 20% in the student's database, we can write the expression [Fee] + [Fee]*0.2 in the expression builder.

Make-table Query

Make-table query retrieves data from one or more tables, and then loads the result set into a new table. These are helpful when we want to copy or archive data.

Previewing and printing reports

Before printing any report, it is advisable to preview the report and make necessary changes to avoid unnecessary waste of the printing cost.

- In the Navigation pane, right-click on the report and select Print Preview as in Fig. 2.39.
- It displays the tab that has commands to modify the report for printing as in Fig. 2.40.

We can set the Page size, Margins, Page Layout, etc. After the changes are done, click on Close Print Preview. Close the report and save the changes.

We can also export the report as Excel file, Text file, PDF or XPS, Word file, HTML file, etc. We can also email the report as an attachment.

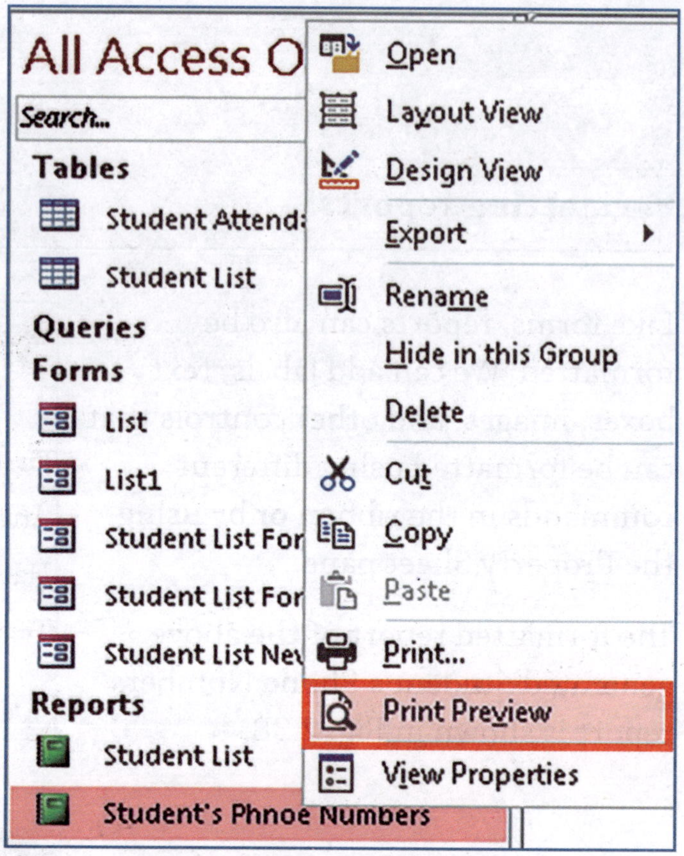

Fig. 2.39: Print Preview

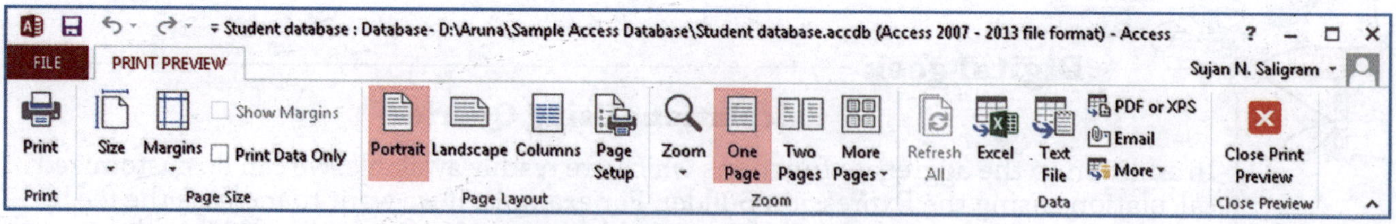

Fig. 2.40: Print Preview Commands

Hands-on practice

1. Open any existing Access database.
2. Open any table/query in the database and create a report.
3. Resize the fields and rows so that all information is visible.
4. Choose a new theme and theme fonts.
5. Add a suitable logo to your report.
6. Export the report as a PDF.

Word web

query: a question about the data stored in the tables, or a request to perform an action on the data

select query: a query that finds records in the database that match the criteria specified and displays those records in a datasheet without changing the data

action query: a query that finds records in the database that match the criteria specified and perform some action with those records

form: an Access database object on which the controls are placed for entering, displaying, and editing data in fields

report: an Access database object that contains well formatted and organised information according to some specifications. It can be printed.

Recall

Access 2013 does not support creating new Data Collection forms although it processes data collection forms that were created in earlier versions. The data collection helps to create the data collection forms that can be sent as emails. When they are returned, the data gets processed and stored in the database.

netsearch

For additional information, visit the link:
https://www.makeuseof.com/tag/libreoffice-free-office-suite-windows-linux-mac/
Base is an equivalent alternative for MS Access which is available in LibreOffice and Apache OpenOffice.

Hands-on practice

1. Create an Access database for the sports club of your school.
2. Create a table to store the details of all the student members, viz, Name, Gender, Class, Roll No., Contact Details, Sports selected, etc.
3. Create records for all the students.
4. Design queries to perform the following tasks:
   a. To display records of students who play a particular sports.
   b. To display records of the position holders.
   c. To display records of the winners of last 3 years.

Write the steps and the queries in the space given below:

Teacher's note

Bring some forms and reports to the class and let the students observe them before learning about forms and reports in Access.

Concepts learnt

1. A query is a statement of question about the data stored in the tables or it can be a request to perform an action on the data.
2. There are two types of queries—Select query and Action query.
3. Select query finds records in the database that match the criteria specified and displays those records in a datasheet, whereas the action query finds records in the database that match the criteria specified and perform an action on them.
4. Queries can be created using Query Wizard or manually using Query Design.
5. We can summarise the data using aggregate functions in queries. Some common aggregate functions are Sum, Average, Count, Minimum, Maximum, Standard deviation and Variance.
6. A form is an Access database object on which the controls are placed for entering, displaying, and editing data in fields.
7. Forms can be created using Form Wizard or manually using Form Design.
8. Reports give the ability to present different elements of the database in an easy-to-read and printable format.
9. Reports can also be created using Report Wizard or manually using Report button.
10. Reports can be previewed and make necessary changes using print preview options before printing the reports.

Exercise

A Fill in the blanks.

1. A ________________ (query/form) is a request to perform an action on the data.
2. ________________ (Show check box/Hide check box) present in the query Design window indicates whether the field is to be displayed in query result or not.
3. ________________ (Average/Sum) is an aggregate function that calculates the total of the values in a field.
4. An input screen designed to make viewing and entering data easier is ________________ (forms/reports).
5. ______________ (Forms/Reports) are created from both tables and queries in MS Access.

B Write T for True or F for False.

1. The query that finds records in the database that match the criteria specified and displays those records in a datasheet is an action query. ☐
2. Update query adds records from one table to the end of another table. ☐
3. We can change the appearance of the form by applying a different theme available in the Design tab. ☐
4. Page footer section prints once at the bottom of every printed page. ☐
5. Report Wizard cannot create groups. ☐

C Choose the correct option.

1. Which among the following is the type of query that can be created using Query Wizard?
   (a) Simple (b) Crosstab
   (c) Find duplicates (d) All the above
2. Which of the following rows in the Design grid helps to set up a condition in a query?
   (a) Field (b) Sort
   (c) Criteria (d) Show

3. Which of the following is NOT an aggregate function that helps to calculate in a query?
   (a) Average (b) Addition
   (c) Count (d) Maximum
4. Which of the following views is used to create and modify the structure of a form?
   (a) Control (b) Datasheet
   (c) Normal (d) Form Design
5. Which of the following statements is not true?
   (a) Queries can include calculated fields that do not exist in table.
   (b) Queries can be used to retrieve data from tables and calculate.
   (c) Queries can be printed in a well-formatted manner and presented as the information.
   (d) Reports and forms are similar but forms are used to display on the screen only but reports are used to print.

D Answer these following questions briefly.

1. What are the different types of queries? Illustrate them with an example.
2. Explain the steps to create a simple query using Query Wizard.
3. Describe the different types of action queries.
4. Explain the steps to create a form using Form Wizard.
5. Distinguish between forms and reports.

E Application-based questions.

1. Saurav has created an EMPLOYEE database in which EMPLOYEE DETAILS and EMPLOYEE ATTENDANCE are the two tables. He wants to display the details of the employees who were absent on a particular day. Explain the steps that Saurav needs to follow to perform this task.
2. Ram is a course facilitator in a university. He has created a database in which the following two tables are included: STUDENT table with fields, Student ID, Student name, Course Enrolled; COURSE table with the fields, Course ID, Course title, Course Fee. Write the steps to display the details of the students enrolled for a course.
3. In the above database, write the steps to find out the total fee collected from all students.
4. Radha is working as the school admin. She has designed a form to collect the details of the new admissions. She wants to add the background image, logo,

change the appearance of the form by changing the font style and colour, Guide Radha to perform this task.

5. Bhavya has prepared a report in MS Access and did the required formatting and made it ready to print. She wants to send it to her manager for approval before proceeding for printing. Help her to perform this task.

Computer is my mentor!

Create sales and customers database.

- Create SALESEMPLOYEE table with the fields: Sales Emp ID (Primary Key), Name, Phone number. Enter at least 5 records.
- Create CUSTOMER table with the fields: Cust ID (Primary Key), Cust Name, Cust City, Cust Phone number, Sales ID(Foreign key same as Sales Emp ID of SALESEMPLOYEE table), Order Value. Enter at least 5 records.
- Create the relationship between the above two tables making Sales Emp ID as foreign key in CUSTOMER table.
- Create forms using Form Wizard for each of the above tables and enter 5 more records into each table using the forms.
- Create queries to do the following:
  → To display sales in a particular city.
  → To display customers related to a particular sales person.
  → To display the total order value of a particular sales person.
- Create a report using Report Wizard which is ready to print.

3 Sorting and Filtering in MS Access 2013

Learning log

- Sort data in tables
- Filter data in tables and forms

Introduction

Observe the tables 3.1 and 3.2 and answer the questions that follow.

Copy Of Student List

ID	First Name	Date of Birtt	Contact Num	City	Locality	Pincode	Fee
1	Aruna	1/16/2009	(809) 572-4288	Bangalore	Ramnagar	560005	$24,000.00
2	Lakshmi	3/4/2012	(912) 546-8213	Hyderabad	Sultanpet	500012	$18,000.00
3	Nachiketh	1/16/2015	(961) 134-9651	Mysore	Hebbal	570006	$12,000.00
4	Tejas	4/7/2015	(987) 531-2641	Mysore	Hootagalli	570018	$18,000.00
5	Shashank	4/1/2008	(947) 861-3235	Hyderabad	Jubilhills	500022	$30,000.00
6	Jagadeesh	10/25/1985	(987) 451-3621	Bangalore	Kodihalli	560015	$21,600.00
7	Nithyashree	6/12/1990	(964) 572-1583	Bangalore	Jayanagar	560030	$22,000.00
8	Seema	5/12/1989	(945) 872-1635	Hyderabad	Amerpet	500002	$12,500.00
9	Sudhir	6/12/1986	(974) 581-3256	Mysore	Vijayanagar	570030	$30,000.00
10	Vijay	6/28/1992	(978) 458-1236	Bangalore	Indiranagar	560008	$15,000.00
11	Dakshayani	3/15/1979	(987) 456-1232	Mysore	Kuvempunagar	570017	$26,000.00
12	Akhila	5/20/1982	(974) 512-8325	Hyderabad	Malakpet	500016	$17,000.00
13	Srinivas	4/25/1995	(951) 347-8621	Bangalore	Peenya	560025	$35,000.00
14	Raghu	3/11/1985	(947) 513-2587	Hyderabad	Kachiguda	500030	$12,000.00
15	Narayan	3/12/1989	(915) 473-2681	Bangalore	Chikpet	560017	$15,000.00

Table. 3.1: Student List

Copy Of Student List

ID	First Name	Date of Birtt	Contact Num	City	Locality	Pincode	Fee
15	Narayan	3/12/1989	(915) 473-2681	Bangalore	Chikpet	560017	$15,000.00
10	Vijay	6/28/1992	(978) 458-1236	Bangalore	Indiranagar	560008	$15,000.00
7	Nithyashree	6/12/1990	(964) 572-1583	Bangalore	Jayanagar	560030	$22,000.00
6	Jagadeesh	10/25/1985	(987) 451-3621	Bangalore	Kodihalli	560015	$21,600.00
13	Srinivas	4/25/1995	(951) 347-8621	Bangalore	Peenya	560025	$35,000.00
1	Aruna	1/16/2009	(809) 572-4288	Bangalore	Ramnagar	560005	$24,000.00
8	Seema	5/12/1989	(945) 872-1635	Hyderabad	Amerpet	500002	$12,500.00
5	Shashank	4/1/2008	(947) 861-3235	Hyderabad	Jubilhills	500022	$30,000.00
14	Raghu	3/11/1985	(947) 513-2587	Hyderabad	Kachiguda	500030	$12,000.00
12	Akhila	5/20/1982	(974) 512-8325	Hyderabad	Malakpet	500016	$17,000.00
2	Lakshmi	3/4/2012	(912) 546-8213	Hyderabad	Sultanpet	500012	$18,000.00
3	Nachiketh	1/16/2015	(961) 134-9651	Mysore	Hebbal	570006	$12,000.00
4	Tejas	4/7/2015	(987) 531-2641	Mysore	Hootagalli	570018	$18,000.00
11	Dakshayani	3/15/1979	(987) 456-1232	Mysore	Kuvempunagar	570017	$26,000.00
9	Sudhir	6/12/1986	(974) 581-3256	Mysore	Vijayanagar	570030	$30,000.00

Table. 3.2: Organized Student List

- How many students are from Bangalore?
- How many students are from Hyderabad?

Using which of the two tables is it easier to assimilate the data?

From Table 3.2, we can understand and analyze the data easily as compared to Table 3.1. The data in Table 3.2 is Sorted by City. Generally, the database contains some thousands of records and multiple tables. It will be useful only when we are able to see the required information in the required format at any point of time. As the database size increases, it would be very complicated to view and analyze the required data.

Access has a variety of tools that help us in achieving this goal. **Sorting** and **Filtering** are such tools that help us to organize and view the required data. In this chapter, we will learn about them in detail.

Sorting

Sorting the data means arranging the data in a logical order. When we sort the records, we arrange them in a logical order with similar data grouped together. The sorted data helps to read and understand the information easily as compared to unsorted data. Sorting can be done either in ascending order or descending order.

Ascending order (Moving up)		Descending order (Moving down)	
Text	Numbers	Text	Numbers
A to Z	Smallest to greatest	Z to A	Greatest to smallest

Sorting in tables

By default, Access sorts the records by ID Number. We can apply sorts to the other fields as well according to our requirement.

Sorting text

Sorting by one field

- Select a field you want to sort by. Let us sort the data sheet in Table 3.3 by 'First Name'.

ID	First Name	Roll N	Date of Birt	City	Locality	Pincode	Fee
1	Aruna	001	1/16/2009	Bangalore	RamNagar	560005	$24,000.00
2	Lakshmi	0002	3/4/2012	Hyderabad	Sultanpet	500012	$18,000.00
3	Nachiketh	00003	1/16/2015	Mysore	Hebbal	570006	$12,000.00
4	Tejas	00004	4/7/2015	Mysore	Hootagalli	570018	$18,000.00
5	Shashank	005	4/1/2008	Hyderabad	Jubilhills	500022	$30,000.00
6	Jagadeesh	000007	10/25/1985	Bangalore	Kodihalli	560015	$21,600.00
7	Nithyashree	0006	6/12/1990	Bangalore	Jayanagar	560030	$22,000.00
8	Seema	0008	5/12/1989	Hyderabad	Amerpet	500002	$12,500.00
9	Sudhir	00009	6/12/1986	Mysore	Vijayanagar	570030	$30,000.00
10	Vijay	0010	6/28/1992	Bangalore	Indiranagar	560008	$15,000.00
11	Dakshayani	11	3/15/1979	Mysore	Kuvempuna	570017	$26,000.00
12	Akhila	0012	5/20/1982	Hyderbad	Malakpet	500016	$17,000.00
13	Srinivas	00013	4/25/1995	Bangalore	Peenya	560025	$35,000.00
14	Raghu	014	3/11/1985	Hyderabad	Kachiguda	500030	$12,000.00
15	Narayan	15	3/12/1989	Bangalore	Chikpet	560017	$15,000.00

Table 3.3: Sorting datasheet

- Click on HOME tab → Sort & Filter group → Ascending or Descending command as shown in Fig. 3.1.

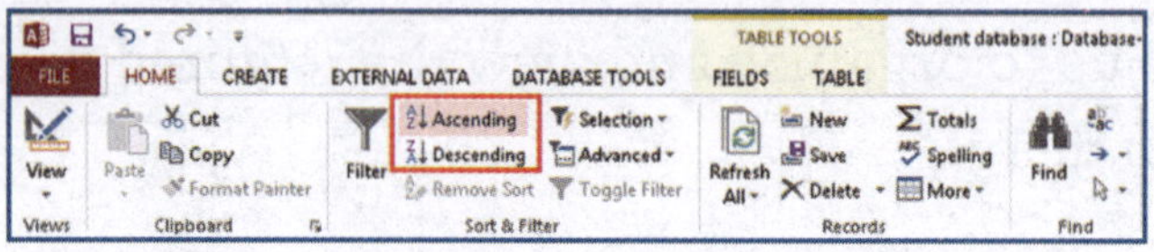

Fig. 3.1: Sort & Filter: Sort options

- Observe that the table is sorted by the selected field. The small upward arrow (↑) near the field indicates that the records are sorted in ascending order as shown in Table 3.4.

ID	First Name	Roll N	Date of Birt	City	Locality	Pincode	Fee
12	Akhila	0012	5/20/1982	Hyderbad	Malakpet	500016	$17,000.00
1	Aruna	001	1/16/2009	Bangalore	RamNagar	560005	$24,000.00
11	Dakshayani	11	3/15/1979	Mysore	Kuvempuna	570017	$26,000.00
6	Jagadeesh	000007	10/25/1985	Bangalore	Kodihalli	560015	$21,600.00
2	Lakshmi	0002	3/4/2012	Hyderabad	Sultanpet	500012	$18,000.00
3	Nachiketh	00003	1/16/2015	Mysore	Hebbal	570006	$12,000.00
15	Narayan	15	3/12/1989	Bangalore	Chikpet	560017	$15,000.00
7	Nithyashree	0006	6/12/1990	Bangalore	Jayanagar	560030	$22,000.00
14	Raghu	014	3/11/1985	Hyderabad	Kachiguda	500030	$12,000.00
8	Seema	0008	5/12/1989	Hyderabad	Amerpet	500002	$12,500.00
5	Shashank	005	4/1/2008	Hyderabad	Jubilhills	500022	$30,000.00
13	Srinivas	00013	4/25/1995	Bangalore	Peenya	560025	$35,000.00
9	Sudhir	00009	6/12/1986	Mysore	Vijayanagar	570030	$30,000.00
4	Tejas	00004	4/7/2015	Mysore	Hootagalli	570018	$18,000.00
10	Vijay	0010	6/28/1992	Bangalore	Indiranagar	560008	$15,000.00

Table 3.4: Sorted Student List

- Save the sorted data by clicking on the Save command in the Quick Access toolbar as in Fig. 3.2.

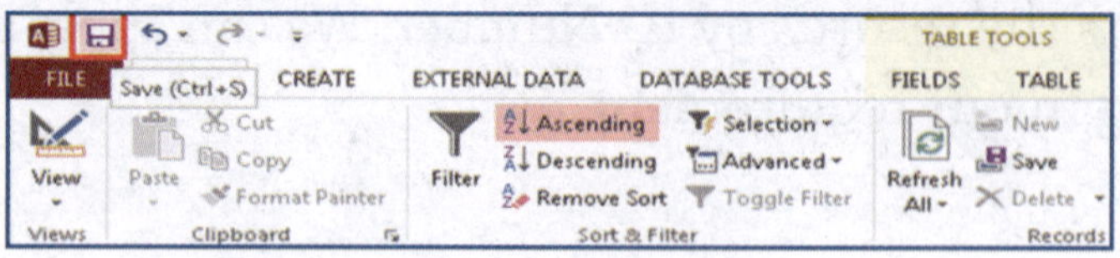

Fig. 3.2: Saving the sorted data

- To clear the sort, click on HOME tab → Sort & Filter group → Remove Sort command as in Fig. 3.3.

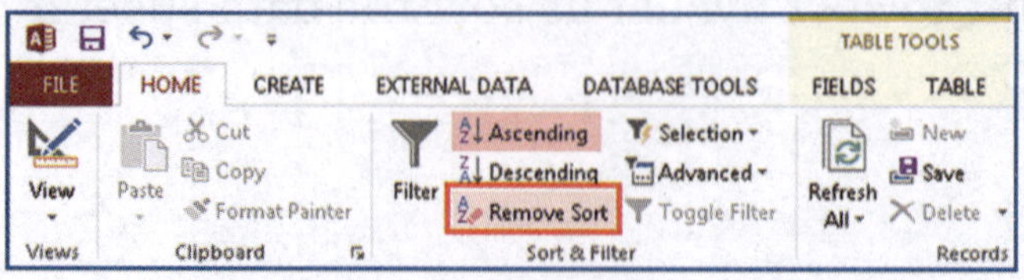

Fig. 3.3: Sort & Filter: Remove Sort

Sorting by more than one field

We can sort the information in a table based on the values in one or more fields. While sorting by more than one field, we must place the fields to be sorted adjacent to each, in the order in which we want to sort them because Access always sorts sequentially from left to right. For example, if we want to sort the students first by their first name and then by the last name, keep those fields adjacent to each other and in the same order in the table.

Let us sort the records first by City field and then by the Locality.

- Select a City field. Hold the Shift Key and select the Locality field as in Table 3.5.

Copy Of Student List

ID	First Name	Roll N	Date of Birth	City	Locality	Pincode	Fee
1	Aruna	001	1/16/2009	Bangalore	RamNagar	560005	$24,000.00
2	Lakshmi	0002	3/4/2012	Hyderabad	Sultanpet	500012	$18,000.00
3	Nachiketh	00003	1/16/2015	Mysore	Hebbal	570006	$12,000.00
4	Tejas	00004	4/7/2015	Mysore	Hootagalli	570018	$18,000.00
5	Shashank	005	4/1/2008	Hyderabad	Jublihills	500022	$30,000.00
6	Jagadeesh	000007	10/25/1985	Bangalore	Kodihalli	560015	$21,600.00
7	Nithyashree	0006	6/12/1990	Bangalore	Jayanagar	560030	$22,000.00
8	Seema	0008	5/12/1989	Hyderabad	Amerpet	500002	$12,500.00
9	Sudhir	00009	6/12/1986	Mysore	Vijayanagar	570030	$30,000.00
10	Vijay	0010	6/28/1992	Bangalore	Indiranagar	560008	$15,000.00
11	Dakshayani	11	3/15/1979	Mysore	Kuvempuna	570017	$26,000.00
12	Akhila	0012	5/20/1982	Hyderbad	Malakpet	500016	$17,000.00
13	Srinivas	00013	4/25/1995	Bangalore	Peenya	560025	$35,000.00
14	Raghu	014	3/11/1985	Hyderabad	Kachiguda	500030	$12,000.00
15	Narayan	15	3/12/1989	Bangalore	Chikpet	560017	$15,000.00

Table. 3.5: Sorting on multiple fields

- Click on HOME tab → Sort & Filter group → Ascending or Descending command as in Fig. 3.4.

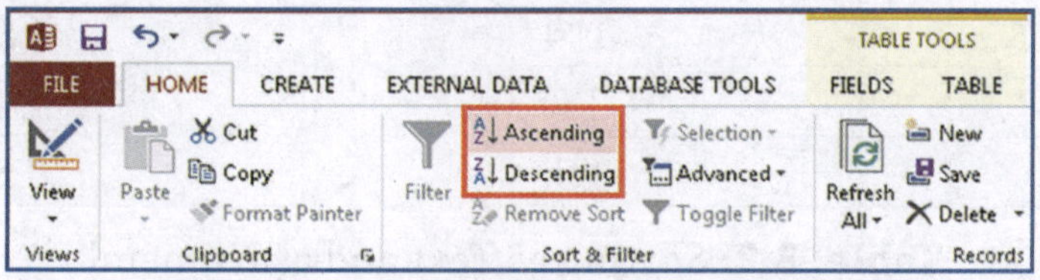

Fig. 3.4: Ascending or Descending Sort

- Observe that the Table 3.6 is sorted by the city and within each city they are sorted locality wise.

Copy Of Student List

ID	First Name	Roll N	Date of Birth	City	Locality	Pincode	Fee
15	Narayan	15	3/12/1989	Bangalore	Chikpet	560017	$15,000.00
10	Vijay	0010	6/28/1992	Bangalore	Indiranagar	560008	$15,000.00
7	Nithyashree	0006	6/12/1990	Bangalore	Jayanagar	560030	$22,000.00
6	Jagadeesh	000007	10/25/1985	Bangalore	Kodihalli	560015	$21,600.00
13	Srinivas	00013	4/25/1995	Bangalore	Peenya	560025	$35,000.00
1	Aruna	001	1/16/2009	Bangalore	RamNagar	560005	$24,000.00
8	Seema	0008	5/12/1989	Hyderabad	Amerpet	500002	$12,500.00
5	Shashank	005	4/1/2008	Hyderabad	Jublihills	500022	$30,000.00
14	Raghu	014	3/11/1985	Hyderabad	Kachiguda	500030	$12,000.00
12	Akhila	0012	5/20/1982	Hyderabad	Malakpet	500016	$17,000.00
2	Lakshmi	0002	3/4/2012	Hyderabad	Sultanpet	500012	$18,000.00
3	Nachiketh	00003	1/16/2015	Mysore	Hebbal	570006	$12,000.00
4	Tejas	00004	4/7/2015	Mysore	Hootagalli	570018	$18,000.00
11	Dakshayani	11	3/15/1979	Mysore	Kuvempunagar	570017	$26,000.00
9	Sudhir	00009	6/12/1986	Mysore	Vijayanagar	570030	$30,000.00

Table. 3.6: Sorted City wise and Locality wise

- Save the sort by clicking on the Save command in the Quick Access toolbar.

Sorting numerals

Sometimes, we may not get the expected results while sorting the fields containing numerals. Access sorts them differently when the field type is given as Short text and as Numeral. While sorting as text, it sorts by each character whereas while sorting as numeral, it considers the whole number as one value. Consider the following example (Table 3.7) and observe the difference in sorting.

Roll No.	Sorted as Text	Sorted as Numeral
001	000007	1
0002	00003	2
00003	00004	3
00004	00009	4
005	00013	5
000007	0002	7
0006	0006	6
0008	0008	8
00009	001	9
0010	0010	10
11	0012	11
0012	005	12
00013	014	13
014	11	14
15	15	15

Table. 3.7: Sorting as Text and as Numeral

- Sorting students table by the 'Pin code' (Table 3.8):

Copy Of Student List

ID	First Name	Roll N	Date of I	City	Locality	Pincode	Fee
8	Seema	0008	5/12/1989	Hyderabad	Amerpet	500002	$12,500.00
2	Lakshmi	0002	3/4/2012	Hyderabad	Sultanpet	500012	$18,000.00
12	Akhila	0012	5/20/1982	Hyderbad	Malakpet	500016	$17,000.00
5	Shashank	005	4/1/2008	Hyderabad	Jublihills	500022	$30,000.00
14	Raghu	014	3/11/1985	Hyderabad	Kachiguda	500030	$12,000.00
1	Aruna	001	1/16/2009	Bangalore	RamNagar	560005	$24,000.00
10	Vijay	0010	6/28/1992	Bangalore	Indiranagar	560008	$15,000.00
6	Jagadeesh	000007	10/25/1985	Bangalore	Kodihalli	560015	$21,600.00
15	Narayan	15	3/12/1989	Bangalore	Chikpet	560017	$15,000.00
13	Srinivas	00013	4/25/1995	Bangalore	Peenya	560025	$35,000.00
7	Nithyashree	0006	6/12/1990	Bangalore	Jayanagar	560030	$22,000.00
3	Nachiketh	00003	1/16/2015	Mysore	Hebbal	570006	$12,000.00
11	Dakshayani	11	3/15/1979	Mysore	Kuvempuna	570017	$26,000.00
4	Tejas	00004	4/7/2015	Mysore	Hootagalli	570018	$18,000.00
9	Sudhir	00009	6/12/1986	Mysore	Vijayanagar	570030	$30,000.00

Table. 3.8: Sorting by Pin code

- Sorting students table by the 'Date of Birth' (Table 3.9):

Copy Of Student List

ID	First Name	Roll N	Date of Birth	City	Locality	Pincode	Fee
11	Dakshayani	11	3/15/1979	Mysore	Kuvempuna	570017	$26,000.00
12	Akhila	0012	5/20/1982	Hyderbad	Malakpet	500016	$17,000.00
14	Raghu	014	3/11/1985	Hyderabad	Kachiguda	500030	$12,000.00
6	Jagadeesh	000007	10/25/1985	Bangalore	Kodihalli	560015	$21,600.00
9	Sudhir	00009	6/12/1986	Mysore	Vijayanagar	570030	$30,000.00
15	Narayan	15	3/12/1989	Bangalore	Chikpet	560017	$15,000.00
8	Seema	0008	5/12/1989	Hyderabad	Amerpet	500002	$12,500.00
7	Nithyashree	0006	6/12/1990	Bangalore	Jayanagar	560030	$22,000.00
10	Vijay	0010	6/28/1992	Bangalore	Indiranagar	560008	$15,000.00
13	Srinivas	00013	4/25/1995	Bangalore	Peenya	560025	$35,000.00
5	Shashank	005	4/1/2008	Hyderabad	Jublihills	500022	$30,000.00
1	Aruna	001	1/16/2009	Bangalore	RamNagar	560005	$24,000.00
2	Lakshmi	0002	3/4/2012	Hyderabad	Sultanpet	500012	$18,000.00
3	Nachiketh	00003	1/16/2015	Mysore	Hebbal	570006	$12,000.00
4	Tejas	00004	4/7/2015	Mysore	Hootagalli	570018	$18,000.00

Table. 3.9: Sorting by Date of Birth

Sorting in other access objects like forms and reports can be done in the similar manner.

Hands-on practice

1. Open Student's database.
2. Create a student table to store the details of all the students of your class. Include the fields: Name, Gender, Location, Phone number, Pin code, Height, Weight, Household expenditure, Mother's occupation, etc.
3. Create at least 15 records.
4. Sort the table by:
   a. Name in ascending order.
   b. Household expenditure in descending order.
   c. Height in ascending order and weight in descending order. (Sorting by more than one field)

Filtering

Filtering helps us to view only the data that is required at that particular moment by hiding the unwanted data. When we create a filter, we set the criteria for data. Only the records that

Word web

sorting: arranging the data in a logical order

satisfy the criteria gets displayed and the other records are temporarily hidden. For locating only the records containing specific information, filtering is more effective than sorting. For example, if we want to see the students who belong to a particular city, who are paying a fee of more than ₹20,000, whose year of birth is greater than 1990, etc.

Creating filters in tables

(a) Simple filters

- Click the drop-down arrow of the field that you want to filter. Let us filter the records by City as in Fig. 3.5.

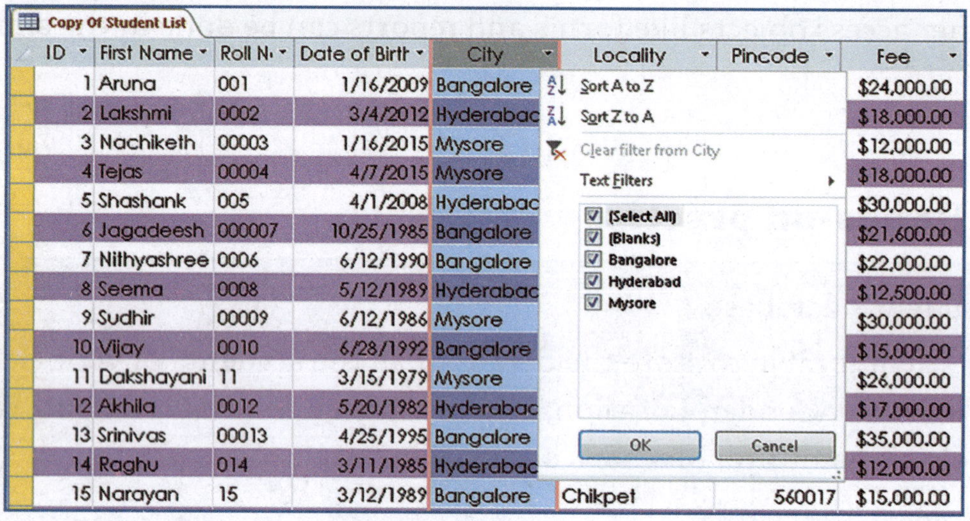

ID	First Name	Roll N	Date of Birtl	City	Locality	Pincode	Fee
1	Aruna	001	1/16/2009	Bangalore			$24,000.00
2	Lakshmi	0002	3/4/2012	Hyderabac			$18,000.00
3	Nachiketh	00003	1/16/2015	Mysore			$12,000.00
4	Tejas	00004	4/7/2015	Mysore			$18,000.00
5	Shashank	005	4/1/2008	Hyderabac			$30,000.00
6	Jagadeesh	000007	10/25/1985	Bangalore			$21,600.00
7	Nithyashree	0006	6/12/1990	Bangalore			$22,000.00
8	Seema	0008	5/12/1989	Hyderabac			$12,500.00
9	Sudhir	00009	6/12/1986	Mysore			$30,000.00
10	Vijay	0010	6/28/1992	Bangalore			$15,000.00
11	Dakshayani	11	3/15/1979	Mysore			$26,000.00
12	Akhila	0012	5/20/1982	Hyderabac			$17,000.00
13	Srinivas	00013	4/25/1995	Bangalore			$35,000.00
14	Raghu	014	3/11/1985	Hyderabac			$12,000.00
15	Narayan	15	3/12/1989	Bangalore	Chikpet	560017	$15,000.00

Fig. 3.5: Simple Filters

- By default, all the options are checked. Uncheck the Select All option and check the city that you want to filter, say 'Hyderabad'. Click OK as in Fig. 3.6.

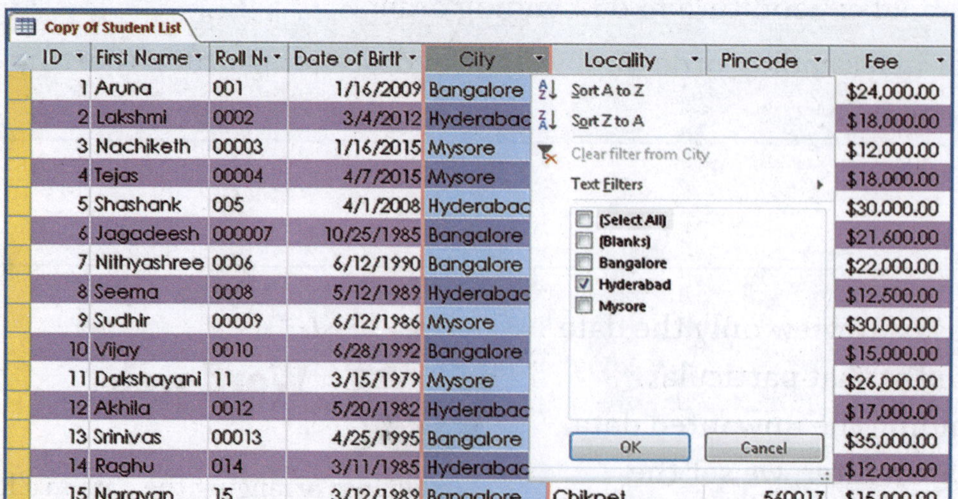

ID	First Name	Roll N	Date of Birtl	City	Locality	Pincode	Fee
1	Aruna	001	1/16/2009	Bangalore			$24,000.00
2	Lakshmi	0002	3/4/2012	Hyderabac			$18,000.00
3	Nachiketh	00003	1/16/2015	Mysore			$12,000.00
4	Tejas	00004	4/7/2015	Mysore			$18,000.00
5	Shashank	005	4/1/2008	Hyderabac			$30,000.00
6	Jagadeesh	000007	10/25/1985	Bangalore			$21,600.00
7	Nithyashree	0006	6/12/1990	Bangalore			$22,000.00
8	Seema	0008	5/12/1989	Hyderabac			$12,500.00
9	Sudhir	00009	6/12/1986	Mysore			$30,000.00
10	Vijay	0010	6/28/1992	Bangalore			$15,000.00
11	Dakshayani	11	3/15/1979	Mysore			$26,000.00
12	Akhila	0012	5/20/1982	Hyderabac			$17,000.00
13	Srinivas	00013	4/25/1995	Bangalore			$35,000.00
14	Raghu	014	3/11/1985	Hyderabac			$12,000.00
15	Narayan	15	3/12/1989	Bangalore	Chikpet	560017	$15,000.00

Fig. 3.6: Text Filter

- Observe that only the students belonging to Hyderabad are displayed. Observe the small funnel icon (⊠) near the field City which indicates that the records are filtered by that field as in Table 3.10.

Copy Of Student List

ID	First Name	Roll N	Date of Birth	City	Locality	Pincode	Fee
8	Seema	0008	5/12/1989	Hyderabad	Amerpet	500002	$12,500.00
12	Akhila	0012	5/20/1982	Hyderabad	Malakpet	500016	$17,000.00
14	Raghu	014	3/11/1985	Hyderabad	Kachiguda	500030	$12,000.00
2	Lakshmi	0002	3/4/2012	Hyderabad	Sultanpet	500012	$18,000.00
5	Shashank	005	4/1/2008	Hyderabad	Jublihills	500022	$30,000.00

Table. 3.10: Filtered Table

- We can apply and remove the filter using the Toggle Filter command in the Sort & Filter group of HOME tab as shown in Fig. 3.7.

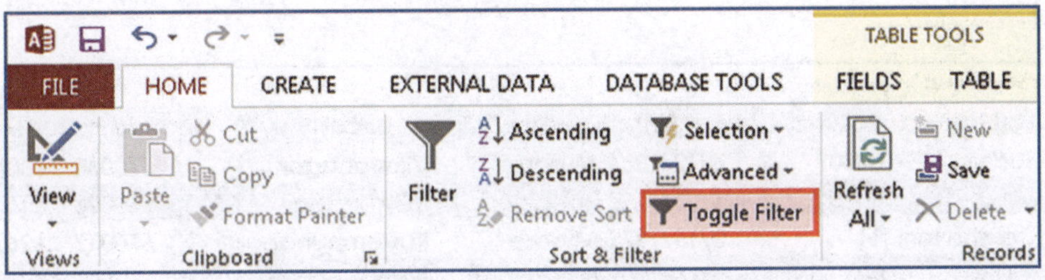

Fig. 3.7: Sort & Filter: Toggle Filter

- Observe that the Toggle Filter changes to Apply Filter when the filter is not applied and Remove Filter when the filter is applied.

(b) Text Filters using selection

We can select a term and filter the records that contain the selected term or do not contain it and so on.

- Select the term on which the filter needs to be created. Let us create a filter that displays the records whose Locality ends with 'Nagar' as in Table 3.11.

Copy Of Student List

ID	First Name	Roll N	Date of Birth	City	Locality	Pincode	Fee
1	Aruna	001	1/16/2009	Bangalore	Ramnagar	560005	$24,000.00
2	Lakshmi	0002	3/4/2012	Hyderabad	Sultanpet	500012	$18,000.00
3	Nachiketh	00003	1/16/2015	Mysore	Hebbal	570006	$12,000.00
4	Tejas	00004	4/7/2015	Mysore	Hootagalli	570018	$18,000.00
5	Shashank	005	4/1/2008	Hyderabad	Jublihills	500022	$30,000.00
6	Jagadeesh	000007	10/25/1985	Bangalore	Kodihalli	560015	$21,600.00
7	Nithyashree	0006	6/12/1990	Bangalore	Jayanagar	560030	$22,000.00
8	Seema	0008	5/12/1989	Hyderabad	Amerpet	500002	$12,500.00
9	Sudhir	00009	6/12/1986	Mysore	Vijayanagar	570030	$30,000.00
10	Vijay	0010	6/28/1992	Bangalore	Indiranagar	560008	$15,000.00
11	Dakshayani	11	3/15/1979	Mysore	Kuvempunagar	570017	$26,000.00
12	Akhila	0012	5/20/1982	Hyderabad	Malakpet	500016	$17,000.00
13	Srinivas	00013	4/25/1995	Bangalore	Peenya	560025	$35,000.00
14	Raghu	014	3/11/1985	Hyderabad	Kachiguda	500030	$12,000.00
15	Narayan	15	3/12/1989	Bangalore	Chikpet	560017	$15,000.00

Table. 3.11: Selecting the text for filter

- Click on HOME tab → Sort & Filter group → Selection command. Select Ends With "nagar" as shown in Fig. 3.8.

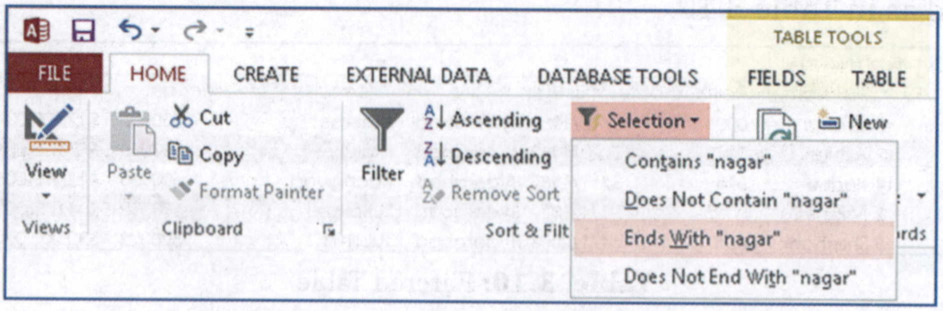

Fig. 3.8: Sort & Filter: Filter by Selection

- Observe that only the records whose locality name ends with 'nagar' are displayed (Table 3.12).

Copy Of Student List

ID	First Name	Roll N	Date of Birth	City	Locality	Pincode	Fee
9	Sudhir	00009	6/12/1986	Mysore	Vijayanagar	570030	$30,000.00
10	Vijay	0010	6/28/1992	Bangalore	Indiranagar	560008	$15,000.00
11	Dakshayani	11	3/15/1979	Mysore	Kuvempunagar	570017	$26,000.00
1	Aruna	001	1/16/2009	Bangalore	Ramnagar	560005	$24,000.00
7	Nithyashree	0006	6/12/1990	Bangalore	Jayanagar	560030	$22,000.00

Table. 3.12: Filtered Table

(c) *Text Filters using search term*

This is like creating the filters using selection. There are some more options in this filter.

- Click the drop-down arrow of the field in which you want to create the filter and again click on small arrow near Text Filters as in Fig. 3.9.

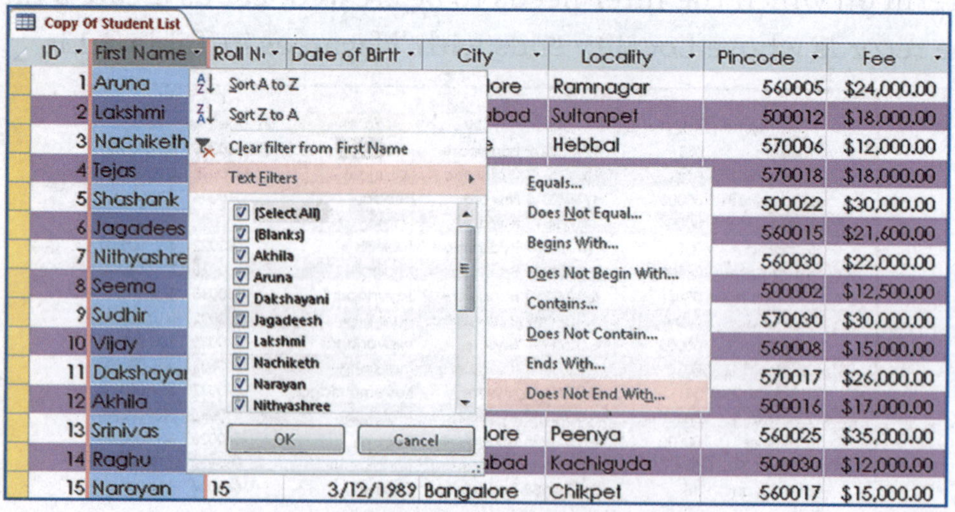

Fig. 3.9: Text Filters More Options

- The options include Equals, Does Not Equal, Begins With, Does Not Begin With, Contains, Does Not Contain, Ends With, Does Not End With. Let us filter the records whose First Name does not end with the letter 'a'. Click on Does Not End With.
- The Custom Filter dialog box as in Fig. 3.10 opens up. Enter 'a' in the text box and click OK.

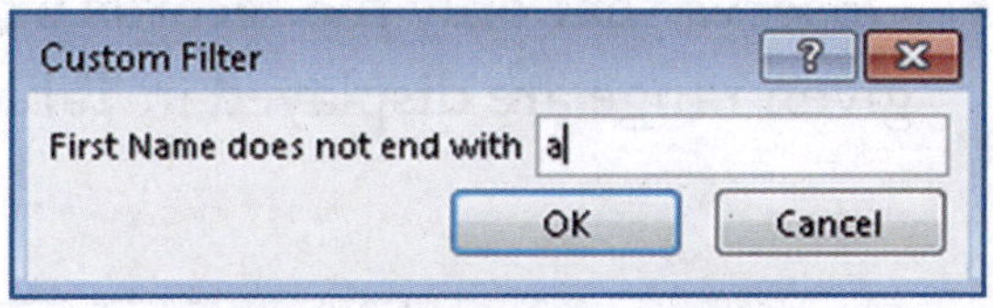

Fig. 3.10: Custom Filter

- Observe that the records whose first names ending with 'a' are not displayed in Table 3.13.

Copy Of Student List

ID	First Name	Date of Birth	Contact Num	City	Locality	Pincode	Fee
2	Lakshmi	3/4/2012	(912) 546-8213	Hyderabad	Sultanpet	500012	$18,000.00
3	Nachiketh	1/16/2015	(961) 134-9651	Mysore	Hebbal	570006	$12,000.00
4	Tejas	4/7/2015	(987) 531-2641	Mysore	Hootagalli	570018	$18,000.00
5	Shashank	4/1/2008	(947) 861-3235	Hyderabad	Jublihills	500022	$30,000.00
6	Jagadeesh	10/25/1985	(987) 451-3621	Bangalore	Kodihalli	560015	$21,600.00
7	Nithyashree	6/12/1990	(964) 572-1583	Bangalore	Jayanagar	560030	$22,000.00
9	Sudhir	6/12/1986	(974) 581-3256	Mysore	Vijayanagar	570030	$30,000.00
10	Vijay	6/28/1992	(978) 458-1236	Bangalore	Indiranagar	560008	$15,000.00
11	Dakshayani	3/15/1979	(987) 456-1232	Mysore	Kuvempunagar	570017	$26,000.00
13	Srinivas	4/25/1995	(951) 347-8621	Bangalore	Peenya	560025	$35,000.00
14	Raghu	3/11/1985	(947) 513-2587	Hyderabad	Kachiguda	500030	$12,000.00
15	Narayan	3/12/1989	(915) 473-2681	Bangalore	Chikpet	560017	$15,000.00

Table. 3.13: Result of Custom Filter

Similarly, we can create filters using any of the filtering options mentioned above.

(d) Number Filters

The filtering options are slightly different when we work with filtering fields that contain numerals or dates.

Let us create a filter using the field 'Fee' which contains numerals.

- Click the drop-down arrow of the field Fee. Observe that the label 'Text Filters' is changed to 'Number Filters'. Also, the filtering options are changed to Equals, Does Not Equal, Less Than, Greater Than and Between as in Fig. 3.11.

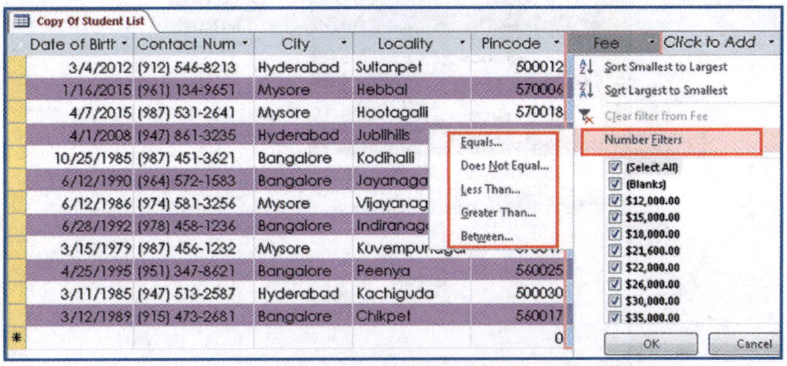

Fig. 3.11: Number Filters

- Select Between and enter the smallest and the largest values and click OK (Fig. 3.12).
- Observe that only the records whose fee is in the given range are displayed in Table 3.14.

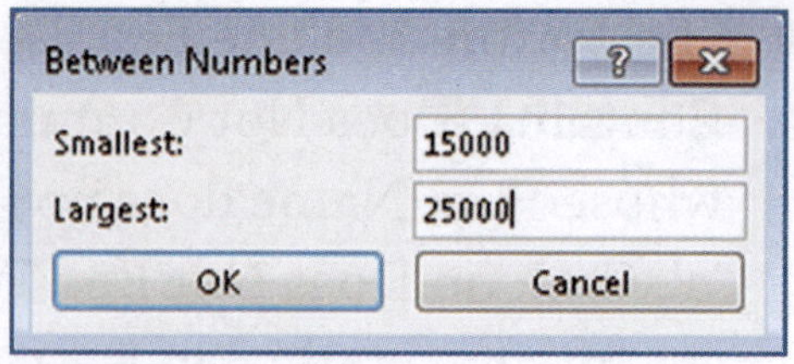

Fig. 3.12: Between Numbers

Copy Of Student List

Date of Birth	Contact Num	City	Locality	Pincode	Fee
3/4/2012	(912) 546-8213	Hyderabad	Sultanpet	500012	$18,000.00
4/7/2015	(987) 531-2641	Mysore	Hootagalli	570018	$18,000.00
10/25/1985	(987) 451-3621	Bangalore	Kodihalli	560015	$21,600.00
6/12/1990	(964) 572-1583	Bangalore	Jayanagar	560030	$22,000.00
6/28/1992	(978) 458-1236	Bangalore	Indiranagar	560008	$15,000.00
3/12/1989	(915) 473-2681	Bangalore	Chikpet	560017	$15,000.00

Table. 3.14: Result of Number Filter

Similarly, we can create filters using any of the filtering options mentioned above.

(e) Date filters

Let us now create a filter using the field 'Date of Birth' which contains dates.

- Click the drop-down arrow of the field Date of Birth. Observe that the label 'Text Filters' is changed to 'Date Filters'. Also, observe the filtering options in Fig 3.13.

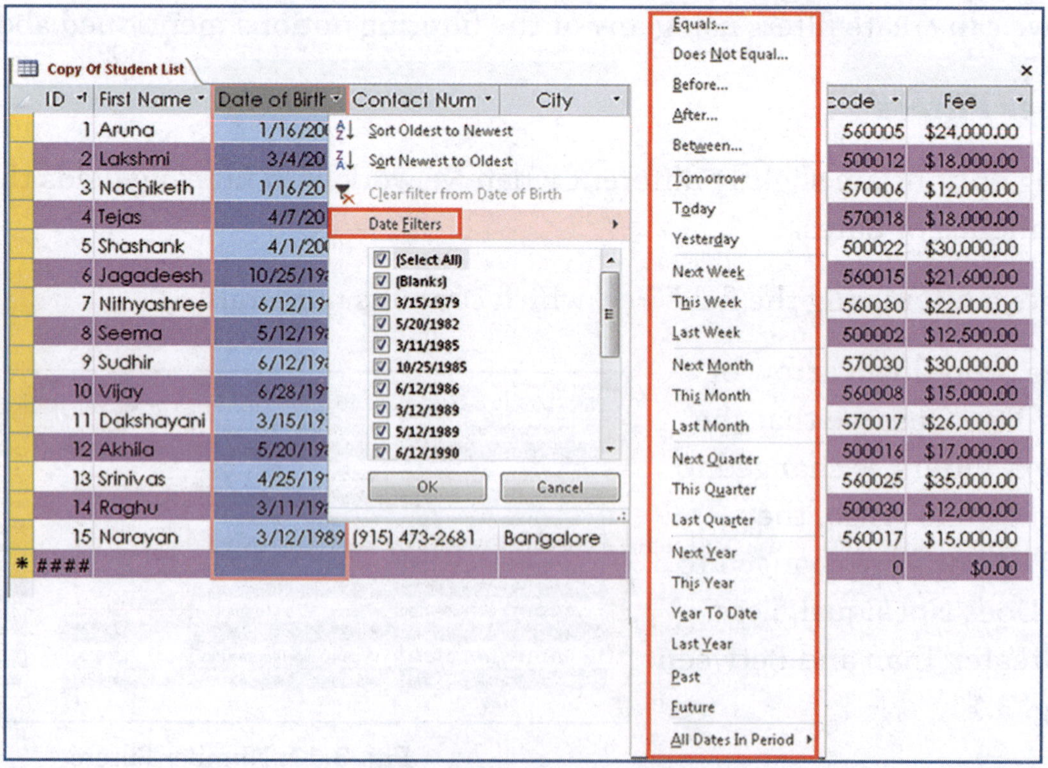

Fig. 3.13: Date Filters

- Select After and enter the date and click OK as in Fig. 3.14.

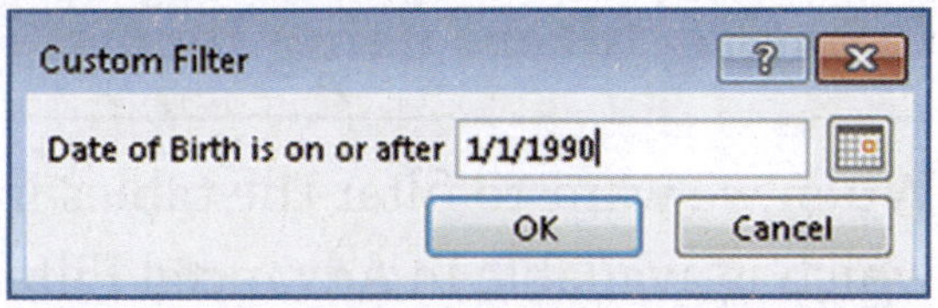

Fig. 3.14: Custom Filter: Date of Birth

- Observe that only the records whose date of birth is on or after 1990 are displayed in Table 3.15.

Copy Of Student List

ID	First Name	Date of Birth	Contact Num	City	Locality
1	Aruna	1/16/2009	(809) 572-4288	Bangalore	Ramnagar
2	Lakshmi	3/4/2012	(912) 546-8213	Hyderabad	Sultanpet
3	Nachiketh	1/16/2015	(961) 134-9651	Mysore	Hebbal
4	Tejas	4/7/2015	(987) 531-2641	Mysore	Hootagalli
5	Shashank	4/1/2008	(947) 861-3235	Hyderabad	Jublihills
7	Nithyashree	6/12/1990	(964) 572-1583	Bangalore	Jayanagar
10	Vijay	6/28/1992	(978) 458-1236	Bangalore	Indiranagar
13	Srinivas	4/25/1995	(951) 347-8621	Bangalore	Peenya

Table. 3.15: Result of Date Filter

Similarly, we can create filters using any of the filtering options mentioned above.

Hands-on practice

1. Open the student's database that is created in the previous practice time.
2. Open the student table containing the fields Name, Gender, Location, Phone number, Pin code, Height, Weight, Household expenditure and Mother's occupation.
3. Create filters to perform the following tasks:
   a. To display the records of only female students.
   b. To display the student's records which contain students who live in 'Location 1' or 'Location 2'. (Note: Location 1 and Location 2 are the location names entered by you).
   c. To display the records of students whose name contains the letter 'i'.
   d. To display the records of students whose mothers are homemakers.
   e. To display the records of students whose household expenditure is in a given range.

Creating filters using forms

When we want to filter the tables in several fields, we can use Filter by Form option which is available in Advanced Filter option (Fig. 3.15).

Let us create a filter on the student's table using the form.

- In the Navigation Pane, double-click and open the form.
- Click on Home Tab → Sort & Filter group → Advanced → Filter By Form.

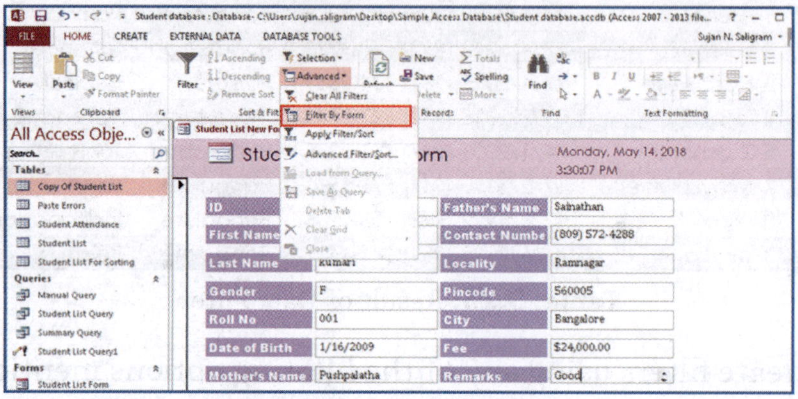

Fig. 3.15: Advanced Filter

- Click the textbox to the right of the First Name label, enter N*, and then press the Enter key as shown in Fig. 3.16.

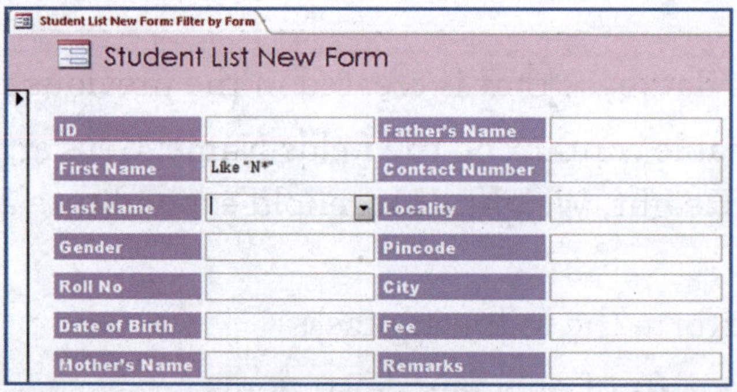

Fig. 3.16: Filter by Form

- Click on Sort & Filter group → Toggle Filter command to apply the filter as shown in Fig. 3.17.

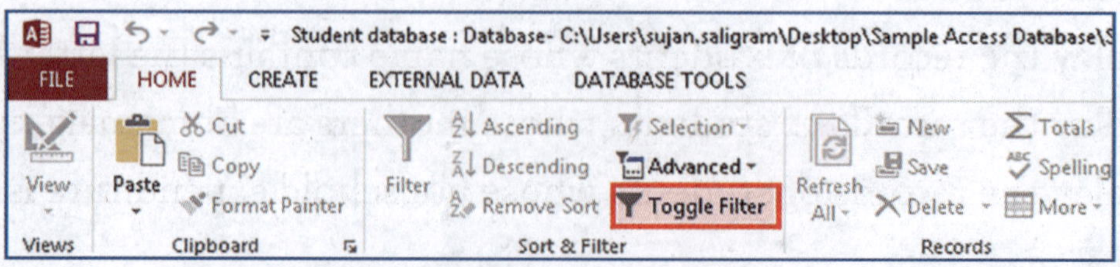

Fig. 3.17: Toggle Filter

- Observe that there are three records whose First Name start with the letter 'N' in Fig. 3.18.

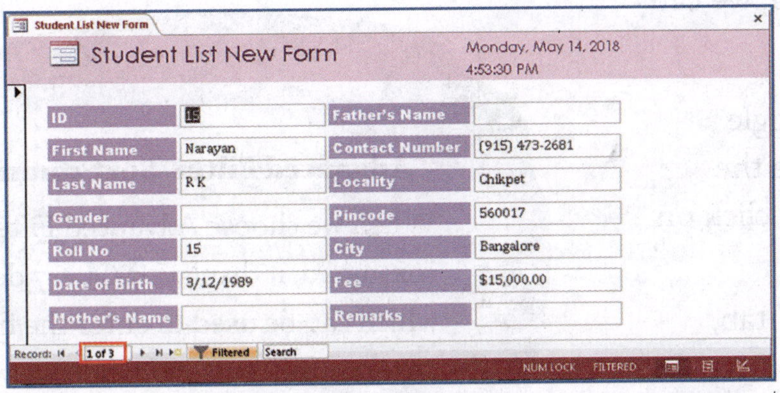

Fig. 3.18: Result Records

- We can enter more than one filtering criteria simultaneously. Let us apply one more criteria to the above filter. Click on Filter By Form again and in the textbox against the field City, select Bangalore from the drop-down box as in Fig. 3.19.

Word web

filtering: a set of criteria applied to the data to display a subset of the data

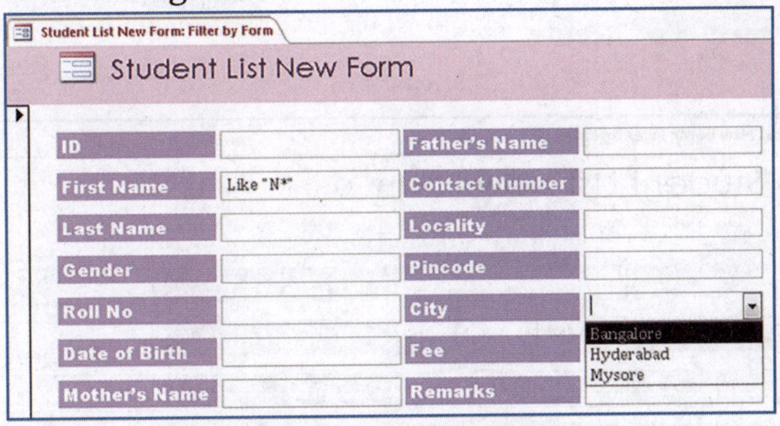

Fig. 3.19: Multiple Filters

- Apply the filter and observe that only 2 records that match both the criteria are displayed as shown in Fig. 3.20.

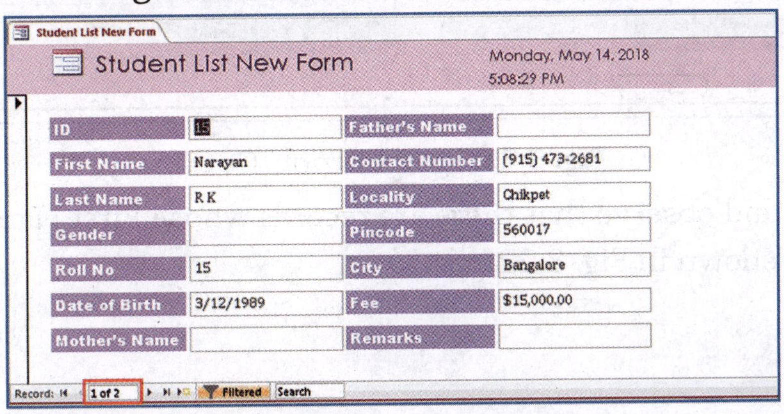

Fig. 3.20: Filtered Records

If we want to apply the alternating criteria, we can use 'Or' tab.

- Click on the Toggle Filter to remove the filter and a gain click on Filter By Form.
- In the 'Look for' tab, type N* against First Name label and press enter. Click on the Or tab and type S* against First Name label and press Enter as shown in Fig. 3.21.

You should know

Advanced Filter/Sort command

When we choose Advanced Filter/Sort command, it displays a Query designer which can be used to enter the filtering criteria. This is useful when we want to search for records that meet multiple criteria in a single table, or when the criteria involve complex expressions.

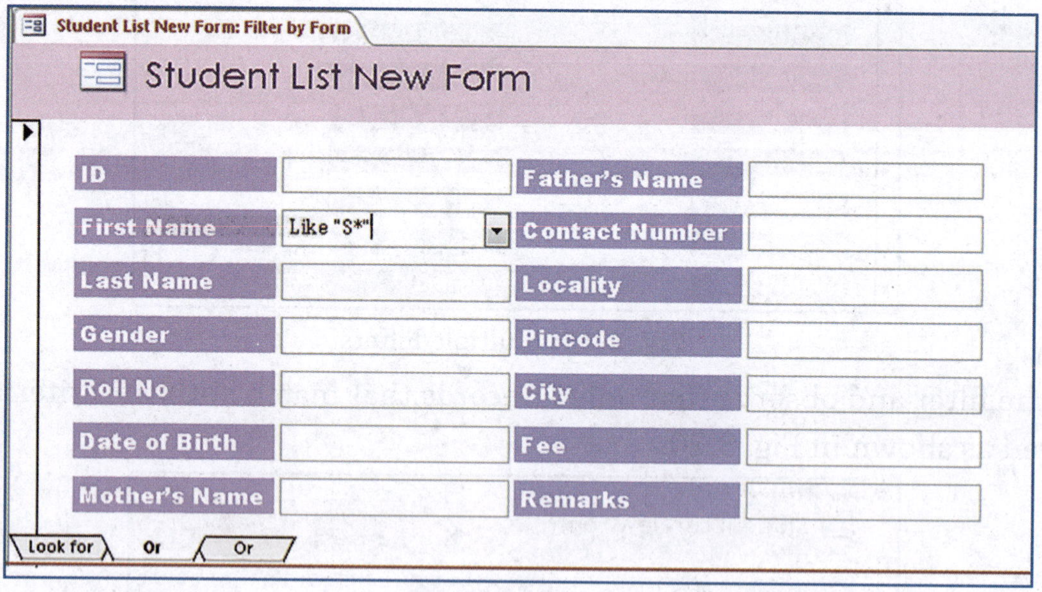

Fig. 3.21: Filter By Form: Or tab

- Apply the filter and observe that there are records whose First Name starts with either N or S as shown in Fig. 3.22.

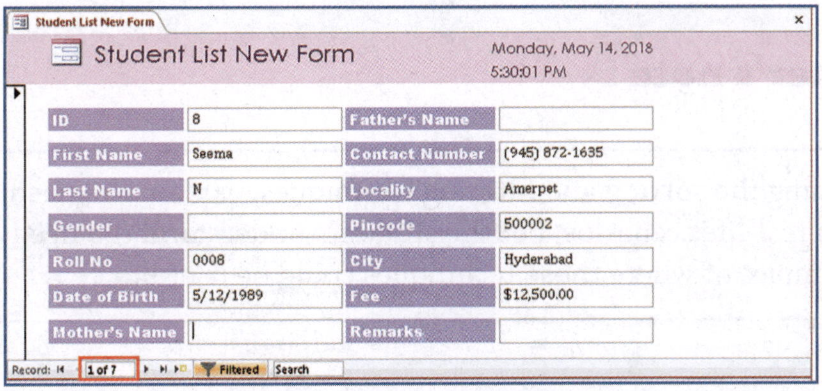

Fig. 3.22: Filtered Records

- Navigate and see whether all the records are matching the criteria.

netsearch

For additional information, visit:
https://www.makeuseof.com/tag/libreoffice-free-office-suite-windows-linux-mac/

Hands-on practice

1. Open the student's database created in the previous practice time.
2. Open the student table containing the fields Name, Gender, Location, Phone number, Pin code, Height, Weight, Household expenditure and Mother's occupation.
3. Create filters using form to perform the following tasks:
   a. To display the records of only male students whose name start with either A or N.
   b. To display the student's records that contain students who live in 'Location 1' or 'Location 2' (Note: Location 1 and Location 2 are the Location names entered by you).
   c. To display the records of students whose mothers are working.

Teacher's note

Before explaining the sorting and filtering techniques, explain the need for them by giving various real-life scenarios. Let the students understand the need and come up with their own examples of where those techniques could be useful.

Concepts learnt

1. Sorting is arranging the data in the logical order by grouping similar data together.
2. There are two types of sorting: Ascending (Moving up) and Descending (Moving down).
   - In Text:
     → Ascending order is arranging from A to Z
     → Descending order is arranging from Z to A.
   - In Numerals:
     → Ascending order is arranging from smallest to greatest.
     → Descending order is arranging from greatest to smallest.
3. By default, Access sorts the records by ID number.
4. Sorting can be done by one field or more than one field at a time. While sorting by more than one field, we must place the fields to be sorted adjacent to each other in the order in which we want to sort them.
5. Access sorts the fields containing numbers differently based on the data type of the field.
6. Filtering is a set of criteria applied to the data to display a subset of the data.
7. Depending on the data type of field that we are filtering, the filtering options change. For example: Text filters, Number filters, Date Filters, etc.
8. When we want to filter the tables in several fields, we can use Filter by Form in Advanced Filter option.

Exercise

A Fill in the blanks.

1. Arranging the data in a logical order by grouping the similar data together is called ______________ (sorting/filtering).
2. Arranging the numbers from largest to smallest is called ______________ (ascending/descending) order.
3. To filter the records that match the selected text, we use ______________ (selection/custom filter) command in Sort & Filter group.
4. The filtering option that should be selected if we want to filter the records in a PURCHASES table whose purchase date is in the given range of dates is ______________ (number/date) filters.
5. The ______________ (toggle/remove) filter command helps to apply and remove filters.

B Write T for True or F for False.

1. Arranging the text from A to Z is called descending order. ☐
2. The filtering option 'Equals' is available in text, number as well as date filters. ☐
3. While filtering the text field, if we do not know the word completely, we enter '&' symbol along with one or two letters. ☐
4. While sorting the tables by multiple fields, the order in which they appear in the table does not matter. ☐
5. Filter by Form option enables to filter the tables in several fields. ☐

C Choose the correct option.

1. Ascending order means
   (a) Arranging the text from A to Z
   (b) Arranging the numbers from smallest to largest
   (c) Both (a) and (b)
   (d) None of the above

2. Which of the following is the correct way to sort a table?
   (a) Click on the field's heading to sort.
   (b) Open the table and select the field to sort and click on Ascending or Descending command in the Sort & Filter group.
   (c) Open the table, click on Ascending or Descending command in the Sort & Filter group and then select the field.
   (d) All the above
3. In which of the following orders should we place the fields to sort the table first by region, then by city and then by name?
   (a) Name, city, region (b) Name, region, city
   (c) Region, city, name (d) City, region, name
4. Which of the following displays the records in a table that matches a criterion?
   (a) Sorting (b) Filtering
   (c) Either (a) or (b) (d) Both (a) and (b)
5. Which of the following is not a filter option on number field?
   (a) Less Than (b) Greater Than
   (c) Between (d) Ends With

D Answer these following questions briefly.

1. Explain the technique 'sorting the text in multiple fields' by giving an illustration.
2. Justify the statement, 'Sorting the field with numerals yields different results when considered them as different data types'.
3. Explain different filtering options available for the field which contains date.
4. What are the different types of filter options that are available to filter records?
5. Distinguish between using a filter and a query to find the records.

E Application-based questions.

1. Naresh is running a start-up company. He has created an EMPLOYEE database to store the details of all his employees. He wants to know the employees who are getting the least salary and those who are getting the highest salary. Help Naresh to quickly view this data from his EMPLOYEE table.
2. Divya is a school teacher. She has prepared a table to analyse the test results of students of a class as shown below. She wants to sort the records in the ascending order of their ranks. But surprisingly she got the results as shown in the second table. Explain the mistake committed by her and how she can correct it.

ID	First Name	Roll No	Rank
1	Aruna	001	First
2	Lakshmi	0002	Third
3	Nachiketh	00003	second
4	Tejas	00004	Fifth
5	Shashank	005	Fifteen
6	Jagadeesh	000007	Sixth
7	Nithyashree	0006	Fourth
8	Seema	0008	Seventh
9	Sudhir	00009	Tenth
10	Vijay	0010	Eleventh
11	Dakshayani	11	Eighth
12	Akhila	0012	Thirteenth
13	Srinivas	00013	Fourteenth
14	Raghu	014	Twelveth
15	Narayan	15	Ninth

Copy Of Student List

ID	First Name	Roll No	Rank
11	Dakshayani	11	Eighth
10	Vijay	0010	Eleventh
5	Shashank	005	Fifteen
4	Tejas	00004	Fifth
1	Aruna	001	First
13	Srinivas	00013	Fourteenth
7	Nithyashree	0006	Fourth
15	Narayan	15	Ninth
3	Nachiketh	00003	second
8	Seema	0008	Seventh
6	Jagadeesh	000007	Sixth
9	Sudhir	00009	Tenth
2	Lakshmi	0002	Third
12	Akhila	0012	Thirteenth
14	Raghu	014	Twelveth

3. A training centre has created a database of the students who have registered for different courses that they offer. They have training centres at various locations. The training coordinator wants to view the students who have registered for a course in a region. Explain how to view those records. (Hint: Use Filter by Form.)
4. Rajesh is working in a credit card company. He has the customer database with credit card bill details. He wants to call all the customers whose due is above ₹50,000. Explain how he can easily view those customer details.
5. Avinash is a sales manager. He has created a database on sales. He wants to view the details of all the sales that have happened in the last three months. Explain the steps to be followed to view those details.

Computer is my mentor!

Create CUSTOMER table with the fields: Cust ID (Primary Key), Name, City, Region, Phone number, Product Purchased, Order Value, Purchase Date, etc. Enter at least 10 records.

- Create a form based on the above table. Enter 10 more records using the form.
- Sort the CUSTOMER table by:
  - Name in ascending order.
  - Cust ID in descending order.
  - City and region in ascending order.
  - Order value in descending order.
- Create filters to:
  - Display customers in a particular region.
  - Display customers in a particular region and city.
  - Display customers who bought a particular product.
  - Display customers whose order value is in between a given range.
  - Display customers whose purchase date is on or before a given date.

4 Working with Images in HTML5

Learning log

- Insert image on a webpage
- Alternate attribute of the image
- Setting width and height of an image
- Image border
- Animated images
- Image as a link
- HTML image maps

Introduction

Alongside is an image showing different webpages. What is it in each webpage that is likely to attract the user to visit it?

It is the images that each web page has in its home page that attracts the user to visit it. Images are very important to make a web page look more beautiful and it also depicts many concepts on a web page in a simple way.

In this chapter, we will learn how to beautify a web page by adding images and styling it using HTML5.

Insert Image on a Web Page

HTML5 multimedia features allows the user to include images, audio clips, video clips and other multimedia element in the web pages. The user can insert the image on the web page by using <img> tag. Attributes are to be declared within quotes. Following is the simple syntax to use this tag.

<img src="url">

Word web

attributes: extra bit of information used along with an HTML tag. It defines a tag's characteristics

In HTML5, images are defined with the <img> tag.

- The <img> tag is used to display image on a web page.
- <img> tag is an empty tag. It contains attributes only and does not contain any closing tag.
- <src> is a necessary attribute that describes the source or path of the image. It also tells the browser to find an image from the server.
- <url> indicates the location of the image where it is stored.

Example: <img src = "Sachin Tendulkar.jpg">

Insert image in the same directory

- Create 'New Folder' in a drive by right-clicking on the mouse and choosing New → Folder as in Fig. 4.1.
- Rename the folder name as 'Image' (Fig. 4.2).

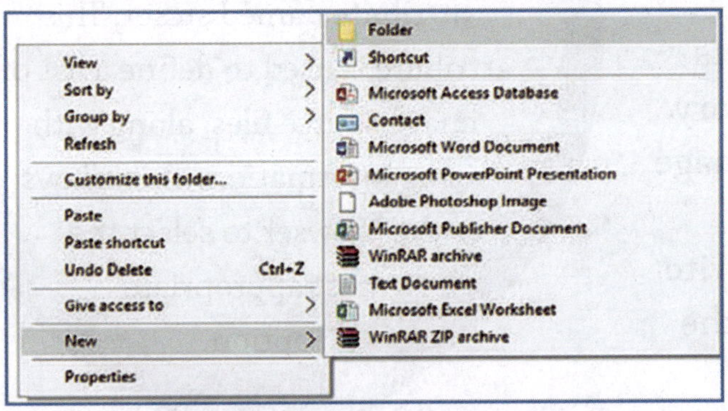

Fig. 4.1: Creating New Folder

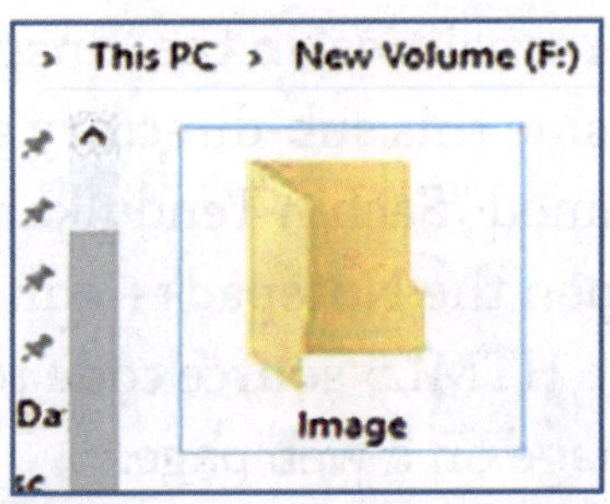

Fig. 4.2: Renaming Folder

- Download an image from a website and paste into Image folder. Here, the name of the image is 'Sachin Tendulkar'.
- Open a Notepad++ editor from the 'Start' menu on the windows.
- Write a HTML source code to insert the image on a web page as shown in Fig. 4.3.
- Save the filename as "Index.html" in Image folder.
- Open the "Index.html" file with the Google Chrome browser to see the image added in the webpage as in Fig. 4.4.

```
Index.html
<!DOCTYPE html>
<<html>
<head>
<title> Image on a same directory</title>
</head>
<body>
<img src="Sachin Tendulkar.jpg">
</body>
</html>
```

Fig. 4.3: HTML to add image to an HTML page

Fig. 4.4: HTML Page

Insert the images in sub-directory or another folder

The steps to add an image to a webpage remains the same while the path for the source code needs to be changed. Following are the steps to change the path in the source code:

- Create a sub-directory called 'Sports Personalities' in the 'Image' directory. Inside this sub-directory add an image named "Sachin Tendulkar.jpg".
- Open the Notepad++ editor and write the HTML5 source code to insert the image on a web page.

You should know

HTML5 has a new image attribute named srcset. This attribute is used to define a list of image source files, along with sizing information. This allows the browser to select the most appropriate option.

```
<!DOCTYPE html>
<<html>
<head>
<title> Image in a sub-directory</title>
</head>
<body>
<img src="C:\Users\Desktop\New folder\Image\Sports Personalities\Sachin Tendulkar.jpg">
</body>
</html>
```

Fig. 4.5: Changing path of the source

- Save the file and run it in the Chrome browser.

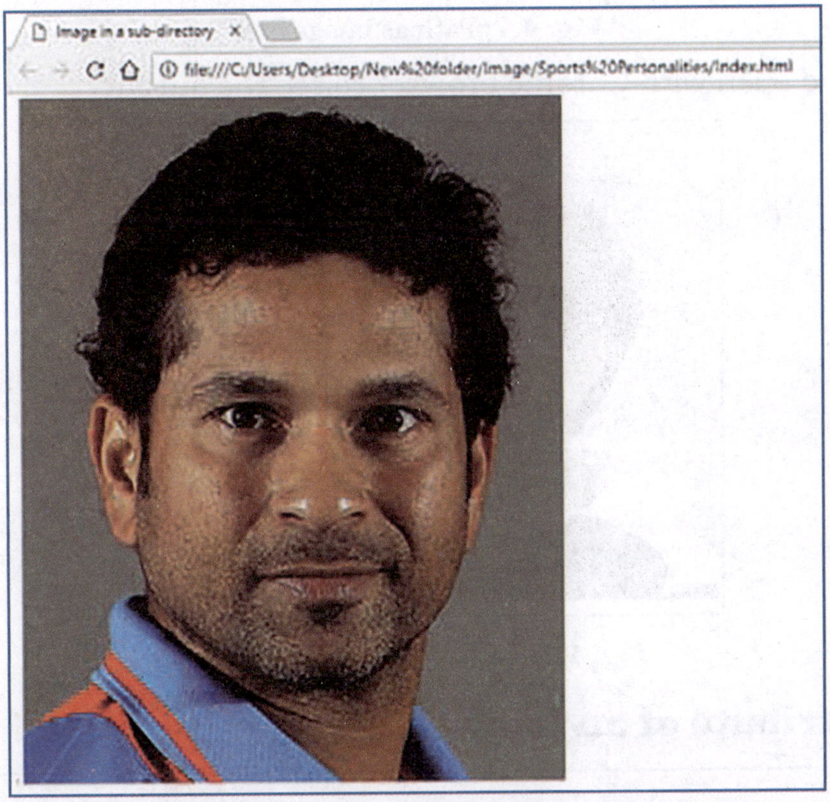

Fig. 4.6: Result after changing the path

Insert the images from server

Images are stored in some of the image servers. User can easily access the images from any of the image servers by accessing through web address.

The steps to add an image to a webpage remains the same while the path for the source code needs to be added from the URL or the path present in the web server. Following are the steps to change the path in the source code.

- Open a Notepad++ editor and write the HTML5 source code to insert the image on a web page.

- Note that the image link can be copied from the image server and pasted next to the source code as in Fig. 4.7.

```
<!DOCTYPE html>
<<html>
<head>
<title> Image from a Server</title>
</head>
<body>
<img src="http://www.spectralhues.com/wp-content/uploads/2013/10/sachin-tendulkar-retires.jpg">
</body>
</html>
```

Fig. 4.7: Path as image link

- Save the file and open with Chrome browser to see the output.

Fig. 4.8: Path as image link result

Alternate Attribute of an Image

The alternate (alt) attribute is the alternative description for an image, if the image cannot be displayed or found. The value of the alt attribute can be defined as:

<img src="C:\Users\Desktop\New folder\Image\Sports Personalities\Sachin Tendulkar.jpg" alt = “God_Of_Cricket”>

In this example,

- <src> attribute searches the image in a path and informs the browser to display.
- <alt> attribute displays when the image is not found in the path.

Follow all the steps as in the previous method but user has to give <alt> attribute in the HTML code.

- Open a Notepad++ editor and write the HTML5 source code to get the value of the alt attribute on a web page.
- The src attribute must have an image in a directory called as Image, having a sub-directory known as Sports Personalities. And the image name is "Sachin Tendulkar" (Fig. 4.9).

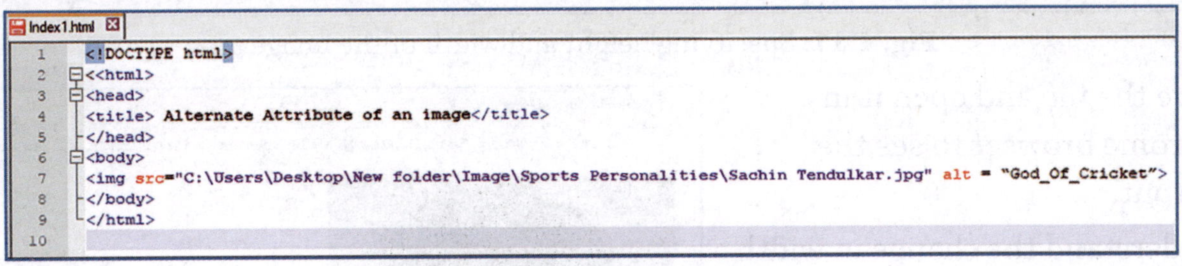

Fig. 4.9: Using alt attribute

- Save the file and open it in Chrome browser to see the output.
- If the given path is devoid of any image with the name given in the source code either in the directory or sub-directory, then the alternate text appears in the web page as in Fig. 4.10.

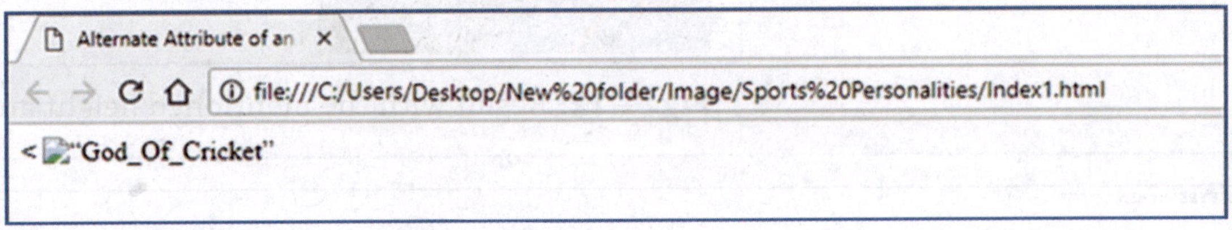

Fig. 4.10: Alt attribute result

Setting width and height of an image

The width and height attributes are used to specify dimension of an image. User can use the width and height attributes to add images with different sizes in a webpage. For example:

<img src="C:\Users\Desktop\New folder\Image\Sports Personalities\Sachin Tendulkar.jpg" alt = "God_Of_Cricket" width ="300" height="350">

In this example,

- <src> attribute searches the image in a path and informs the browser to display.
- <alt> atrribute displays when the image is not found in the path.
- Width and height gives the dimension of the image to be displayed in the web browser. Along with the code, the user needs to give specific width and height of the image in the HTML5 code.
- Open a Notepad++ editor and write the HTML5 source code to get the value of the alt attribute and dimensions on a web page.

```html
Index2.html
<!DOCTYPE html>
<<html>
<head>
<title> Setting Width and Height of an Image</title>
</head>
<body>
<img src="C:\Users\Desktop\New folder\Image\Sports Personalities\Sachin Tendulkar.jpg" alt = "God_Of_Cricket" Width="300" Height="350">
</body>
</html>
```

Fig. 4.11: Specifying height and width of the image

- Save the file and open it in Chrome browser to see the output.

To understand the change in width and height of an image, a program with images of different dimensions is given in Fig. 4.13 and output in Fig. 4.14.

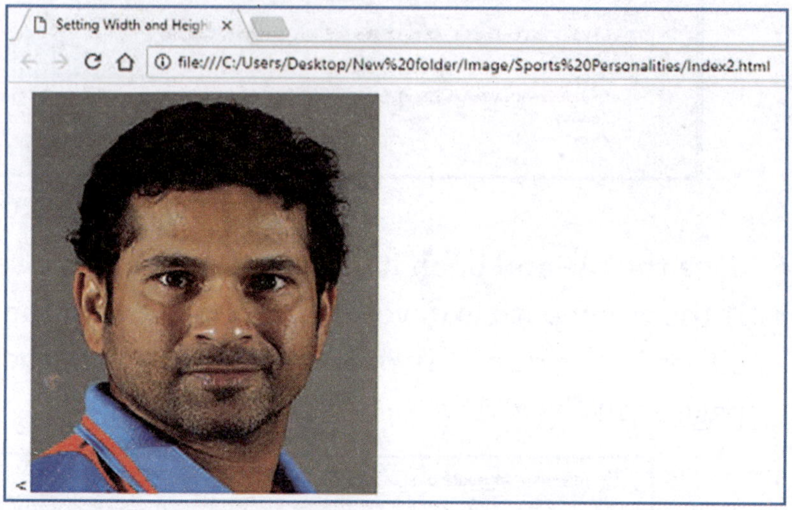

Fig. 4.12: Result with the mentioned height and width

```html
Index3.html
<!DOCTYPE html>
<<html>
<head>
<title> Setting Width and Height of an Image</title>
</head>
<body>
<img src="C:\Users\Desktop\New folder\Image\Sports Personalities\Sachin.jpg" alt = "God_Of_Cricket" Width="300" Height="400" >
<img src="C:\Users\Desktop\New folder\Image\Sports Personalities\Sachin Tendulkar.jpg" alt = "God_Of_Cricket" Width="400" Height="550">
<img src="C:\Users\Desktop\New folder\Image\Sports Personalities\Sachin-Tendulkar.jpg" alt = "God_Of_Cricket">
</body>
</html>
```

Fig. 4.13: Images with various sizes

Fig. 4.14: Output of images with various sizes

Image border

User can set the border for an image by using border attribute. With the help of border element, user can specify the border thickness for an image.

- Open a Notepad++ editor and write the html source code and mention the value of the attribute "border" as in Fig. 4.15.

```
Index4.html
<!DOCTYPE html>
<<html>
<head>
<title> Image Border</title>
</head>
<body>
<img src="C:\Users\Desktop\New folder\Image\Sports Personalities\Sachin.jpg" alt = "God_Of_Cricket"
Width="300" Height="400" border="5">
</body>
</html>
```

Fig. 4.15: Image with border

- Save the file and open it in Chrome browser to see the output.

Fig. 4.16: Image with border output

Animated images

HTML5 multimedia features allow the user to include animated GIF's in a web page.

Example: <img src="C:\Users\shruthi.l\Desktop\New folder\Image\Sports Personalities\Sachin batting.gif" alt = "God_Of_Cricket_Batting" Width="300" Height = "400" border="5">

Follow all the steps as earlier but the user has to give an animated image source in the HTML code.

- Open a Notepad++ editor and write the html source code to get the value of the attribute on a web page.

```
<!DOCTYPE html>
<<html>
<head>
<title> Animated Image </title>
</head>
<body>
<img src="C:\Users\Desktop\New folder\Image\Sports Personalities\Sachin batting.gif" alt = "God_Of_Cricket_Batting"
Width="600" Height="400" border="5">
</body>
</html>
```

Fig. 4.17: Adding Animated Images

- Save the file and open it in Chrome browser to see the output.

Fig. 4.18: Adding Animated Images result

Image as a link

The href attribute represents Hypertext Reference. It is an attribute of the anchor tag used to create a link to another web page.

For example, <a href ="http://www.sachintendulkar.in"> <img src="C:\Users\Desktop\New folder\Image\Sports Personalities\Sachin.jpg" alt = "God_Of_Cricket" width ="300" height="400"border="5"></a>

In this example,

- <a href> attribute links to the website mentioned in the given URL. It has to be closed with a closing tag.
- <src> attribute searches the image in a path and informs the browser to display. Follow all the steps which is similar to previous method, but the user has to give a link in the source code of HTML5.

- Open a Notepad++ editor and write the html source code to get the value of the attribute on a web page.
- Save the file and open it in Chrome browser to see the output.

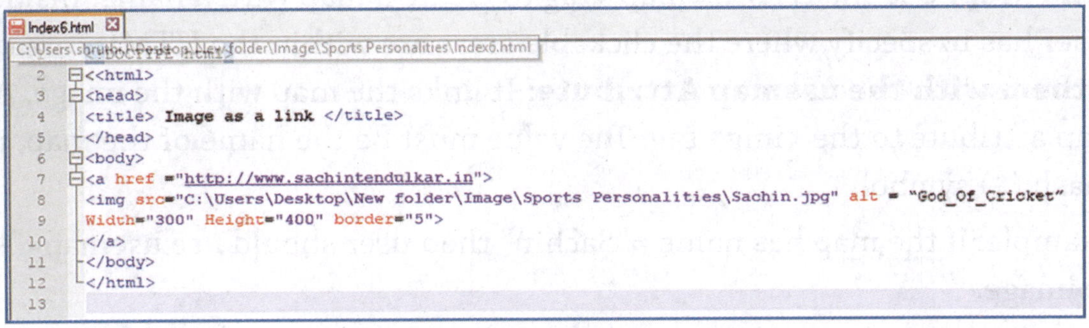


```
<!DOCTYPE html>
<<html>
<head>
<title> Image as a link </title>
</head>
<body>
<a href ="http://www.sachintendulkar.in">
<img src="C:\Users\Desktop\New folder\Image\Sports Personalities\Sachin.jpg" alt = "God_Of_Cricket"
Width="300" Height="400" border="5">
</a>
</body>
</html>
```

Fig. 4.19: Setting image as a link

- Clicking on the image, will redirect the user to the webpage linked along with the source code, i.e., href attribute.

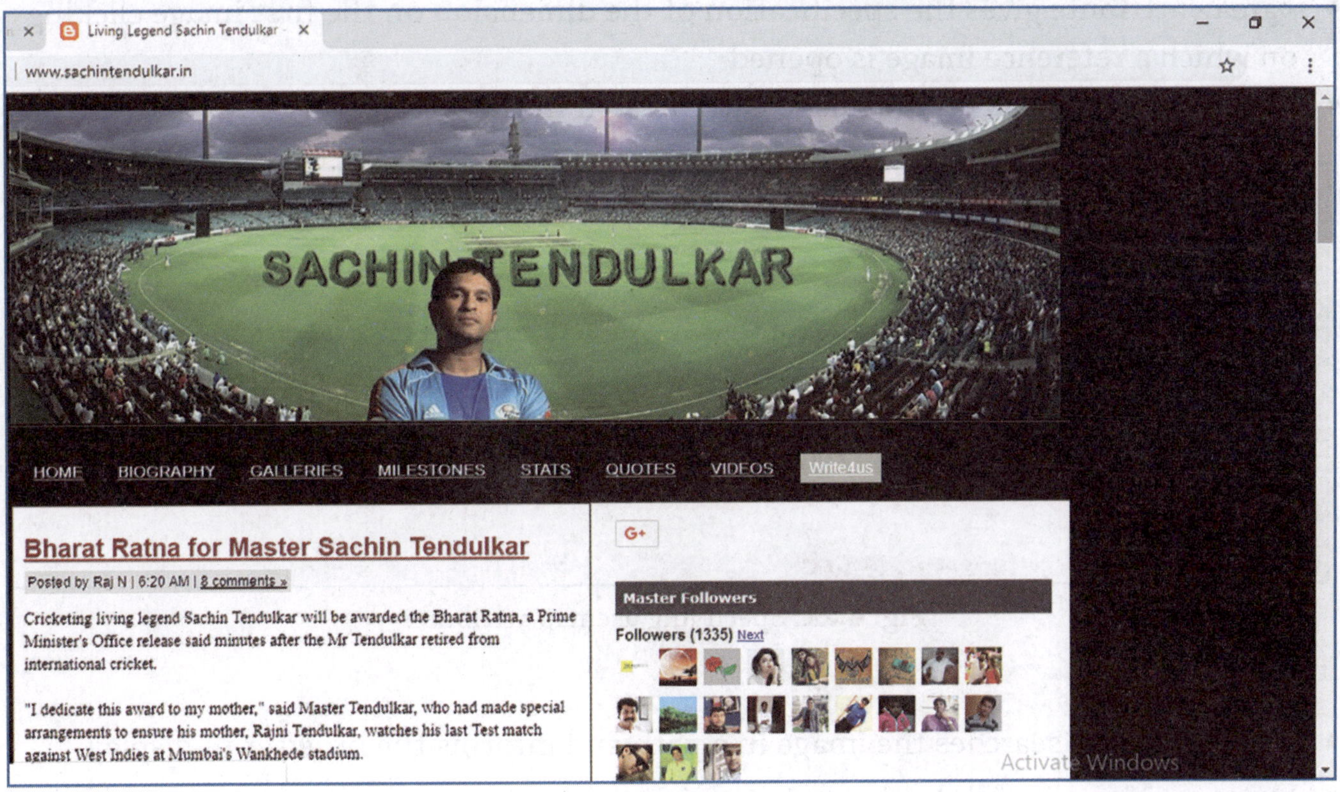

Fig. 4.20: Output on clicking the image as a link

HTML Image Maps

Image maps are clickable areas that usually link to another page. To create an image map, the prerequisites are discussed below.

- **Add the <img> Tag:** Embed the image into the web page by using <img> element. The image can be any source file available in a directory or it can be available on the web or internet. Any image, icon, logo, etc., can be added in the element.
- **Add the Map:** Use the HTML <map> tag to create a map with a name. Inside this tag, user has to specify where the clickable areas are within the HTML <area> tag.
- **Link them with the usemap Attribute:** It links the map with the image. Add the usemap attribute to the <img> tag. The value must be the name of the map, preceded by a hash (#) symbol.

  For example: if the map has name =“Sachin” then user should use usemap=”#Sachin” in the image.

Following are the steps to create an Image map for a HTML5 web element.

- Open a Notepad++ editor and write the HTML source code and specify the value of the attribute usemap.
- <area> attribute gives the specification of the dimension on the first image clicking on which a reference image is opened.
- <href> gives the link on the image path present in the web server.

```
<!DOCTYPE HTML>
<html>
<head>
<title> Image Maps </title>
</head>
<body>
<img src= "C:\Users\Desktop\New folder\Image\Sports Personalities\Sachin First Match.jpg"
alt= "Sachin Tendulkar"
usemap= "#mapping">
<map name= "mapping">
<area shape= "rect" coords= "0,0,600,400" alt= "God_of_Cricket_Tribute"
href= "https://i.ytimg.com/vi/6daz7Vut_nc/maxresdefault.jpg">
</area>
</map>
</body>
</html>
```

Fig. 4.21: Specifying usemap attribute

In this example,

- <src> attribute searches the image in a path and informs the browser to display.
- Usemap=“#maping” links the map with image
- <map name=“mapping”> specify the clickable areas.
- Save the file and open it in Chrome browser to see the output.

Fig. 4.22: Output

- User has to click the image once to see the next clickable areas. User may then find the next area in the web page.

Fig. 4.23: Output after clicking

Hands-on practice

Write the descriptions of the tags and attributes given below.

1. <img>
2. <img scr>
3. alt
4. usemap
5. <href>

netsearch

For additional information, visit:

http://www.dummies.com/web-design-development/site-development/how-to-add-an-image-to-your-html5-web-page/

https://www.w3schools.com/html/html_images.asp

https://www.tutorialrepublic.com/html-tutorial/html-images.php

https://resource-centre.net/html5-tutorials/html5-images/

https://learnwebcode.com/how-to-insert-an-image-in-xhtml/

Hands-on practice

Create a sample webpage for your school. Insert images of various places in the school that are worth noticing. Set each image as a link and add description/details of the place in the linked page. Give border to each of the images too. Now in the space given below, write the code for the webpage and paste the print-out of the webpage too.

Mastering keyboard

Shift + Alt + I: Insert image

Teacher's note

Brainstorm with the students the need to have images in a webpage. Review multimedia tags with them.

Concepts learnt

1. Inserting an image on the web page by using <img> tag.
2. <img src= "url"> syntax allows the user to use an image present in a sub-directory or a folder.
3. Images stored in some of the websites on image servers can also be used to add an image in a webpage.
4. Alternate (Alt) attribute is the alternative description for an image, if the image cannot be displayed or found.
5. Width and height attributes are used to specify the dimentions of an image.
6. Border for an image is set by using border tag in the HTML element.
7. HTML5 multimedia features allows user to include animated GIF's in a web page.
8. href attribute represents Hypertext Reference.
9. Images can be mapped linking it to the another web page.

Exercise

A Fill in the blanks.

1. ____________ (Program/Images) in a webpage beautify and depict many concepts in a simple way.
2. HTML5 ____________ (existing/multimedia) features allow user to include images and video clips elements in the web page.
3. ____________ (<img>/<alt>) attribute displays when the image was not found in the path.
4. Image maps are clickable areas that are usually linked to ____________ (another/same) page.
5. ____________ (<img>/<href>) gives the link on the image path present in the web server.

B Write T for True or F for False.

1. The <img> tag is used to display image on a web page. ☐
2. Saved HTML document can be run by using web server. ☐
3. Attributes is to be declared within quotes. ☐
4. Width and height attributes are used to specify the dimensions of an image. ☐
5. <map> tag allows the user to specify clickable areas with the HTML <area> tag. ☐

C Choose the correct option.

1. Which of these indicate the location of where the image is stored?

   (a) <url> (b) <img>
   (c) <src> (d) <href>

2. Images from which of these sources cannot be used to design a webpage?

   (a) Web pages (b) Digital cameras
   (c) Websites (d) Image servers

3. Which of these tags is used to create a map with a name?
   (a) <img> (b) <href>
   (c) <src> (d) <usemap>
4. Which of these attributes of the anchor tag is used to create a link to another web page?
   (a) <alt> (b) <href>
   (c) <img> (d) <src>
5. Images in which of these formats supports animated images in the creation of a webpage?
   (a) GIF (b) JPG
   (c) Bitmap (d) PNG

D Answer these following questions briefly.

1. Write the steps to insert an image on a web page?
2. How can one insert the image in a sub-directory or another folder?
3. How to insert an image from server?
4. Explain the 'alt' attribute of the image. How can one set the width and height of the image?
5. Explain what is usemap attribute.

E Application-based questions.

1. Anita wants to insert a gif image using html code by adjusting the width and height of the image. Write the necessary steps required?
2. Shilpa wants to link a website to an image she has added in the webpage. What should she do to achieve the same?
3. Ram coded a program with an image in it and when he ran the program in the Chrome browser the image was not getting displayed. What could be the possible issue here?

Computer is my mentor!

Write an HTML code to insert an image by setting its height, width and border by linking the image to the webpage.

5 Internet Protocol

Learning log

- Network protocols
- Types of network protocols
- Internet protocol (IP)
- Transmission Control Protocol (TCP)
- Implementation of Internet Protocol
- Advantages of Internet Protocol

Introduction

We have learnt about the Internet and its purposes in the previous classes. Internet is a large network of interconnected computers on which the connected computers exchange information.

Do you know how computers communicate and what enables them to communicate on the Internet?

For computers to understand the communication, they need a medium. This medium is provided by protocols. In this chapter, we will learn about the protocols used in computer networking, primarily the protocol that is widely used on the Internet called **Internet Protocol**.

Network Protocol

Computers that are connected in a network need a method of communication to function. Just like how we humans communicate using various languages, which have several rules and conditions, computer communicates through a language on the network. These communication languages are called **network protocols**. Network protocol is a set of guidelines that define communication between two or more devices over a network.

Without protocols, devices would lack the ability to understand the electronic signals they send to each other over the network. Protocols specify the rules governing the transmission of information and communication between computers. A protocol defines what is communicated, how data and information is communicated and when it is communicated.

Types of Network Protocol

There are several network protocols that are used for a specific purpose to communicate. Following are some of the commonly used protocols.

1. **IP or Internet Protocol:** A protocol used to communicate on the Internet. Data is sent from one computer to another computer on Internet through this protocol.
2. **FTP or File Transfer Protocol:** A protocol that is used to transfer and manipulate files on the Internet.
3. **HTTP or HyperText Transfer Protocol:** An Internet-based protocol for sending and receiving webpages.
4. **IRC or Internet Relay Chat:** A protocol used for Internet chat and other communications.
5. **SMTP or Simple Mail Transfer Protocol:** A protocol for sending e-mail messages on the Internet.

You should know

In May 1974, the Institute of Electrical and Electronic Engineers (IEEE) published a paper entitled "A Protocol for Packet Network Intercommunication". The paper's authors, Vint Cerf and Bob Kahn, described an Internet working protocol for sharing resources that came to be known as network protocols.

Vint Cerf and Bob Kahn

Internet Protocol

Internet Protocol (IP) is the communication protocol which contains the formats of digital message and rules for exchanging messages between computers across a single network or a series of interconnected networks. Every computer that uses IP in the network to communicate, has an Internet Protocol address (IP address) which is a numerical label assigned to each device connected to a computer network. An IP address serves two principal functions:

- Unique identification of every device/user on the Internet
- Identify the location of the device.

The basic functions of IP are (Fig. 5.1):

- Send data to the correct recipient(s)
- Transmit data from source to destination.

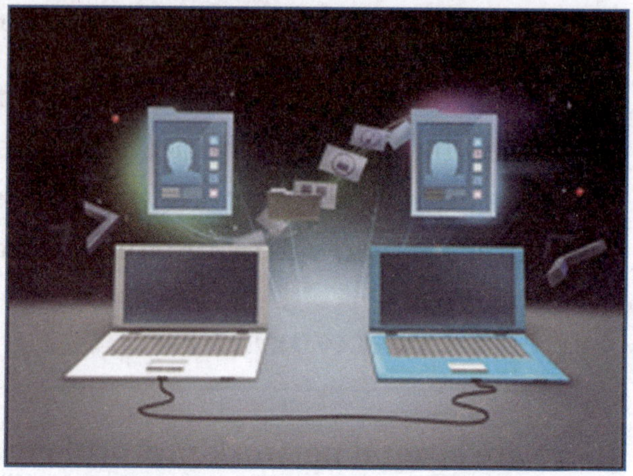

Fig. 5.1: Transfer of data

IP transports data in packets called **datagrams**, also known as **data packets**, which is a basic transfer unit. Each datagram has two components: a header and a payload. The IP header includes source IP address and destination IP address. The payload is the data that is transported.

Transmission Control Protocol

Transmission Control Protocol (TCP) is a network protocol used as a communication standard that defines how to establish and maintain communication in the network through which computer programs can exchange data. (Fig. 5.2) TCP works with the Internet Protocol (IP), which defines how computers send packets of data to each other.

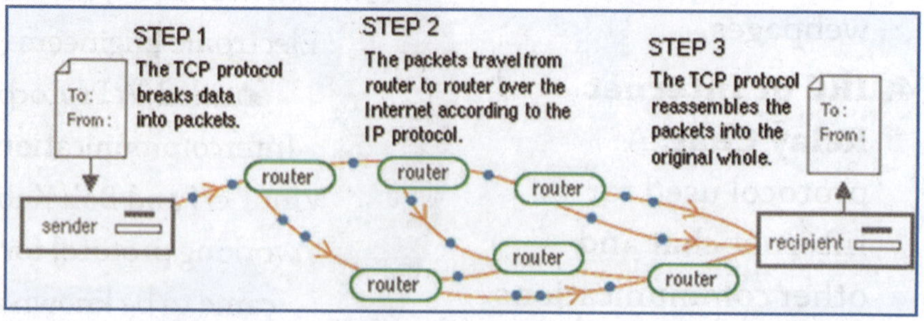

Fig. 5.2: Data transfer travels over Internet

Together, TCP and IP form the basic guidelines that govern the exchange of data on the Internet and are often referred to as TCP or IP since these two protocols are always present together to transmit data.

Following are the functions of TCP:

- It establishes the connection and maintains it until the application programs at each end have finished exchanging information.
- It determines how to break the data into packets that networks can deliver and send and accept data packets in the network.

You should know

Internet Assigned Number Authority (IANA) is a nonprofit private American corporation that manages IP addresses.

iana
Internet Assigned Numbers Authority

IANA logo

Implementation of Internet Protocol

To implement a network protocol, first a standard document that contains all the rules of communication needs to be prepared. Once the standard has been established, a software that allows communication between the computers in a network is developed. This software is developed such that it obeys the rules described in the standard document.

Word web

standard: the main guideline that provides all the necessary information

Advantages of Internet Protocol

- IP can coexist with other network protocols, thus different services can share a common network infrastructure at the same time.
- IP as a transport protocol can operate on various networks.
- IP assigns each computer on the network a unique address called its IP address. Thus, every computer on the network is uniquely identifiable and information could be sent to it by simply addressing its IP address.
- It is the most widely used protocol for communication on the Internet and hence, it is easier for new devices to join the network.

netsearch

For additional information, visit:
https://www.lifewire.com/Internet-protocol-explained-3426713
https://www.lifewire.com/structure-of-ip-packet-3426715
https://www.lifewire.com/transmission-control-protocol-and-Internet-protocol-816255

Teacher's note

Brainstorm prerequisites of Internet communication and possible operations on the Internet. Use the responses from the students to build the introduction to the concept of protocols.

Concepts learnt

1. Computers that are connected in a network communicate using network protocols.
2. Network protocol is a set of guidelines that define communication between two or more devices over a network.
3. Without protocols, devices would lack the ability to understand the electronic signals they send to each other over the network.
4. There are several types of network protocols. Some of the commonly used network protocols are IP, FTP, HTTP, TCP, IRC and SMTP.
5. Internet Protocol (IP) is the communication protocol which contains the formats of digital message and rules for exchanging messages between computers in a network.

Hands-on practice

1. Create a presentation that describes all the protocols in details. Discuss the same with your classmates and show it to your teacher.
2. Now prepare a report on the history of development of all the protocols read in this chapter. Write the main points in the space given below.

Exercise

A Fill in the blanks.

1. Without ____________ (protocols/hardware) computers would lack the ability to understand the electronic signals over the network.
2. A numerical label assigned to each device connected to a computer network is known as ____________ (IP/HTTP) address.
3. ____________ (FTP/IRC) is a protocol that is used to transfer and manipulate files on the Internet.
4. ____________ (Payload/Header) is the data that is transported through datagrams.
5. ____________ (IP/TCP) is the communication protocol which contains the formats of digital message and rules for exchanging messages between computers across a network.

B Write T for True or F for False.

1. Internet Protocol cannot coexist with other network protocols. ☐
2. Internet Protocol transports data in packets called quantum. ☐
3. Some standards need to be established to implement protocols. ☐
4. Internet Protocol assigns one address to three devices in the network. ☐
5. Internet Protocol can operate on various networks. ☐

C Choose the correct option.

1. Which of the following specify the rules governing the transmission of information and communication between computers?
   (a) Network protocols (b) Software protocol
   (c) Hardware protocols (d) Industry Protocol
2. Which of the following is a part of IP header?
   (a) Source IP address (b) Destination IP address
   (c) Both (a) and (b) (d) Neighbouring IP address

Exercise

3. With which of the following protocols does TCP always work?
   (a) HTTP (b) IP
   (c) FTP (d) SMTP
4. Which of the following protocols determines how to break the data into packets that networks can deliver?
   (a) IP (b) TCP
   (c) IMAP (d) Datagram
5. Which of the following is not a function of IP?
   (a) Unique identification of every device/user on the Internet.
   (b) Send data to the correct recipient(s).
   (c) Transmit data from source to destination.
   (d) Establishing and maintaining the connection between computers on the network.

D Answer these questions briefly.

1. What are network protocols? Briefly describe FTP, HTTP and SMTP protocols.
2. What are datagrams? What do datagrams comprise of?
3. What is the function of IP and TCP?
4. How is IP implemented?
5. What are the advantages of IP?

E Application-based questions.

1. A network of computers has been established in a school. What are the protocols needed for file transfer and communication between the computer?
2. A start-up company starts its web page. Which protocol is needed for its users to view the web page?

Computer is my mentor!

Find out other commonly used protocols. List their function and usages and present it to your class.

6 Introduction to Java

Learning log

- History and features of Java
- Types of Java applications
- Java platforms
- Java editors
- Program in Java
- Keywords and identifiers
- Data types and variables

Introduction

Below is a list of computer programs and program file extensions jumbled.
Sort and match them in the table given below.

JAVA	C	C++	.CPP	C#	.CS	.JS	.JSE	.CC
PHP	.HTML	Java	.JAV	J#	.JSL	.PHP	JavaScript	.C

Programs	File extension

In this chapter we will be learning simple programming using Java.

Java

Java is a general-purpose programming language which produces software for multiple platforms. Java is an object-oriented, class-based, concurrent, imperative, reflective, general-purpose computer programming language and a widely used technology. (Fig: 6.1) The intention of this application is to 'write once, run anywhere' (WORA). This means that the compiled Java code can run on all platforms that support Java without the need for recompilation. Java has its own runtime environment (JRE) and API (Application Program Interface).

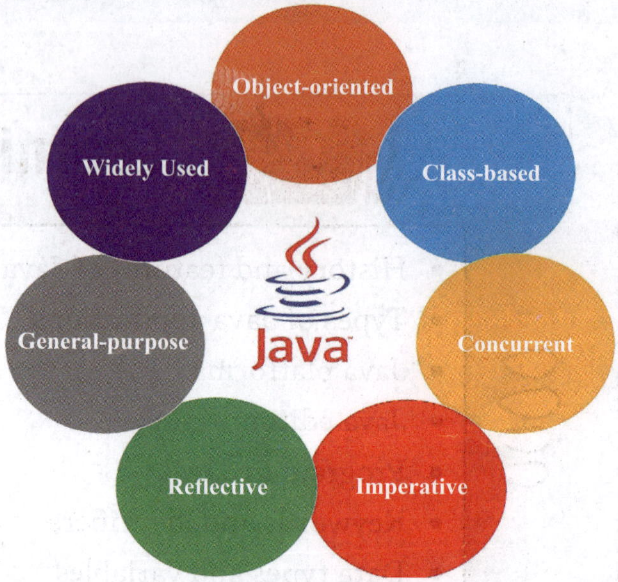

Fig. 6.1: Java

There are two basic types of Java programs—Application Program and Applet program. Java applications don't require a browser to run, it runs on its own just executing the main ( ) routine. Applet is a program written in the Java programming language that can be included in an HTML page. these programs are created especially to work on the Internet. They run through Java enabled web browsers such as Internet Explorer, Firefox, Opera, etc.

Java is a highly popular programming language that has dominated the programming field from early 2000's till date. Java has been used in different domains. (Fig: 6.2) Some of them are listed below:

1. **Banking:** Transaction management is supported with applications built using Java.
2. **Retail:** Billing applications are written using Java.
3. **Information Technology:** Implementation dependencies are solved with Java.

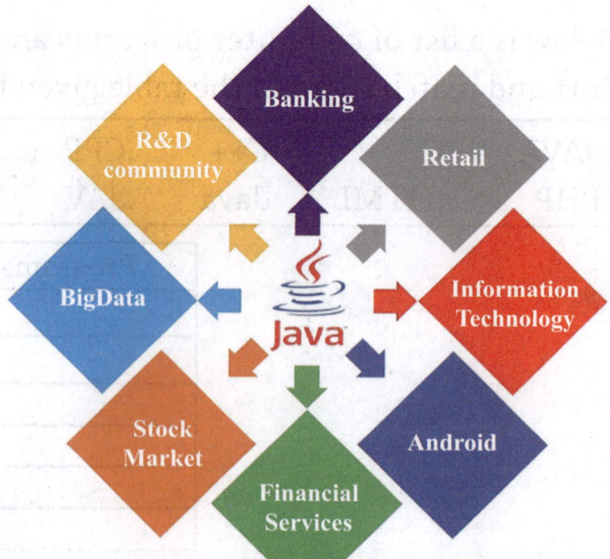

Fig. 6.2: Uses of Java

4. **Android:** Mobile applications are either written in Java or use Java API.
5. **Financial services:** Server-side applications are coded in Java.
6. **Stock market:** Algorithms of different companies are written with Java.
7. **Big data:** Hadoop MapReduce framework is written using Java.
8. **Scientific and research community:** Java can handle volumes of data for scientific research.

Word web

platform: a software or hardware environment in which a program executes, or runs
object-oriented: it is a way of classifying computer program based on the concept of objects (a variable, data, function, etc.)
class-based: it is a style of object-oriented programming (OOP) in which the process of creating new class is achieved by defining classes of objects
concurrent: several computer operations performed during an overlapping period
imperative: it is a way of classifying computer programs that use statements that changes a program's state
hadoop mapreduce: it is a software program used for distribution processing of large data sets

History of Java

The initial development of Java was meant to have interactive television programs. Java is a programming language developed by James Gosling with other team members named Mike Sheridan and Patrick Naughton also called as Green Team in 1995 for Sun Microsystems. This project was to develop a language for digital devices such as set-top boxes, televisions, etc. But, it was suited for Internet programming, mobile devices, games, e-business solutions, etc.

Fig. 6.3: (a) Java logo (b) James Gosling

Initially this programming language was called **Green talk** by James Gosling and all the file extension had .gt. It was later named 'Oak' and was developed as a part of Green project. In 1995, Oak was renamed as 'Java'.

Java name is given to this programming language because Java is an island of Indonesia where first coffee was produced. Hence, the logo of Java has a cup of coffee. This was again suggested by James Gosling.

Features of Java

The main objective of Java programming language is to create portable, simple and secure programming language. Some of the important features of Java are listed below:

Simple	It has removed all the complexities such as pointers and operator overloading like in C++, etc.
Portable	It is a "write once, run anywhere" (WORA) application.
Object-oriented	Everything is an 'object' and all the operations are performed using these objects.
Secured	All the code is converted in bytecode after compilation. This is not readable by a human. There is no pointer concept to run the program inside the sandbox. This prevents any activities from untrusted sources. It enables development of virus-free, tamper-free applications.
Dynamic	It supports dynamic memory allocation with the change in working environment. Memory wastage is reduced and performance of the application is increased.
Distributed	It provides Remote Method Invocation (RMI) and Enterprise JavaBeans (EJB) features to create distributed applications.
Robust	It has a strong memory management system. It auto checks the codes and eliminates the error during compilation and runtime.
High performance	It is easy to translate bytecode into native machine code. With the use of JIT (Just-In-Time) compilers. Java enables high performance.
Interpreted	Bytecodes are interpreted by a Java run-time environment.
Multi-threaded	A thread is a small, separate program, executing concurrently. Java supports multiple threads execution simultaneously.

Word web

pointers: it is a programming language object, whose value refers to another value stored in some other place in the computer memory

bytecode: it is the computer object code that is processed by a program as a virtual machine

sandbox: set of rules that are used when creating a small application

Types of Java applications

There are four main types of applications that can be used in Java.

1. **Standalone application:** This application is also known as *desktop application*. This needs to be installed on every machine. Examples are antivirus, media player, etc.

2. **Web application:** This is an application that runs from the server side and creates a dynamic web page. Examples are servlet, jsp, etc.
3. **Enterprise application:** This is a distribution application. Examples are banking applications.
4. **Mobile application:** This application is mainly designed for mobile devices. Examples are Android and Java ME.

Java platforms and editions

There are four platforms or editions in Java.

1. **J2SE (Java Standard Edition):** It is a Java programming platform which is used to develop standalone and client-server applications.
2. **J2EE (Java Enterprise Edition):** It is a Java enterprise platform which is used to develop web and enterprise applications.
3. **J2ME (Java Micro Edition):** It is a Java micro platform which is used to develop embedded and mobile applications.
4. **JavaFx:** It is a Java library used to build on rich Internet applications. These applications can run across a wide variety of devices.

You should know

For all the editors, Java Development Kit (JDK) 8 or 10 is required for installing and running the Java applications.

To write a Java program a text editor is essential. Notepad, Notepad++, Notebeans and Eclipse are some of the popular text editors.

Programming in Java

To write a simple program of Java it is important to install a Java Development Kit (JDK). A class needs to be created and it should also include a main method to execute a simple Java program. This program is then compiled and run to check its output. (Fig. 6.4)

Input	Output

`public class Simple{`
`public static void main(String args[]){`
`System.out.println("hello world");`
`}}`
	Compile by: javac Simple.java
	Run by: java Simple
	hello world

Fig. 6.4: Input and Output of a simple Java program

Parameters used in a Java program

1. **Public:** It is an access that specifies who can use it outside the class.
2. **Class:** It is a keyword used to declare a class in Java. Everything needs to be there inside the class only.
3. **Static:** It is a keyword that creates only one copy in the memory.
4. **Void:** It is the return type of the method, which doesn't return any value.
5. **Main:** Indicates the starting point of the program.
6. **String args[]:** It is used for command line argument.
7. **System.out.println ():** It is used to print the values in console.

   System→Built in class

   Out→Static reference variables of Print stream class

   Println→Instance method of PrintStream class

It is important to note that all the parameters or codes in Java are case sensitive and have to be coded consciously. Example: A & a.

ASCII value of 'A' and 'a' is 65 and 97 respectively.

Steps to execute a simple Java program

1. Open notepad application and write the below (Fig. 6.5) given simple program:
2. Save the document from the File menu after writing the program.
3. Save the document in a path with the file name 'Sample.java' and select the save as type to 'All files'. Click Save button to save your file.

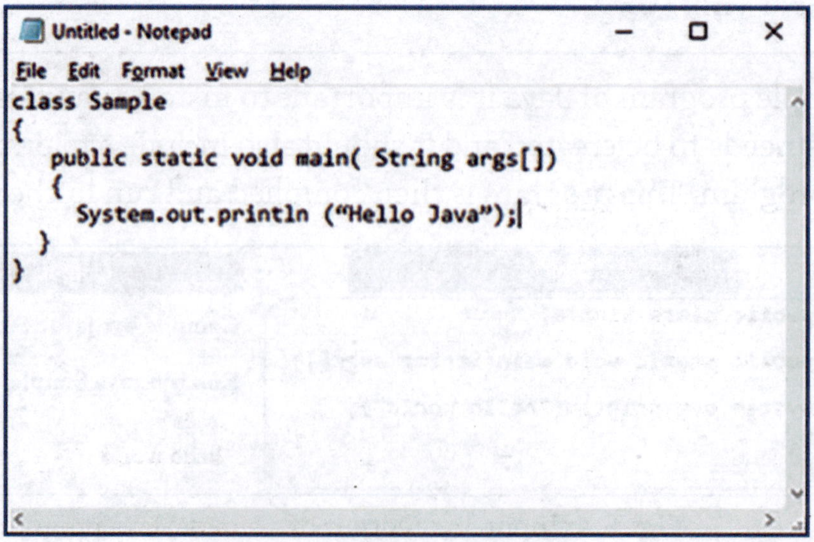

Fig. 6.5: Java program

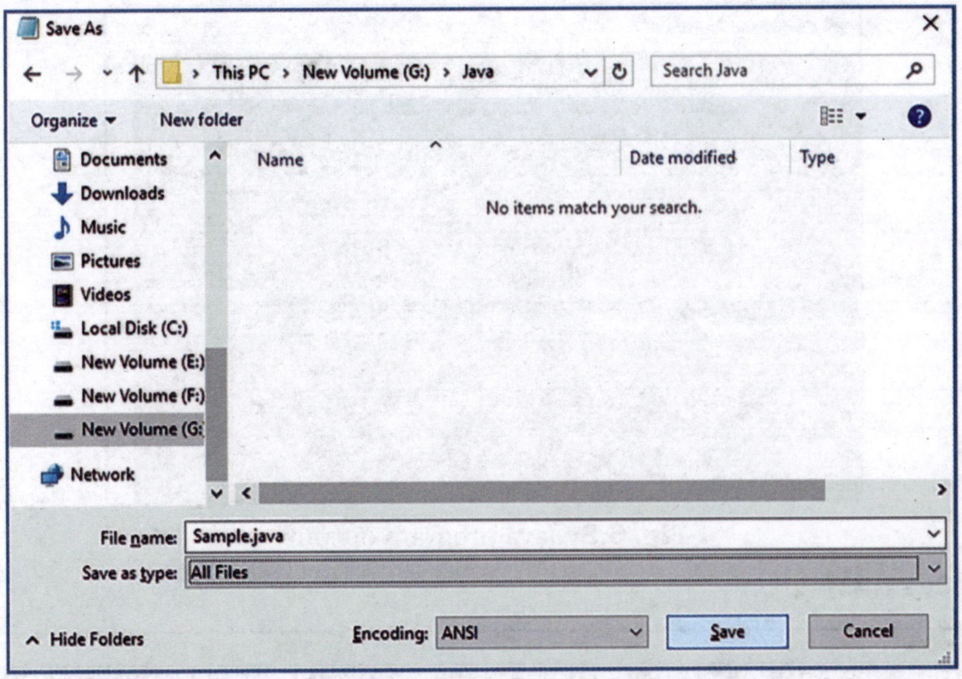

Fig. 6.6: Saving a Java file

4. To compile and run this program, open command prompt from the following path Start Menu → All Programs → Accessories → Command Prompt.
5. To compile and run the above program, go to the current directory and follow the command prompts.

```
Cd\
G:
Cd Java
```

Fig. 6.7: Command prompt

Once current directory is entered the Java program needs to be compiled using the format 'Javac Filename.java'.

```
Javac Sample.java
```

Once the source code file is compiled it gets converted into bytecode and the resultant is a file with the type 'filename.class' with the extension same as in directory. To execute a Java program, a command 'Java Filename' needs to be run.

```
Java Sample
```

The output is displayed in the command prompt.

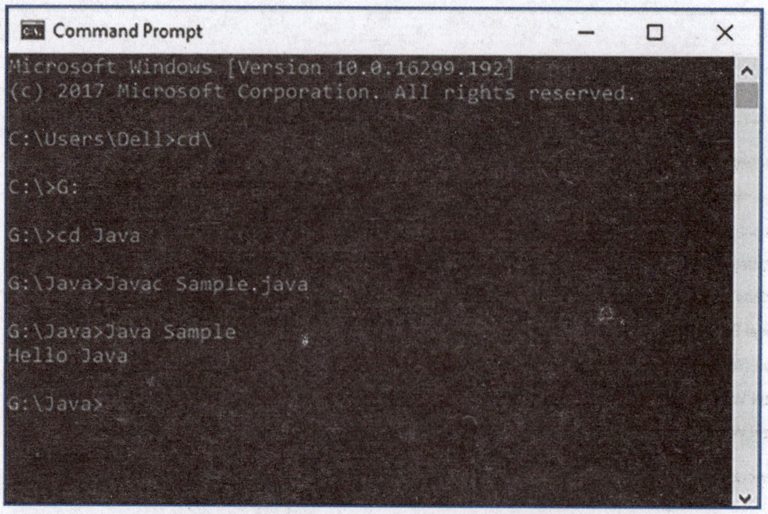

Fig. 6.8: Java program output

Program internal

At compile time a Java file is compiled by a Java compiler. This compiler converts the Java code into bytecode.

Fig. 6.8: Working of Java Compiler

At run-time following events occur:

- A class file is loaded into a classloader, a subsystem of Java Virtual Machine (JVM) is used to load class files. Files from this are sent to a Bytecode Verifier which checks the code fragments for illegal code that can violate access right to objects. Once verified at this stage, it is sent to an interpreter which reads bytecode stream and then executes the instructions. These steps are shown in Fig. 6.9.

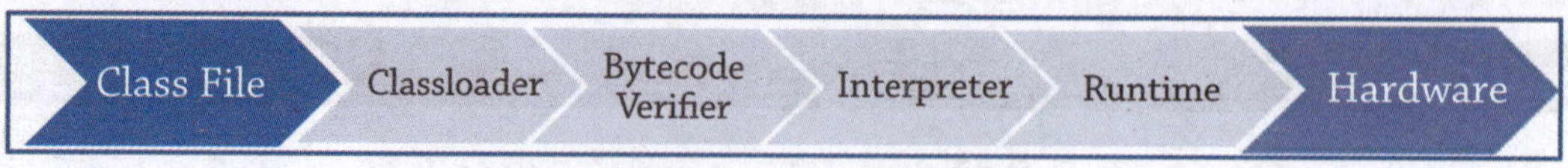

Fig. 6.9: Working of Java Runtime

Keywords and Identifiers

Keywords

A keyword has a predefined meaning in the language and is reserved for a specific command action. There are 53 keywords included in Java. Some of these are public, static, void, class, int, extends, if, else, this, etc.

Identifiers

Identifiers are used to name conventions for class, methods, variables, etc. An identifier should never begin with a digit (number), special character other than underscore (_) and dollar ($).

It follows camelcase syntax for naming the class, interface, method and variable. Example: actionPerformed(), firstName, ActionEvent, ActionListener, etc.

Standard Java naming conventions make the code easier to read by the programmers. Some of the naming conventions are listed below:

Name	Convention
Class name	It starts with uppercase letter and a noun, e.g., String, Color, etc.
Interface name	It starts with uppercase letter and an adjective, e.g., Remote, ActionListener, etc.
Method name	It starts with lowercase letter and a verb, e.g., actionPerformed(), main(), etc.
Variable name	It starts with lowercase letter, e.g., firstName, orderNumber, etc.
Package name	All the letters should be in lowercase, e.g., Java, lang, sql, util, etc.
Constants name	All the letters should be in uppercase, e.g., RED, MAX_PRIORITY, etc.

Data Types and Variables in Java

Data types

Data types indicate the kind of values that are stored in a variable. There are two types of data types:

1. **Primitive data types:** some of the primitive data types and their values are listed below.

- byte→1 byte
- short→2 byte
- int→4 byte
- long→8 byte
- float→4 byte
- double→8 byte
- char→2 byte
- Boolean→1 bit

You should know

JVM is the component of Java architecture that provides the cross platform functionality.

2. **Non- Primitive data types:** Some of the non-primitive data types are array, string, etc.

Variables

Variable is the name of memory location used to store data or value. It is a reserved area allocated in the memory of the system. The values here can vary or change as the name explains vary+able. There are three types of variables in Java:

1. **Local variable:** A variable declared in this method is called *local variable*.
2. **Instance variable:** A variable declared inside the class but outside the method, is called *instance variable*.
3. **Static variable:** A variable which is declared as static is called *static variable*. A single copy of static variable is created in the memory shared among all the instances of the class.

Operators in Java

Operators in Java are the symbols that are used to perform operations. Some of the operators are listed in the table on next page.

Operator type	Category	Precedence
Unary	Postfix	Expr++, expr--
	Prefix	++expr, --expr, +expr, -expr, ~ !
Arithmetic	Multiplicative	* / %
	Additive	+ -
Shift	Shift	<<>>>>>
Relational	Comparison	<><= >= instanceof
	Equality	== !=
Bitwise	Bitwise and	&
	Bitwise exclusive or	^
	Bitwise inclusive or	|
Logical	Logical and	&&
	Logical or	||
Ternary	Ternary	? :
Assignment	Assignment	= +,= -,= *.= /.= ,%= &= ^= |= <<= >>= >>>=

Java array

An **array** is a collection of similar type of elements that have shared memory location. A Java array is an object that contains elements of similar data type. Only fixed set of elements can be stored in a Java array. Java arrays are index based and the first element of the array is stored at 0 index.

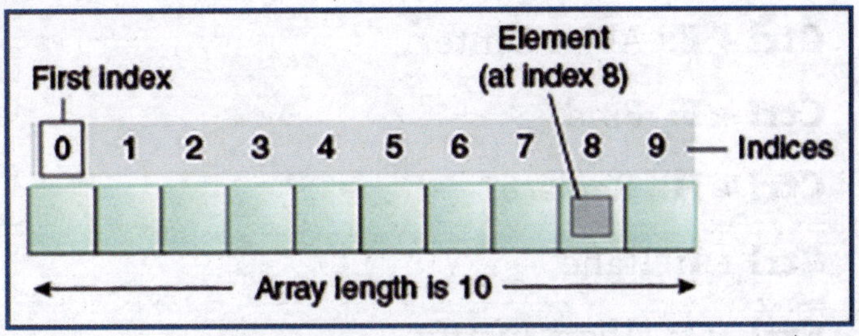

Fig. 6.10: Java array index

Advantage

Code retrieval or sorting of data is easy with the code optimisation. And data from any remote and random location at any index position can be located easily.

Disadvantage

Only fixed size of elements can be stored in an array.

netsearch

For additional information, visit:
https://www.java.com/en/
https://www.guru99.com/java-tutorial.html
https://go.java/index.html
https://www.edx.org/course/learn-to-program-in-java

Mastering the keyboard

Ctrl + A: Select All

Ctrl + B: Bold

Ctrl + C: Copy

Ctrl + E: Align Center

Ctrl + F: Find

Ctrl + H: Replace

Ctrl + I: Italic

Ctrl + J: Align Justify

Ctrl + L: Align Left

Ctrl + N: New

Ctrl + O: Open

Ctrl + R: Align Right

Ctrl + S: Save

Ctrl + U: Underline

Ctrl + V: Paste

Ctrl + W: Close

Ctrl + X: Cut

Ctrl + Y: Redo

Ctrl + Z: Undo

Alt + Left/Right/Up/Down Arrow: Back/Forward/Up/Down

Shift + F1: Contextual Help

F1: Help

Home: Home

Delete: Delete

Teacher's note

Introduce the students to the basics of C/C++ programming languages.

Concepts learnt

1. Java is a general purpose programming language and this produces software for multiple platforms.
2. Java is a programming language developed by James Gosling with other team members, Mike Sheridan and Patrick Naughton in 1995 for Sun Microsystems. They were also called the Green Team.
3. J2SE (Java Standard Edition), J2EE (Java Enterprise Edition), J2ME (Java Micro Edition) and JavaFx are four platforms in Java.
4. Notepad, Notepad++, Notebeans and Eclipse are some of the popular text editors.
5. To write a simple program of Java it is important to install a Java Development Kit (JDK).
6. A compiler converts the Java code into bytecode. At run time, bytecode stream is read to execute the instructions.
7. Identifiers are used to name conventions for class, methods, variables, etc.
8. Java follows camel case syntax for naming the class, interface, method and variable.
9. Variable is a name of memory location used to store data or value.
10. Operators in Java are the symbols that are used to perform operations.
11. A Java array is an object that contains elements of similar data type.

Exercise

A Fill in the blanks.

1. Software or hardware environment in which a program executes, or runs is known as a_________ (platform/path).
2. ______________ (J2SE/J2EE) is a Java programming platform which is used to develop client-server applications.
3. __________ (Static/Void) is a keyword that creates only one copy in the memory.
4. An identifier should never begin with a _______________ (underscore/ digit).
5. _______________ (float/array) is a non-primitive data type.

B Write T for True or F for False.

1. A thread is a small, separate program, executing concurrently. ☐
2. Java programming platform is mainly used to develop Standalone and client-server applications. ☐
3. Java codes or parameters are not case sensitive. ☐
4. On compiling source code gets converted in bytecode. ☐
5. Variable which is declared as static is called static variable. ☐

C Choose the correct option.

1. Which of the following is not a Java application?
   (a) Standalone Application (b) Web Application
   (c) Mobile Application (d) Cloud Application
2. Which of the following is generated on compilation of a source code?
   (a) Code (b) Binary code
   (c) Bytecode (d) Bits
3. Which of the following is not a parameter in Java?
   (a) Static (b) Void
   (c) Main (d) Javac

4. Which of the following checks the code fragments for illegal code that can violate access right to objects?
   (a) Classloader
   (b) Bytecode Verifier
   (c) Interpreter
   (d) Runtime
5. Which of the following names all the letters should be in lowercase?
   (a) Class name
   (b) Method name
   (c) Package name
   (d) Variable name

D Answer these questions briefly.

1. What are the features of Java?
2. Explain how a Java program is compiled and run.
3. What are Java keyword and identifiers?
4. Explain Data types and variables in Java?
5. Write a note on Java array.

E Application-based questions.

1. Smith is learning the basics of Java programming. Help him script a simple program saying, 'This is my first program in Java'.
2. Suzy is struggling to run the program that Smith has written. Write the steps to compile and run the program.
3. John is struggling to understand how a program written in a text editor can be read in command prompt. Explain him the internal programming protocol in your own words.

Computer is my mentor!

Write a simple program with a simple paragraph stating what you have learnt about Java in the chapter.

7 Consolidating Cloud Computing

Learning log

- Cloud computing
- Types of cloud computing
- Cloud computing architecture

Introduction

You already know about storing data on various storage devices and accessing them whenever necessary. Identify the data storage devices among the pictures given below.

Cloud computing is a method of storing and delivering information with the help of Internet. Cloud-based storage uses remote database storage devices and makes them accessible for the people through Internet, rather than storing the files on a local hard drive or local storage devices. Cloud Computing provides a means by which we can access the applications as utilities, over the Internet. Services like Software development platforms are made easy on Internet with cloud computing. Some of the popular cloud computing systems are AWS, Azure and Google Cloud.

Cloud computing plays an important role in accessing the data and services, including storage and application through the Internet. Cloud computing evolved from its roots in 1950s when mainframe computers were introduced. The cost of maintaining these mainframe computers was large and hence was not affordable. Then the concept of shared access to a single computer was introduced. This idea helped the companies to reduce the cost to a great extent.

You should know

By 2020, cloud computing will cross the $270 billion mark.

IBM introduced an OS (Operating System) called VM (Virtual Machine) in 1970. This made simultaneous operations of more than one OS.

Later in 1990s, telecom operators offered virtualized private network connections, which provided the quality of service as good as that of dedicated connections at a lower cost. Also, the introduction of grid computing contributed much to the same, which addressed major challenges through parallel computing.

Cloud Computing

Now, we know that cloud computing is the Internet-based computing that uses shared servers to provide software, infrastructure, and other resources to the users. (Fig. 7.1)

Fig. 7.1: Cloud computing

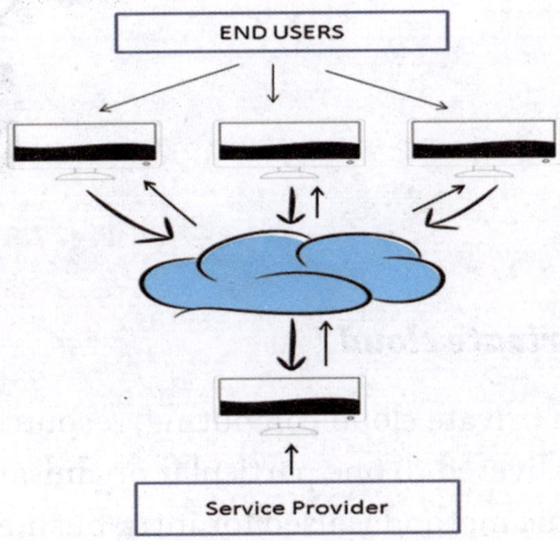

Fig. 7.2: Stages in cloud computing

The origin of the term 'cloud' came from the network design that was used to represent the location of various network devices and the network connection between them. The shape of this network design was like a cloud, and hence the name came into existence. (Fig. 7.2)

With the development of Internet, computer networks and increased mobile users, data storage and accessibility became very much essential for the people for their daily life communication and transaction. Some of the popular cloud services that we use are mail services like Gmail, Hotmail, Yahoo, etc.

When we use email services, our information is stored on a cloud server not on our personal computers or mobile devices.

Types of Cloud Computing

Cloud computing can be mainly classified into private cloud, community cloud, public cloud and hybrid cloud as depicted in Fig. 7.3.

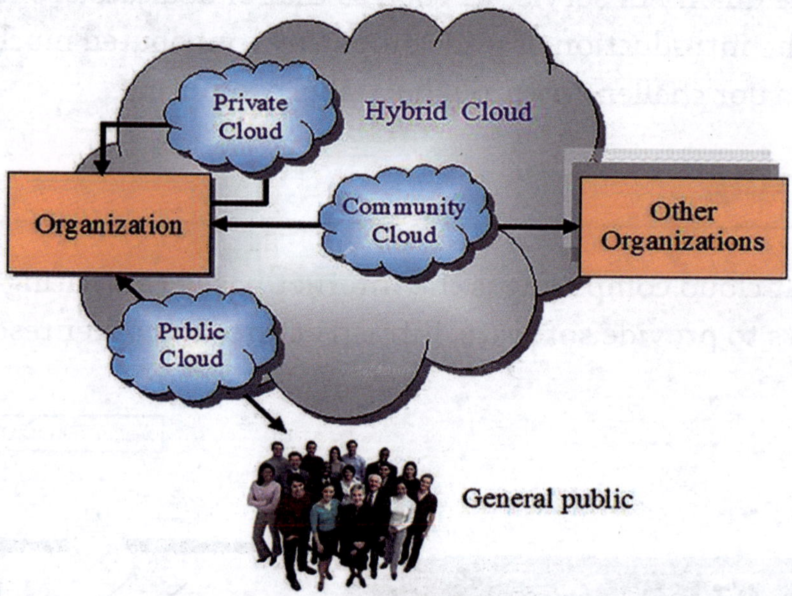

Fig. 7.3: Types of cloud computing

Private cloud

In private cloud computing, resources are delivered to one particular organisation. This method is used for intra-business interaction. In this type, the server and other resources are owned and operated by the same organisation. (Fig. 7.4)

Fig. 7.4: Private cloud

Community cloud

In this type of cloud computing, the information and resources stored in the server are shared and made accessible for community organisations. (Fig. 7.5)

Fig. 7.5: Community cloud

Public cloud

In public cloud computing, the information in the server is made accessible to the public. This type of cloud is usually used in B2C (Business to Consumer) type of interaction. In this case, the server and the other resources are owned and operated by an academic or business organisation. (Fig. 7.6)

Fig. 7.6: Public cloud

Hybrid cloud

Hybrid cloud computing is used for both B2B (Business to Business) or B2C (Business to Consumer) interaction. (Fig: 7.7)

Fig. 7.7: Hybrid cloud

Cloud Computing Architecture

Cloud computing system constitutes a front-end part that consists of client part of the cloud system and a back-end part that consists of cloud storage and resources required for providing the services. While the front-end part deals with interfaces and applications that are required to provide the service, the back-end part consists of servers, data storage and security, etc.

Advantages and Disadvantages of Cloud Computing

Cloud computing provides wide range of possibility to share and access the data across the world. It is useful for communication as well as online transactions. It improves the performance and reduces the cost of maintenance to the users. It increases the data storage capacity and backup. Though cloud computing has lot of advantages, it also has some disadvantages such as security and privacy issues, online scams, etc. We must be careful in giving our private information such as bank account details and passwords while carrying out online transaction.

Concepts learnt

1. Cloud computing is a method for delivering the information by storing the data in a server and making it accessible to the user.
2. Cloud computing decreases the hardware and software demand for the user.
3. Different types of cloud computing are: private, public, community and hybrid.
4. Cloud computing systems have mainly two parts: front-end part and back-end part.

Hands-on practice

1. With the permission of your teacher, search the Internet for more details on Cloud Computing. Also, try to find the details on PaaS, SaaS and IaaS. Use the space given below to document your observations.

____

____

____

____

2. Research on the Internet to find more details on the companies that provide web services. Prepare a comparative report in the space given below.

Exercise

A Fill in the blanks.

1. Cloud computing is a method for delivering _____________ (hardware/information) technology services.
2. Business units use some or all the components of cloud services for their _____________ (service/users).
3. Improved performance is one of the _____________ (benefits/challenges) of cloud computing.
4. Cloud computing comprises of two components, namely _____________ end and _____________ (front and back/front and rear) end.
5. _____________ (Hybrid/Front end) is a type of cloud computing.

B Write T for True or F for False.

1. Cloud computing network supports only private and hybrid clouds. ☐
2. Private computing is more useful for intra-business interaction. ☐
3. In community cloud, computing resources are provided only for organisation. ☐
4. Security and privacy issues are the challenges of cloud computing. ☐
5. Cloud computing facilitate to share and access data across the world. ☐

C Choose the correct option.

1. _____________ type of cloud is usually used in B2C.
   (a) Public (b) Private
   (c) Hybrid (d) Community
2. _____________ cloud can be used in both types of interaction like B2B and B2C.
   (a) Public (b) Private
   (c) Hybrid (d) Community
3. Which of the following is not an advantage of cloud computing?
   (a) Improved performance (b) Online transaction
   (c) Privacy security (d) Accessing information

4. Back end part of cloud computing consists of ____________.
   (a) cloud storage
   (b) resources
   (c) Both (a) and (b)
   (d) None of these

D Answer these questions briefly.

1. What is cloud computing?
2. Explain different types of cloud computing.
3. Mention some of the benefits and challenges of cloud computing.

E Application-based questions.

1. Briefly explain the architecture of cloud computing.
2. Mention some of the examples of cloud computing services.
3. Give examples on different types of cloud computing.

Computer is my mentor!

Search more on cloud computing and collect more information on cloud computing system and its application. Draw a sketch of cloud computing in a chart and present it in your class.

8 More on Synfig Studio

Learning log

- Morphing and cutout animation
- Basics of animation
- Animating shapes
- Basic bone tutorials

Introduction

Below is a set of images. How many people are there in these images?

Yes, these are the images of two people with their faces mixed and matched to make it appear as one. We have learnt that Synfig Studio can be used to create animations frame by frame. It can also be used to morph images and create cutout animation.

Morphing Images

Morphing is a technique of creating a smooth transition between two images. In this process, one shape is deformed into another and is defined by its control points. Morphing in Synfig studio is done automatically allowing the user to create animation by drawing only key positions at right intervals of time.

Fig. 8.1: Morphing images

Cutout Animation

An object is split into different parts and simple transformation is applied onto it at different intervals of time. This is known as cutout animation. The values defined for each part for the movement in Synfig Studio interpolates the motion for in-between frames.

Fig. 8.2: Cutout animation

Basics of Animation

To change a drawing into animation in Synfig Studio means to create the first stage and last stage of a change and the steps in between is automatically programmed by Synfig.

For example: Consider a moving light. To create this, it requires the following three steps:

1. The circle of light is on the left.
2. The circle of light is on the right.
3. The circle of light is back on the left.

To perform any animation, the following steps need to be followed:

1. Setting up the workspace
2. Adding movement

3. Understanding the Timeline
4. The Keyframes
5. Rendering your animation

Setting up the workspace

Following are the steps to set a workspace:

1. Click the canvas menu and select Canvas Properties.
2. The Canvas Properties Dialog (Fig. 8.3) will appear.
3. Give a name and description for the canvas and click 'Apply'.
4. Go to the 'Time' tab and edit 'End Time' to '2s' and click 'OK'.
5. Create a background to the canvas by drawing a simple black rectangle with the help of a Rectangle Tool.
6. Now, draw a circle of different color with the help of a circle tool.
7. Select the Transform Tool and click the circle to adjust and fit it inside the black rectangle.

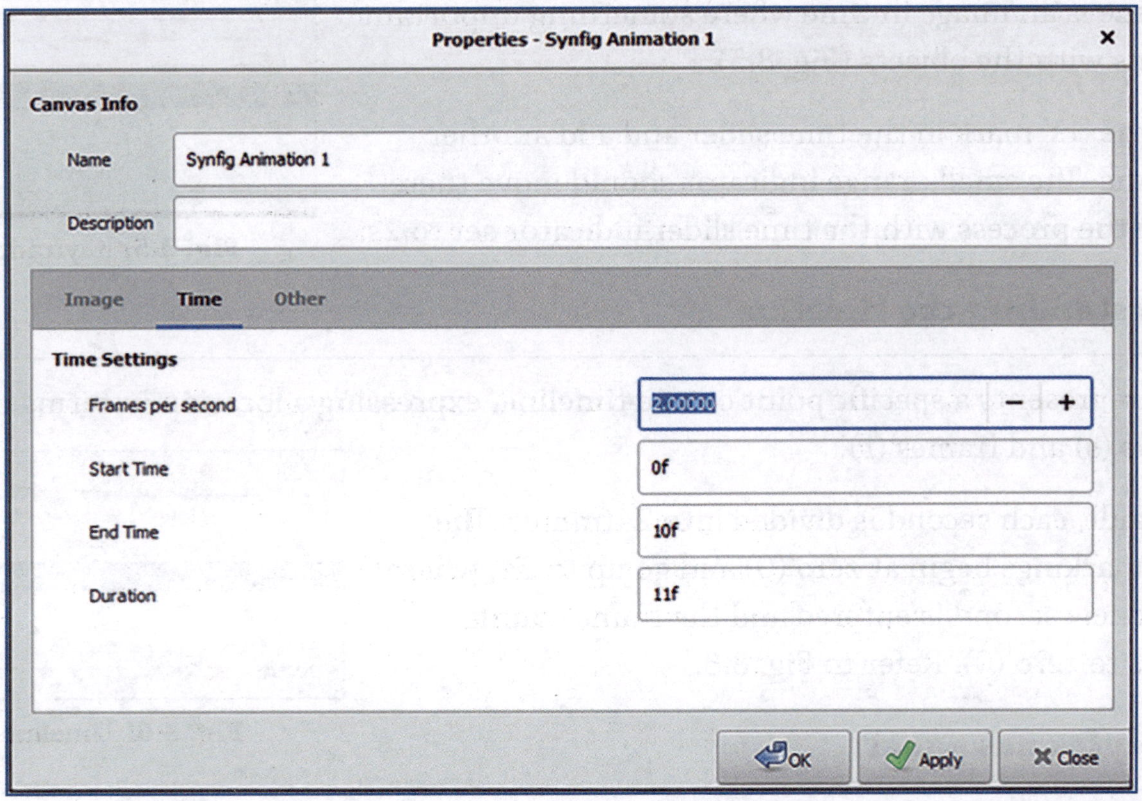

Fig. 8.3: Canvas properties

Adding movement

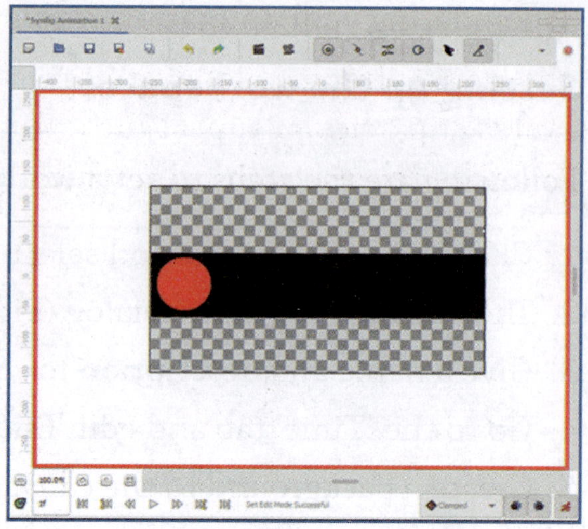

Fig. 8.4: Adding movement

The canvas window has a time slider at the bottom called the Time Bar. Clicking on it, a small orange indicator appears indicating the position in time. The position on the time slider can be set by changing the values in the field. For example, if you enter 1s and press Enter, the orange indicator will move to the middle of the time slider and entering 2s will move it to the end of the time slider. Switch to Animate Editing Mode by clicking the green man button to the right of the time slider. The canvas will display a red outline.

In animate editing mode, every change made in the objects' parameters creates a waypoint that is associated with the change in current time. Synfig creates a smooth intermediate change between waypoints. The three 'steps' mentioned earlier are represented by keyframes. A keyframe is an image in time where something important happens with the objects (Fig. 8.5).

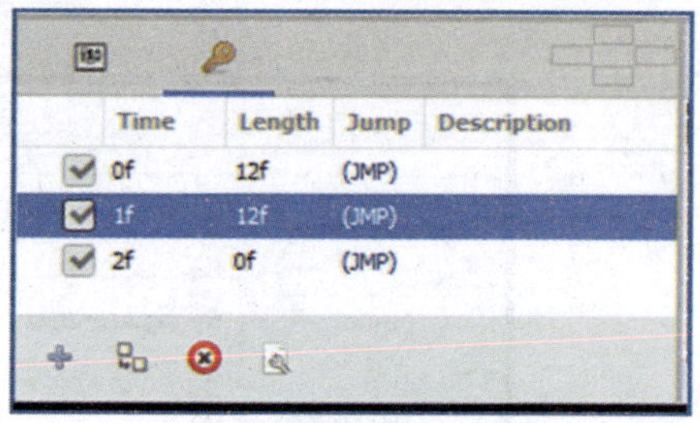

Fig. 8.5: Keyframes

Go to the '1s' mark in the time slider and add another keyframe. The small orange indicator should move there. Repeat the process with the time slider indicator set to 2s.

Understanding the timeline

1s 10f represents a specific point on the timeline, expressing a location in terms of seconds (s) and frames (f).

By default, each second is divided into 24frames. The frame markings begin at zero (0) and go up to 24, where upon a new second is entered and the frame count returns to zero (0). Refer to Fig. 8.6.

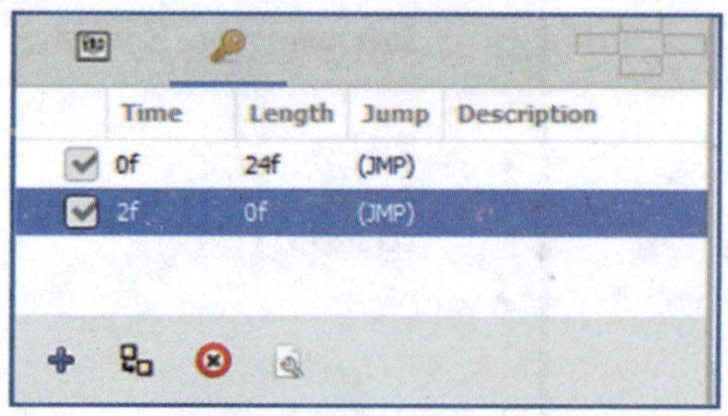

Fig. 8.6: Timeline

The keyframes panel

The Keyframes Panel displays start time, length, jump and description. (JMP) are the links just like weblinks. Clicking on them will jump the indicator in the time slider to the correct time. This can be used to edit an image for a given moment in time.

The user need not go to the last keyframe at 2s and move the circle back to the left as the last keyframe is set default to zero (0). Keyframes make Synfig remember the image states at particular times. The green dots on the Timetrack Panel are called Waypoints, and they represent times at which they are instructed to take on specified new values.

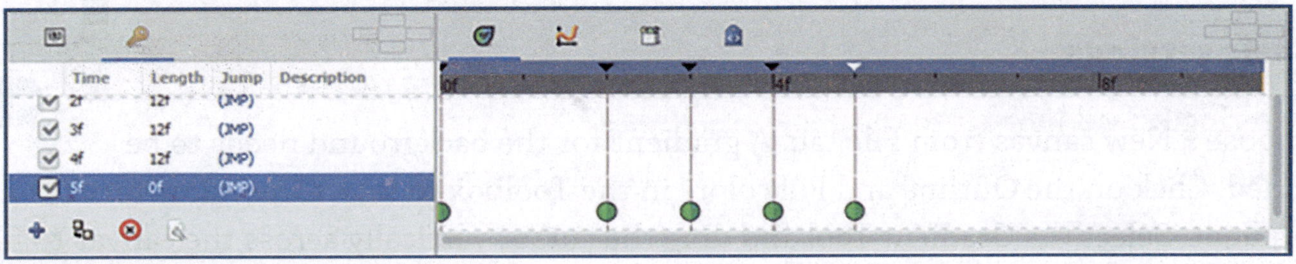

Fig. 8.7: Keyframe panel

Rendering the animation

There are two ways to render the work:

(a) Using the Synfig Studio: Leave the Animate Editing Mode and save the file. Then go to file menu and click render. A dialog box appears. Change the file format to GIF and click 'Render'. The output of the same can be seen in any of the browsers.

Word web

render: it is an automatic process of generation of animations by means of computer program

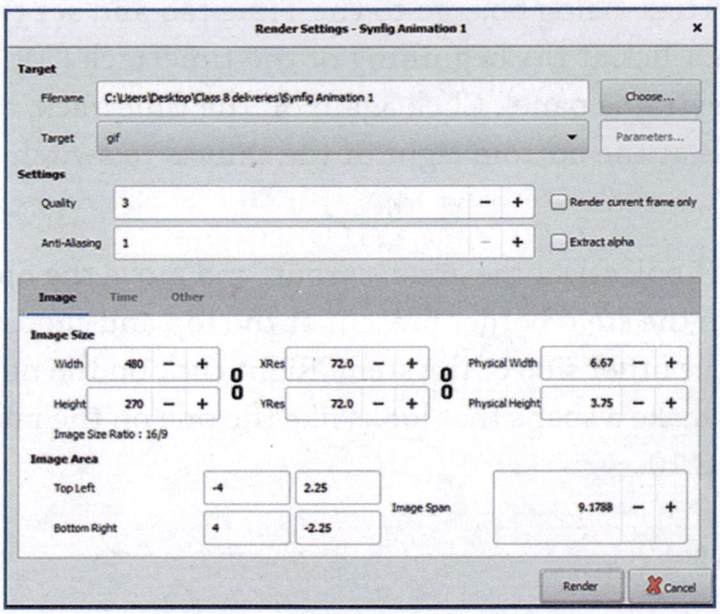

Fig. 8.8: Rendering a video

(b) Command-line program called 'Synfig': To use the command line instead of the menu to render your animation, open the windows terminal and enter the file name you have entered and run. Animated gif can be viewed in Firefox or another browser.

Animating Shapes

Basic settings

Choose a New canvas from File tab. A gradient for the background needs to be added. Click on the Outline and Fill colors in the Toolbox to select the colors for gradient. Select the Gradient Tool and drag the cursor vertically across the canvas to fill it with the gradient.

Select the Spline Tool from the Tool Options Panel. Draw a kind of triangle with the Spline tool. To close the shape after drawing the 3 vertices, right click on the first vertex and choose Loop Spline. Now the trace of the form is closed, select the Transform tool to generate the proper form. This will be the base of the stem.

Word Web

spline: it is a curve that connects two or more points

Animate the stem

In the Canvas properties dialog box, go to the Time tab and set the End time and click OK button. Click at the beginning of the timetrack ("0f") and then add Keyframes in the Keyframe panel. Click again on the timetrack, at "4s 12f", and press the green circle at the bottom right of the canvas to switch to the Animate Editing Mode.

Using the Transform Tool, select the green sprout, and move the upper vertex to make a stem. Right-click on the stem border present at the top and choose Insert Item. Repeat the same to the other side of the stem. Right click on the new points and choose Split Tangents. Now make a shape that looks like the one on the image, to create the flower bud as in Fig. 8.10.

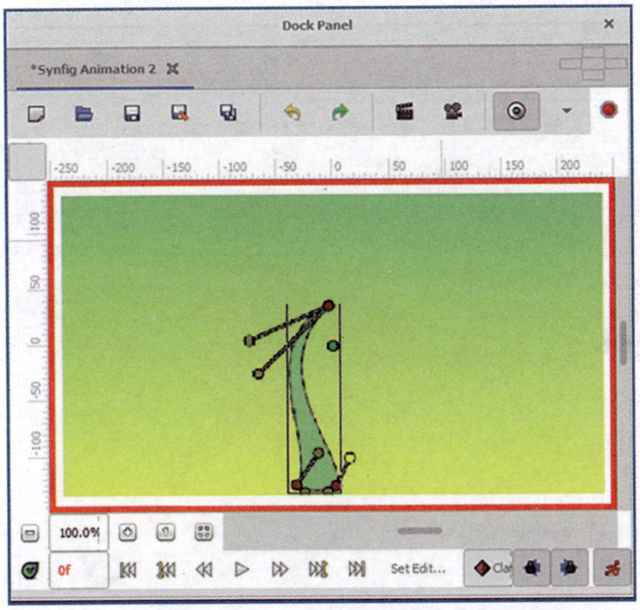

Fig. 8.9: Drawing of stem

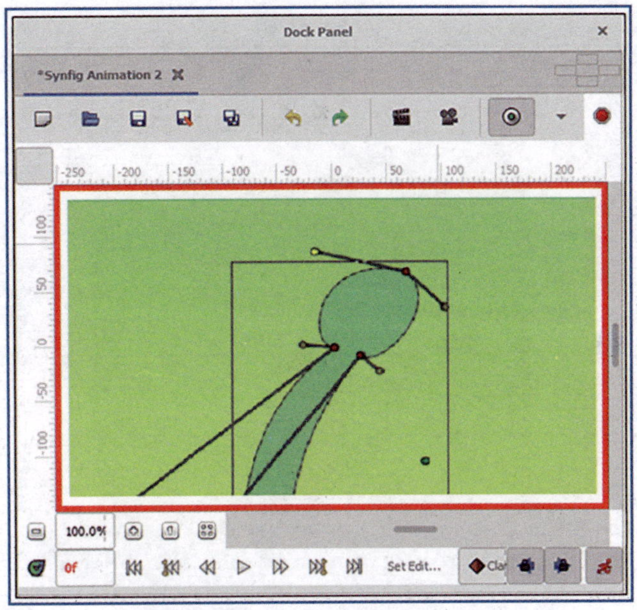

Fig. 8.10: Animation of stem

Each waypoint stands for a recorded value. The two vertices we added to make the bud are marked with green and red vertical line on their 0s and 4s waypoints. Right-click on them in the parameters list, and select Mark Activepoint as Off.

Adding the petals

Leave the Animate Editing Mode and change the fill color to pink. Create petals with the Spline Tool. Select all the vertices of the petal using the shortcut keys Ctrl + A and move them close to the green handle. Then drag the green handle very close to the top of the bud. Press Ctrl + A again to select all vertices of the petal and tweak it a bit with Rotate Tool.

Now click on the vertex at the top of the stem and ctrl-click on the green handle of the petal. Then right-click on the stem top vertex and select Link. The petal will move a bit as the green handle is snapped on the stem vertex. As there is a link between the petal and the top of the stem, the petal will follow the movement shown by the stem.

In the Layers Panel, select the newly created Petal layer and duplicate it. Similarly, add all the petals as shown in Fig. 8.12 and link them to the bud of the flower.

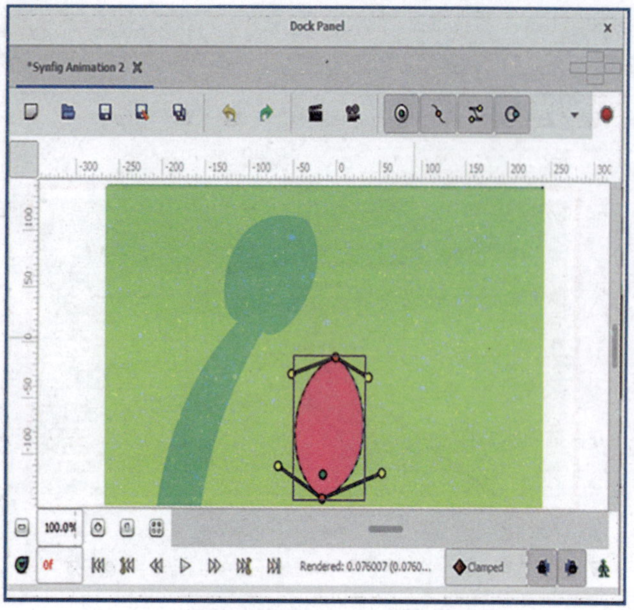

Fig. 8.11: Drawing petals

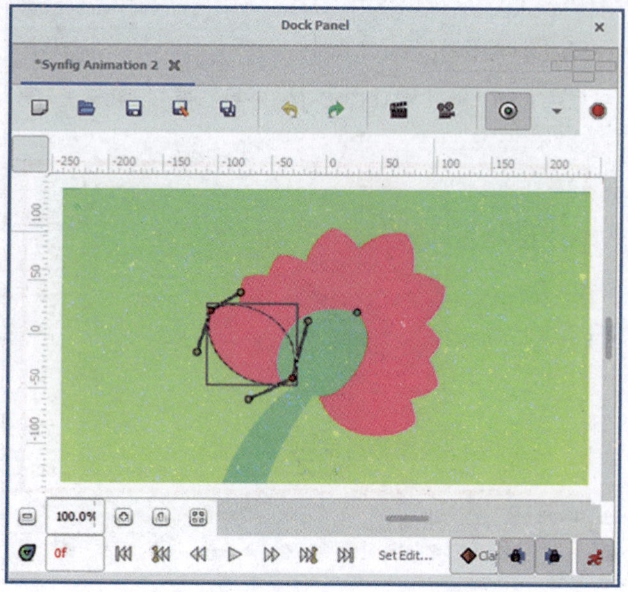

Fig. 8.12: Adding petals

Hiding the petals

To show blossom of a flower, each petal should appear one after the other. For this, let us set 4 seconds of transition time in the animation. To achieve this, switch to Animate Editing Mode and go to 4s and modify. A keyframe at 5s needs to be added on the timetrack to show full blossom of the flower.

Scale down the image with the Scale Tool and move them inward, so they are hidden by the stem. From 4s to 5s, the petals will now appear and bloom. The petals should be made tiny and hidden tweaking their size on every frame from 0s to 4s so that petals do not appear in 0s or the petals should be made invisible in this interval. Group the petal layers into a Group Layer by right-clicking on them on the Layers Panel and select Group. Select the Petals Group Layer and jump to the first keyframe. In the Parameters Panel, set the Amount value to '0'. The petals are now invisible on that keyframe (Fig. 8.13).

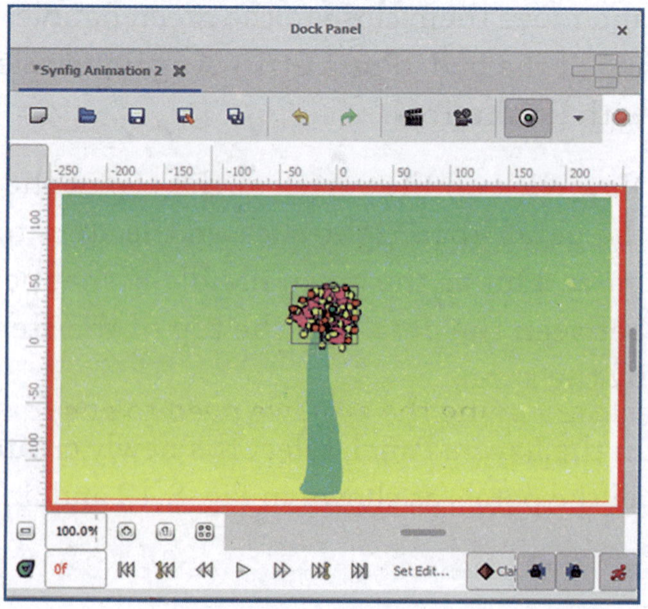

Fig. 8.13: Hiding petals

The opacity of petals from 0s to 4s should slowly increase, making the petals visible. To achieve this, change the Amount interpolation method. Right click on the Amount waypoint at 0f and select Edit. A new dialog box will appear, in which you can choose the In and Out interpolation. Set the Out Interpolation to Constant.

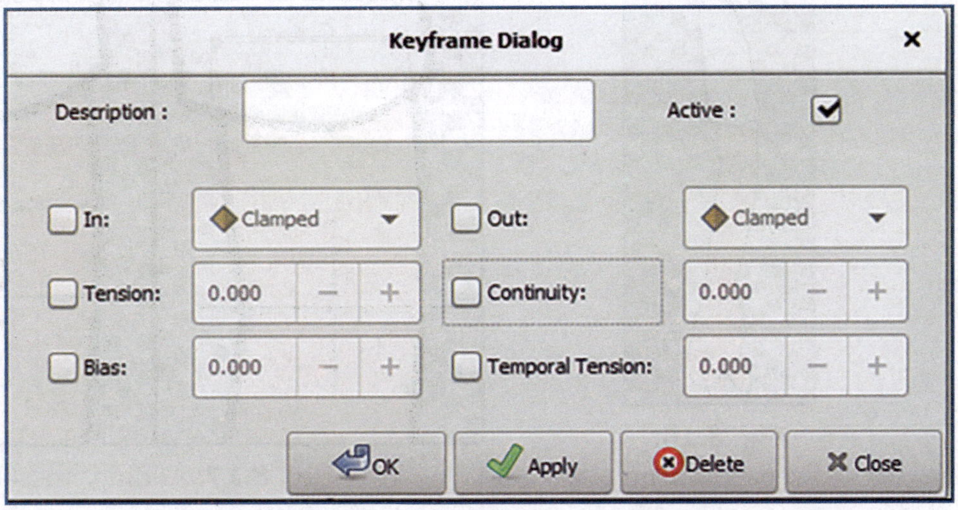

Fig. 8.14: Keyframe dialog box to set interpolation

With this change, the stem grows for 4.5 seconds and then stays still the last 1.5 seconds. The petals are hidden until 4 seconds and then grow quickly between 4 and 5 seconds and stay till the last 1 second. Render the animation by ensuring that Use current frame option is unchecked.

Basic Bone Structures in an Animation

This kind of animation is used to show movement in locomotive organisms like humans and animals. To understand the basics of bone movement, we shall take the examples of an arm with fixed joints using the Skeleton Layer and three bones.

The arm consists of three parts: the upper arm, the lower arm and the hand. Each part is grouped in a layer called arm (Fig. 8.15).

Prepare the joints

Before rigging the arm, we need to ensure that the joints rotate properly. It is to be noticed that the lower side of the upper arm is straight and does not have an outline, while the upper part of the lower arm has an outline. The joint of the hand is also curved with an outline. To make sure that the joint parts of the arm rotate correctly, it is made with the help of a couple of crosshairs as in Fig. 8.16.

The horizontal crosshair line should match the straight line of the bottom of the upper arm and at the same time, the outline of the circle of the crosshair matches the top curved outline of the lower arm as in Fig. 8.17.

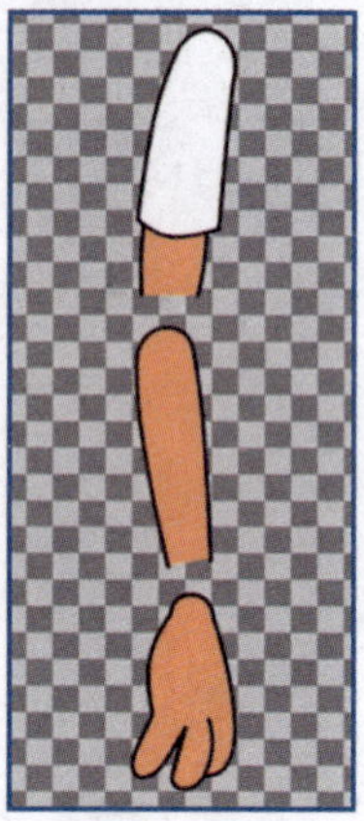

Fig. 8.15: Parts of an arm

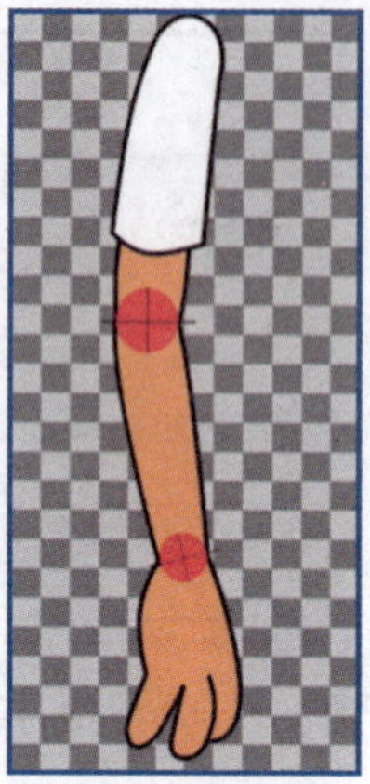

Fig. 8.16: Preparing arms

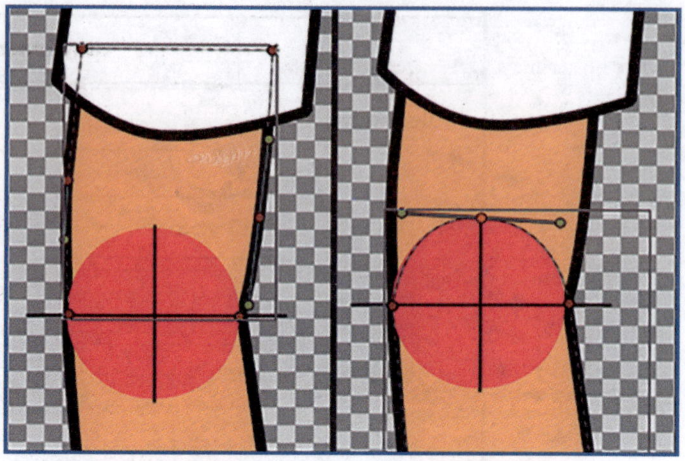

Fig. 8.17: Adding crosshair

The same principle is applied to the hand and the bottom part of the lower arm. The crosshairs also mark the centre of the rotation point. This will later be used when placing the bones. Before placing the bones, we can align the Group Transformation Widget of the lower arm group and the hand group with the crosshair of the elbow and the wrist to check if the joints rotate correctly.

Word web

rigging: ropes and wires that support a structure

Adding the bones

To add the bones, the arm has to be rigged by adding a Skeleton Layer. To add this, right-click on any layer in the Layers Panel and choose New Layer. A new Skeleton Layer will appear in the Layers Panel alongside with a small bone in the canvas.

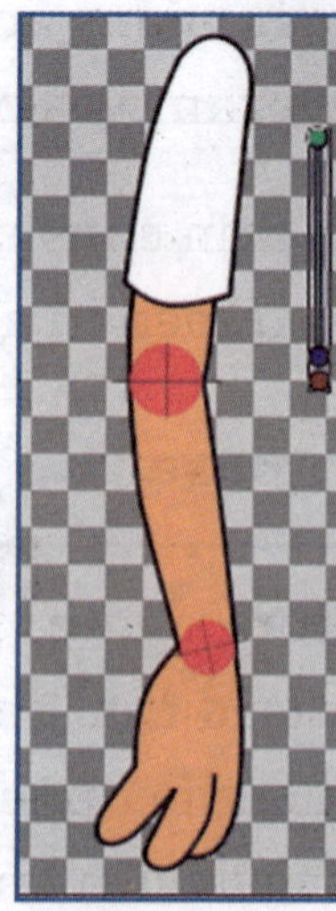

Fig. 8.18: Adding bones

Put the Skeleton Layer above the arm and group it. The green handle of the bone is the origin of the bone and is used to move the bone in place. The blue handle can be used to rotate the bone and green handle acts as the centre of rotation. The orange handle determines the length of the bone. The bone should be moved towards the shoulder and stretched to meet the outlines of the first crosshair of the elbow. Right-click on any of the handles of the parent bone and select Create Child Bone. Move the green origin point of the child bone to match the crosshair of the elbow and stretch it until it reaches the crosshair of the wrist. Right click on any of the handles of the child bone and create another child bone. Move the green origin point of the second child bone so that it matches the crosshair of the wrist. Stretch the bone until it reaches the end of the fingers.

Attaching the bones

With the completion of Skeleton Layer, it is now to attach the bones to the parts of the arm. To achieve this, from the Layers Panel, click on the upper arm group, right-click and select Child Layers. Then press Ctrl + A in the canvas window. With everything in the upper arm group being highlighted, Ctrl - click on any bone in the canvas window and right-click on any of the handles of the parent bone and click Link to Bone. The upper arm group is now linked to the parent bone. Repeat the same with the lower arm and fingers.

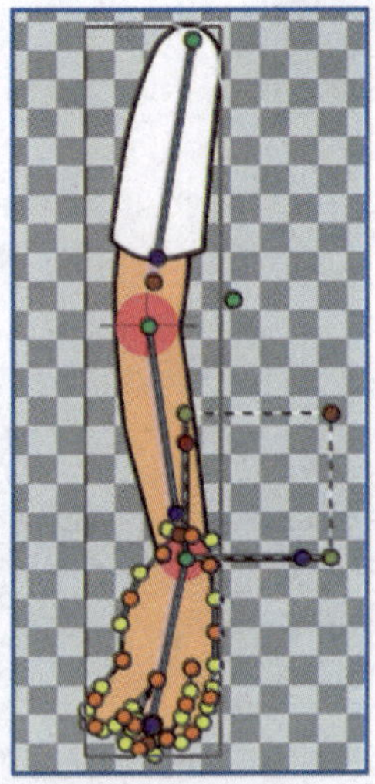

Fig. 8.19: Attaching bones

You should know

All the major components in Synfig are buildable, installable and runnable. Build is not tested without the installation of ETL. Following are the list of libraries on which Synfig is dependent: boost (system, filesystem, program_options, chrono), zlib, libsigc++-2.0, glibmm-2.4, giomm-2.4, cairo, libxml++-2.6, mlt++, fftw3, pango, gtkmm-3.0 (only for studio), gettext (optional), some threading support (e.g. pthread), etc.

netsearch

For additional information, visit:

https://www.youtube.com/watch?v=15aVx7k3xqg

https://www.youtube.com/watch?v=zVFbYm4EnlA

https://www.youtube.com/watch?v=P65_ACqWxbQ

https://www.youtube.com/watch?v=f8bCahcjg84

Mastering the keyboard

Ctrl + A: Select all Handles
Ctrl + C: Copy currently selected layer(s) and put them in the clipboard
Ctrl + D: Deselect all Handles
Shift + Ctrl + D: Deselect all layers
Ctrl + N: New composition
Ctrl + O: Open composition
Ctrl + P: Play the current animation in the WorkArea
Ctrl + V: Paste the layer(s) from the clipboard above the currently selected layer
Ctrl + X: Cut currently selected layer(s) and put them in the clipboard
Ctrl + 0...9: Change the current rendering quality (lower is better, but 0==10)
Ctrl + ,: Move backward one frame
Ctrl + .: Move forward one frame
Ctrl + <: Move backward one second
Ctrl + >: Move forward one second
Ctrl + [: Move backward to previous Keyframe
Ctrl +]: Move forward to next Keyframe
Home: Jump to beginning of timeline
End: Jump to end of timeline
Ctrl + (: Decrease Workarea pixel size
Ctrl +): Increase Workarea pixel size
Alt + A: Select Transform Tool
Alt + T: Select Rotate Tool
Alt + C: Select Circle Tool
Alt + R: Select Rectangle Tool
Alt + G: Select Gradient Tool
Alt + P: Select Polygon Tool
Alt + B: Select Spline Tool
Alt + X: Select Text Tool
Alt + F: Select Fill Tool
Alt + D: Select Draw Tool
F8: Canvas Properties
F9: Render
F11: Preview
F12: Canvas Options (Grid size, etc.)
Escape: Deselect the last Tool and select Transform Tool
Backspace: Select the immediate parent Group Layer (if any) of the current selected layer.

Teacher's note

Refresh the basics of Synfig studio and begin the class by asking them some of the simple animations they have come across.

Concepts learnt

1. Morphing is a technique of creating a smooth transition between two images.
2. An object is split into different parts and simple transformation is applied onto it at different intervals of time. This is known as cutout animation.
3. To change a drawing into animation in Synfig Studio means to create the first stage and last stage of a change and the steps in between are automatically programmed by Synfig.
4. To perform a simple animation: Workspace needs to be set, movement should be added to the objects, timeline should be fixed, the keyframes should be added, and the animation needs to be rendered.
5. To animate shapes, example flower—Stem and the petals of the flower need to be drawn independently and joined together before animation.
6. Basic bone structures are used to show movement in locomotive organisms like humans and animals.
7. To add bones to the skeletal structure of an animation, following are the steps: Preparing the joints, adding the bones and attaching the bones.

Hands-on practice

Consider an image of your favourite vehicle. Try to animate it using the concepts learnt in this chapter. Write the steps in space given on next page.

Exercise

A Fill in the blanks.

1. The green dots on the Timetrack Panel are called ________________ (Waypoints/Keyframes).
2. The keyboard shortcut to select a circle tool is ________________ (Ctrl + C / Alt + C).
3. ________________ (Rotate/Transform) tool can be used to select the green bud and move the upper vertex to make a stem.
4. ________________ (Group Transformation Widget/Create Child Bone) can be used to check the movement of the bones.
5. The ________________ (orange/green) handle determines the length of the bone.

B Write T for True or F for False.

1. Switching between the animation editing modes will add and remove a red border around the canvas. ☐
2. In a keyframe, by default each second is divided into 12 frames. ☐
3. Command-line program cannot be used to render Synfig animation. ☐
4. "1f" is the default beginning of the timetrack. ☐
5. Blue handle of the bone acts as a centre of rotation. ☐

C Choose the correct option.

1. Which of the following is not included in Render settings dialog box?
   (a) File name (b) Image size
   (c) Image area (d) Frames per second
2. What is the default length of the last keyframe in an animation?
   (a) 0f (b) 1f
   (c) 2f (d) 3f

Exercise

3. Identify the spline tool.

(a) 

(b) 

(c) 

(d) 

4. Which of the following tools can be used to tweak the petals of the flower and fit it into bud?

(a) Rotate (b) Transform

(c) Spline (d) Polygon

5. Which of the following is the keyboard shortcut to render an animation?

(a) F8 (b) F9

(c) F11 (d) F12

D Answer the questions briefly.

1. Write the steps to setup a workspace.
2. In an animation, the user need not set the last keyframe back to zero. Why?
3. What is the function of the tool “Loop Spline?
4. Explain how to draw a flower bud in Synfig studio.
5. Write a note on how to attach bones.

E Application-based questions.

1. Suzy wants to demonstrate a simple animation in Synfig Studio. Suggest a simple animation to help her achieve the same.
2. John has added crosshairs to his animation character. He wants to check if he has added it correctly by checking its movement. What should he do?
3. Mike wants to draw a freehand character and add animation to it. Which are the tools needed to draw the same.

Computer is my mentor!

Prepare a simple animation of a ball bouncing twice on a ground.

9 More on OpenShot Video Editor

Learning log

- Working with files and clips
- Understanding transitions and animations
- Setting titles and profiles

Introduction

Movies and videos that we see in our day-to-day life are mostly edited and formated. From the below image which do you think is the most apt method of editing a video?

Yes, digital editing is the most apt method of editing a video. Now, list a few basic editing requirements you would want to have in a video editor.

____

____

____

Features of OpenShot video editor are:

1. It is opensource video Editor for different platforms like Mac, Linux, Windows.
2. It supports many format of video, audio and image.
3. Titles and Subtitles can be created along with 3D animated titles and effects.
4. Audio mixing and video mixing can be done.

In this chapter, we will be learning some of the simple editing options which are available in OpenShot Video Editor.

Files

It is important to import files into OpenShot before video making is initiated. Imported files can be viewed and managed in the Project Files panel. Media files can be imported either by dragging and dropping to the Project File panel or from the File tab.

Media files have certain file options included with it. To explore these options, right click on the media file and see the drop list of options as in Fig. 9.1.

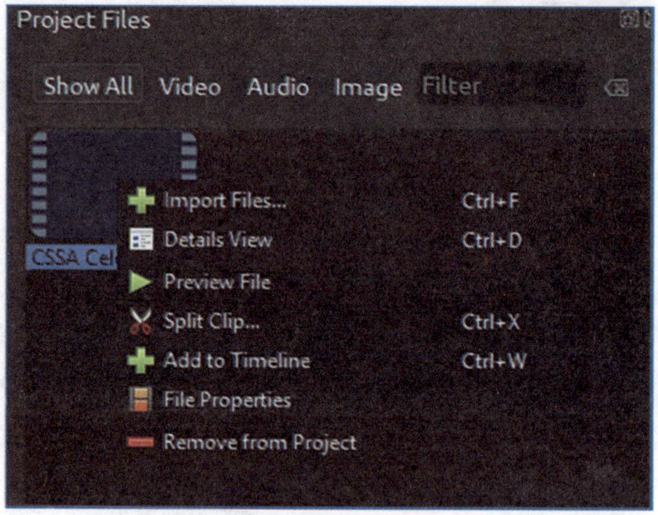

Fig. 9.1: File option of media files

Following are the actions performed by media file options:

- **Import Files:** Imports files into the user's project
- **Detail:** Toggle the view between details and thumbnails
- **Preview File:** Preview a media file
- **Split Clip:** Split a file into many smaller clips
- **Add to Timeline:** Add many files to the timeline in one step
- **File Properties:** View the properties of a file
- **Remove from Project:** Remove a file from the project

Word Web

timeline: a period of time represented graphically on a line

Split clips

This option is used to cut a file into many smaller clips before editing. To perform this option right click on a file and choose Split Clip from the File menu. This opens the Split Clip dialog as in Fig. 9.2.

Use this dialog to cut out as many small clips as you need. Click Create to make the video clip. The dialog box remains open allowing the user to create as many clips as required. Once finished with splitting videos for different clips close the dialog box.

Fig. 9.2: Split Clip

Add to timeline

This option can be used to add a large number of files to the timeline at the same time. For example, a photo slide show or a large number of short video clips. The Add to Timeline dialog can automate this task for you. First, select all files you need to add, right click and choose Add to Timeline. The order of the files selected, Timeline Position, Fading and Zooming Options and transitions can be performed on this timeline.

Fig. 9.3: Add to timeline dialog box

File properties

To view the properties of any imported file the user needs to right click on the file and choose File Properties. This launches the File Properties dialog (Fig. 9.4) displaying information about the media file chosen.

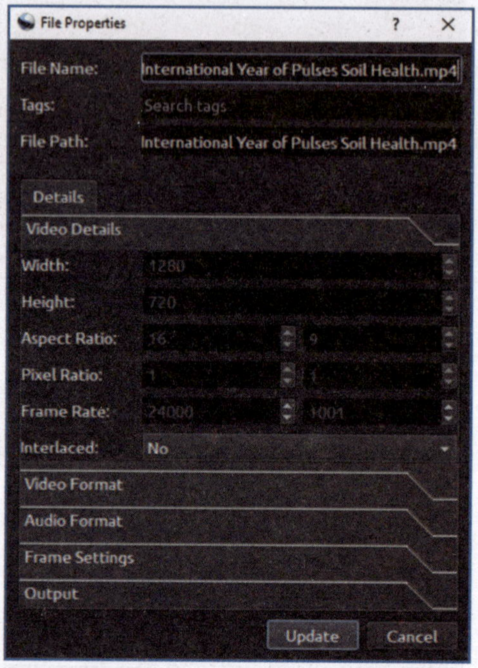

Fig. 9.4: Properties dialog box showing properties of a media file

Clips

Any media file added to the OpenShot timeline is called a clip. These files are shown by a dark, rounded rectangle. A clip has many properties such as scale, location, rotation and alpha. These properties affect how the clip is rendered and composited.

Word Web

transitions: the period of changing from one form to another

OpenShot has many easy ways to adjust the start and end positions of a clip. The most common method is simply grabbing the left edge of the clip and dragging. It also has pre-set animations and clip properties, such as fading, sliding, zooming, etc. Right clicking on the clip will give the user numerous options to run a video. Refer to Fig. 9.5.

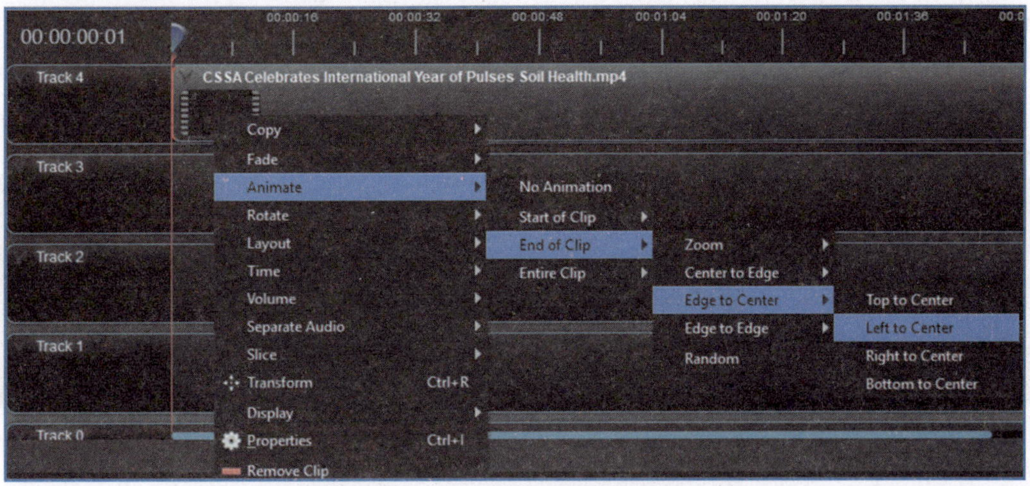

Fig. 9.5: Pre-set options for animations

Transform

To adjust the location and scale of a clip, transform tool can be used from the timeline on right clicking. Hold the small blue handles to adjust scale and hold the middle circle to move the image (Fig. 9.6).

Fig. 9.6: Transform a clip

Transitions

Gradual fade between two clips can be imparted by transition option. Transitions are represented by blue, rounded rectangles on the timeline. They are automatically created when two clips overlap. This can also be added manually by dragging one onto the other in the timeline as in Fig. 9.7.

Fig. 9.7: Transition between clips

Transitions adjust the alpha or transparency of the clip. Transition can either fade from opaque to transparent or transparent to opaque. To change the direction of fade right click and choose Reverse Transition (Fig. 9.8).

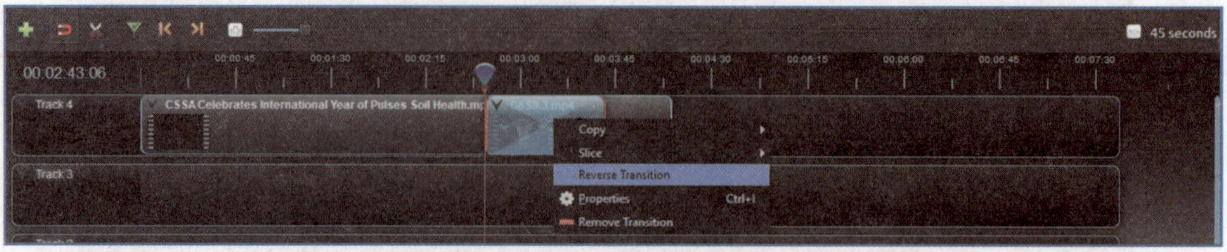

Fig. 9.8: Reverse transition

Following are the methods for cutting transitions in a video clip.

Name	Description
Slice	Choose Slice when the play-head is overlapping a transition by right clicking on the transition.
Slice All	Choose Slice All when the play-head is overlapping many transitions by right clicking on the play head.
Resizing Edge	Move mouse over the edge of a transition and resize the edge.
Razor Tool	The razor tool cuts a transition wherever the user clicks.

Animation

The curve-based animation framework of OpenShot handles most animation tasks with ease. It is a flexible application to create any kind of animation. Keyframes specify values at certain points on a clip and OpenShot interpolates the in-between values.

To create a keyframe, position the play-head at any point over a clip and edit properties from the clip property dialog. If the clip property supports keyframes, it turns green. Repeat the same in different positions. Any animation requires at least 2 keyframes, but it can support numerous keyframes.
Right click on the small graph icon next to a property value to adjust the interpolation mode as in Fig. 9.9.

To adjust the interpolation mode, right click on the small graph icon next to a property value.

Word web

keyframe: a drawing that defines starting and ending points for smooth transition

bézier: it is a parametric curve frequently used in computer graphics

Name	Description
Bézier	Interpolated values use a quadratic curve for Ease In and Ease Out
Linear	Interpolated values are calculated linear values
Constant	Interpolated values stay the same until the next key frame and change to the new value

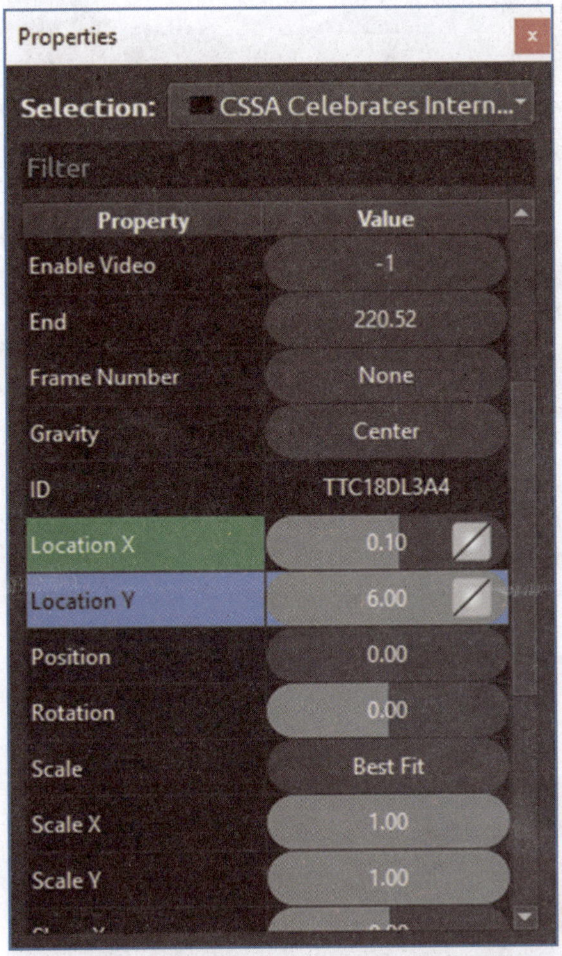

Fig. 9.9: Clip Properties with changed Keyframe

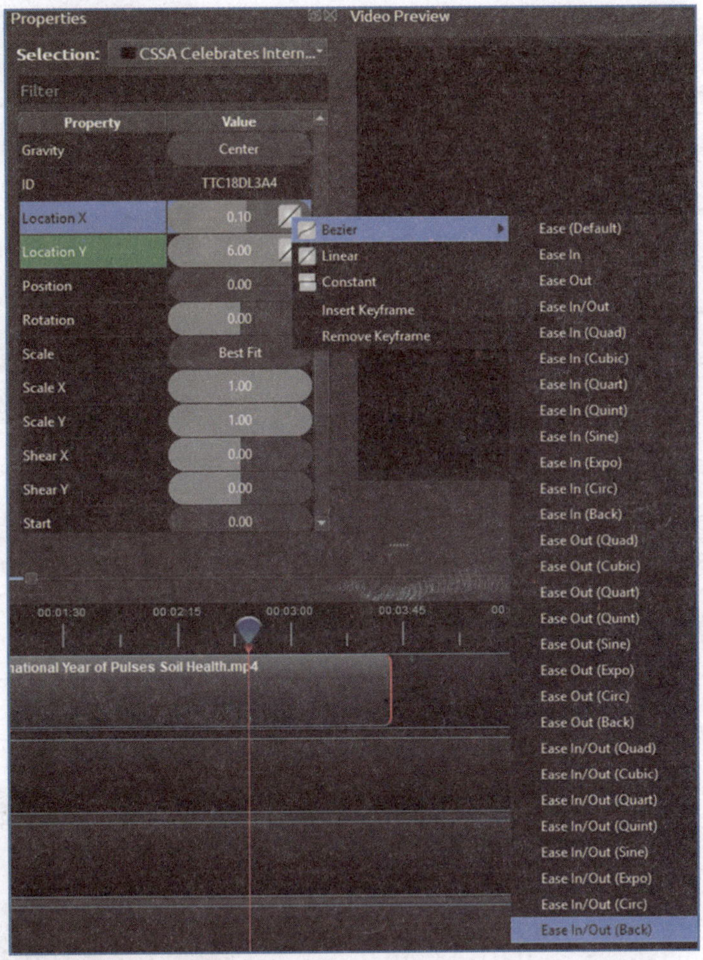

Fig. 9.10: Pre-set interpolation modes

A Bézier curve for animation includes more than 20 curve pre-sets. For example, Ease In has a more gradual slope at the beginning, making an animation move slower at the beginning and faster at the end. To choose a curve pre-set, right click on the small graph icon next to a keyframe and choose Bézier option as in Fig. 9.10.

Titles

OpenShot comes with an easy to use Title Editor as adding text and titles is an important aspect of video editing. Title Editor can be launched from the Title menu.

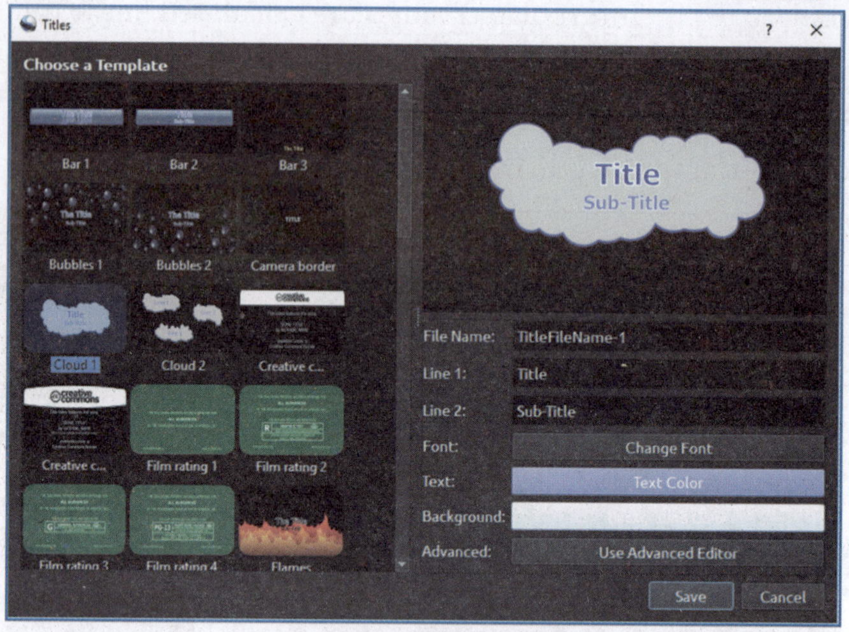

Fig. 9.11: Titles dialog box

3D animated titles can also be added to the video clip by choosing Animated Titles option from the Title menu.

Titles and Animated Titles dialog boxes provides a pre-set template of tiles. It also has a preview available with the properties of the title type choose for the animation. Once the desired animation is selected click Save for titles and click Render for animated titles.

Profiles

A collection of common video settings like size, frame rate, aspect ratio, etc., is called a profile. Profiles are used for a quick switch between common combinations and their settings during editing, previewing and exporting a video clip.

Fig. 9.12: Animated Titles dialog box.

The project profile is used for previewing a project and editing it. The default project profile is HD 720p 24fps. It is suggested to switch to the target profile specifications before the commencement of editing by choosing the same from the Choose Profile option in File tab. For example, if the video is targeted to be in 1080p 30fps, switch to that profile before commencing the editing the project as in Fig. 9.13.

Word web

HD 720p 24fps: high Definition 720 pixels 24 frames per second

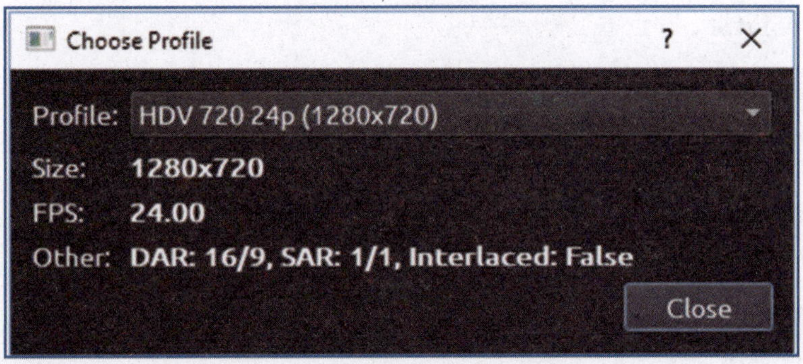

Fig. 9.13: Profile options dialog box

netsearch

For additional information, visit:
https://www.omgubuntu.co.uk/2017/11/openshot-2-4-1-released-various-improvements
https://www.archlinux.org/packages/community/any/openshot/
http://openshotusers.com/forum/

Mastering keyboard

Ctrl + Shift + T: Add Track

Ctrl + W: Add to Timeline

Ctrl + B: Animated Title

Ctrl + P: Choose Profile

Ctrl + C: Copy

Ctrl + D: Details View

Ctrl + F: Import Files

Ctrl + N: New Project

Right: Next Frame

Ctrl + Right: Next Marker

Ctrl + V: Paste

Left: Previous Frame

Ctrl + Left: Previous Marker

Ctrl + I: Properties

Ctrl + A: Select All

Ctrl + Shift + A: Select None

Ctrl + K: Slice All: Keep Both Sides

Ctrl + L: Slice All: Keep Left Side

Ctrl + J: Slice All: Keep Right Side

Ctrl + G: Toggle Snapping

Ctrl + X: Split Clip

Ctrl + T: Title Editor

Ctrl + Scroll: Zoom In/Out

Teacher's Note

Refresh the basics of OpenShot and begin the class. Ask them if they can crop and morph a video, collect the answers and direct them to the chapter.

Concepts Learnt

1. Imported files can be viewed and managed in the Project Files panel.
2. Split Clip is used to cut a file into many smaller clips before editing.
3. To add many files to the timeline at the same time 'Add to timeline' option can be used.
4. Any media file added to the OpenShot timeline is called a clip.
5. OpenShot has many easy ways to adjust the start and end positions of a clip.
6. To adjust the location and scale of a clip transform tool can be used from the timeline on right clicking.
7. Gradual fade between two clips can be imparted by transition option.
8. Transitions adjust the alpha or transparency of the clip.
9. The curve-based animation framework of OpenShot handles most animation tasks with ease.
10. To create a keyframe, position the play-head at any point over a clip and edit properties from the clip property dialog.
11. A Bézier curve for animation, includes more than 20 curve pre-sets.
12. OpenShot comes with an easy to use Title either plain or in animated format.
13. A collection of common video settings like size, frame rate, aspect ratio, etc., is called a profile.

Exercise

A Fill in the blanks.

1. __________________ (Transformations/Transitions) adjust the alpha or transparency of the clip.
2. _______________ (Clip/Image) files in OpenShot are shown by a dark, rounded rectangle.
3. If the clip property supports keyframes, it turns____________ (blue/green).
4. ____________________ (Linear/Bézier) interpolated values use a quadratic curve for Ease In and Ease Out.
5. A collection of common video settings like size, frame rate, aspect ratio, etc., is called a _________________ (profile/project profile).

B Write T for True or F for False.

1. Split Clip dialog box closes once the clip is cut as per requirement. ☐
2. Transition can only fade from opaque to transparent. ☐
3. A Bézier curve for animation includes more than 20 curve pre-sets. ☐
4. Titles dialog box has a preview window. ☐
5. Animated titles need to be rendered to the video clip. ☐

C Choose the correct option.

1. Which of the following options is not available under file options?
   (a) Import files (b) Split Clip
   (c) Add to timeline (d) Animate
2. Which of the following is used to cut the transition wherever the user clicks?
   (a) Razor tool (b) Resizing edge
   (c) Slice (d) Slice all
3. Which of the following can be performed from a clip in timeline?
   (a) Add to timeline (b) Check file properties
   (c) Reverse transition (d) Toggle the view

4. Which of the following is not an interpolation mode?
   (a) Bézier (b) Keyframe
   (c) Linear (d) Constant
5. Which of the following is the default output of a project profile?
   (a) HD 720p 24fps (b) HD 1080p 30fps
   (c) HD 720p 25fps (d) HD 1080p 50fps

D Answer these questions briefly.

1. List the options that can be performed under media file options?
2. What are the different methods that can be used to cut a transition in a video clip?
3. Write a note on different interpolation modes in animation.
4. Write a note on titles.
5. Write a note on profiles.

E Application-based questions.

1. Smith wants to edit and show a small portion of the video he captures while he was travelling to his country side. He was worried if he can do it with the OpenShot Video Editor application he has in his Linux OS. What do you think should he be worried or not?
2. John wants to add title to his video project created on the topic magic. He wants to beautify the same by adding attractive title styles to the video. What would you suggest him to use and why?
3. Joseph wants his video output in the high quality. What should he do to obtain the same?

Computer is my mentor!

Prepare a video clip from a huge video and add animated title to the animation. Also add transition between the clips.

10 Introduction to Web 2.0 Education Tools

Learning log

- Introduction to World Wide Web
- Introduction to Web 2.0
- Elements of Web 2.0
- Comparison of Web 1.0 with respect to Web 2.0
- Content classification of Web 2.0
- Features and techniques of Web 2.0
- Advantages and disadvantages of Web 2.0
- Social media marketing—advantages and disadvantages
- Web 3.0—introduction

Introduction

Have you ever heard about World Wide Web? Where have you used the WWW URL? Yes, it is related to web and the Internet. But do you know what is the purpose of using it and how did the different versions evolve?

Introduction to World Wide Web

Also, abbreviated as WWW or the web, it is an information space where documents and other web-related resources are identified by URLs, interlinked by hypertext links and accessed via the internet. In other words, it is a way of exchanging information between computers on the internet.

Web 2.0

It is the second stage of development of the internet. The main characteristics are the change from static web pages to dynamic pages.

Word web

interactivity: it is a way the computer responds to user's input

Web 2.0 is the current stage of online technology. As compared to the early days of the web it is characterized by greater user interactivity and collaboration, more pervasive network connectivity and enhanced communication channels.

You should know

Sir Tim Berners-Lee is a computer scientist, best known as the inventor of the World Wide Web. He wrote the first web client and server in 1990. His specifications of URIs, HTTP and HTML were refined as web technology spread. Sir Tim presently of Technology at CSAIL (Computer Science and Artificial Intelligence Lab), (USA) and the University of Oxford (UK).

The most significant difference between Web 2.0 and the traditional World Wide Web referred to as Web 1.0 is greater collaboration among internet users, content providers and enterprises. The social nature of Web 2.0 is the

other difference between it and the original, static Web. Nowadays, websites enable community-based input, interaction, content-sharing and collaboration. The types of social media sites and applications include forums, microblogging, social networking, social bookmarking, social curation, and wikis. (Fig. 10.1)

Fig. 10.1: Microblogging and social networking sites

File properties

- Wikis: Websites that enable users to contribute, collaborate and edit the site content. Wikipedia is one of the oldest and best-known wiki-based sites. (Fig. 10.2)

Fig. 10.2: Wiki

- The increasing popularity of Software as a Service (SaaS), web apps and cloud computing rather than locally-installed programs and services. (Fig. 10.3)

Fig. 10.3: Software as a Service and cloud computing

- Mobile computing is the trend towards users connecting from wherever they want. This is usually done using smart phones, tablets and other mobile devices using data or Wi-Fi networks. (Fig. 10.4)

Fig. 10.4: Mobile computing

- Mash-ups: Web pages or applications that integrate complementary elements from two or more sources.
- Social networking: The practice of expanding the number of one's business and/or social contacts by making connections through individuals.
- Social networking sites include Facebook, Twitter, LinkedIn and Google+. (Fig. 10.5)
- Collaborative efforts based on the ability to reach large number of participants and their collective resources such as crowdsourcing, crowdfunding and crowdsource testing.
- User-Generated Content (UGC): Writing, images, audio and video content, among other possibilities, made freely available online by the individuals who create it.

- Unified Communications (UC): Unified communication is a business and marketing concept describing the integration of enterprise communication services such as instant messaging, presence information, voice, mobility features, audio, web & video conferencing, fixed-mobile convergence, desktop sharing, data sharing, call control and speech recognition with non-real-time communication services such as unified messaging.

Fig. 10.5: Social networking sites

- Social curation: The collaborative sharing of content organized around one or more themes or topics. Social content curation sites include Reddit, Digg, Pinterest and Instagram.

Comparison of Web 1.0 to Web 2.0

It is not an easy task to differentiate Web 1.0 and Web 2.0 as there is not much difference between them. Web 2.0 is just a jargon that cumulatively describes the changes on how people interact with the Web. The only discriminating feature of Web 2.0 is the rate at which information changes. In Web 1.0, the information that is displayed is mostly static and the data is updated occasionally. But in Web 2.0, the information is very dynamic and the rate at which the information is updated is extremely fast. Sites like Twitter are an example of how dynamic Web 2.0 is. (Fig. 10.6)

Fig. 10.6: Twitter

The change is not restricted to what you see, but the improvement is also on what you can do. A part of Web 2.0 is the introduction of web applications that are software not located on the computer hosted in online servers. Services like Google Docs provide an office suite that does not require one to install any software on the computer other than a browser. (Fig. 10.7)

Fig. 10.7: Google docs

Another major difference seen between the two is in the flow of information as there is a strict structure in Web 1.0 where webmasters determine uploaded information on their sites, which are then viewed or downloaded by end users. Every single control over the content lies with the webmaster. In Web 2.0, control over the content is shifted towards the user. Social sites like Facebook, MySpace, Orkut, etc. are example for this.

These sites provide a blank slate to their users so that they can configure the web pages to their liking and upload their own content for others to see. Blogging is also one of the major additions as it has made the task of broadcasting online easier for the masses. Examples include sites like Wordpress that lets user to build a simple site with a given structure. (Fig. 10.8)

Fig. 10.8: Examples for some blogging sites

Content Classification of Web 2.0

Web 2.0 can be described in three parts:

- Rich Internet Application (RIA) is the experience brought from the desktop to the browser, from the graphical point of view to the usability/interactivity or features point of view.
- Web-oriented Architecture (WOA) – shows how the applications expose their functionality to leverage and integrate richer applications. Examples include feeds, RSS feeds, web services and so on.
- Social web, defines how the websites tend to interact with the end user. The things that include are adding profiles, adding comments on content, uploading new contents or user–generated content.

Features and Techniques of Web 2.0

The following are the features and techniques, referred to as SLATES.

Word web

webmaster: a person who maintains a website
leverage: control or influence
syndication: the transfer of something to control

- **Search:** Finding information through keyword search
- **Links to other websites:** Connects information together
- **Authoring:** Ability to create and update content
- **Tags:** Categorization of content by users
- **Extensions:** Software that makes the web an application platform.
- **Signals:** The use of syndication technology, such as RSS feeds to notify users of/about content changes.

Few examples of extensions are Adobe Reader, Silverlight, Active, Quicktime, and Windows Media.

Advantages of web 2.0

Web 2.0 has its own pros and cons. Some of these includes that we can communicate, work cooperatively and collaboratively online, do research, share information and ideas, play games, ask questions and so on. Few of the added advantages are:

- Availability, at any time and place
- Variety of media
- Ease of usage
- Involvement of the learners in knowledge building
- Can create dynamic learning communities
- Anyone can be an author and an editor; every single edit can be tracked.
- User friendly
- Updates in wiki are immediate and it offers more resources for researchers
- Provides real-time discussion
- Blog and Google are the most important addition for any student

Disadvantages of web 2.0

Due to many disadvantages of Web 1.0, Web 2.0 came into existence. Following are few disadvantages of Web 2.0.

- Information overload which creates confusion for the readers and affects the quality, reliability of the content.
- Freedom to post views and comments provides good opportunities for the competitors to give negative comments on other companies.
- Too many fake IDs and spam emails, messages.
- Breach in the privacy and security of individual user.

Social Media Marketing

One of the biggest and significant results of Web 2.0 is the social media marketing. The top websites like Facebook, LinkedIn, Twitter, MySpace, YouTube, Instagram are included in this domain. This serves as a boon because networking is one of the essential needs of the present world. Two-third of the total internet users visit the social media website daily. As any Web 2.0 tool has its advantages and disadvantages, even social media marketing does. Few examples for social media websites are shown in Fig. 10.9.

Fig. 10.9: Social media marketing

Advantages

- Creates a strong network and increases the number of virtual/real friends.
- There is a higher exchange of knowledge because of more interactions.
- People tend to build up relationships.

Word web

paradigm: a pattern or a model

Disadvantages

- People are very much dependent on internet for networking purpose.
- Lot of time is wasted.
- There is a huge increase in the number of frauds and hackers.

Web 3.0 – Introduction

This is said to be the new paradigm shift in web interaction. This will change not only how developers create websites, but also how people interact with those websites. It is predicted that web 3.0 will change how the web will make people's online lives easier and more intuitive with the addition of smarter applications and better search functions. Integration of artificial intelligence which understands context rather than simply comparing keywords would also be an added feature.

You should know

Artificial intelligence is said to be a boon. Many robots have been developed using AI. The latest robot is Sophia. It is a social humanoid developed by a Hong Kong based company, Hanson Robotics.

Artificial intelligence is the theory and development of computer systems that will be able to perform tasks that require human intelligence such as visual perception, speech recognition, decision-making, and translation between languages.

netsearch

For additional information, visit:

- https://en.wikipedia.org/wiki/Sophia_(robot)
- https://acodez.in/artificial-intelligence-web-design/
- https://science.howstuffworks.com/robot6.htm
- https://www.youtube.com/watch?v=BXKfi1Ubly8

Teacher's note

Ask learners to submit a report on Web 3.0 and on integration of AI technology in Web 3.0.

Concepts learnt

1. Web 2.0 is the World Wide Web websites that are created for end users.
2. Web 2.0 is the evolution of Web 1.0.
3. Web 2.0 is called the second stage of development of the internet.
4. The new features that can be seen in Web 2.0 are referred to as SLATES.
5. There are many advantages and disadvantages of Web 2.0.
6. Web 3.0 is said to be the paradigm shift in the web interaction from Web 2.0.

Hands-on practice

Research the Internet to find the detailed features on web 3.0. Prepare a short report and discuss the same with your classmate and teachers. In the space given, paste the print-out of the report.

Exercise

A **Fill in the blanks.**

1. The information in Web 2.0 is said to be ______________ (dynamic/static).
2. The experience brought from the desktop to the browser is ______________ (Rich Internet Application/Web-Oriented Architecture).
3. Social web defines how the websites tend to ______________ (discuss/interact) with the end user.
4. WORDPRESS is an example of ______________ (social media marketing site/ blogging site).
5. ______________ (UC/UGC) is a business concept describing the integration of enterprise communication services.

B **Write T for True or F for False.**

1. Blogging is one of the major additions in Web 1.0. ☐
2. There is a risk of frauds and hackers while using social media marketing. ☐
3. Artificial intelligence is the development of computer systems that can replace human beings in every field. ☐
4. User Generated Content is available free, online by the content developers. ☐
5. Real time discussion is not possible on web 2.0. ☐

C **Choose the correct option.**

1. Categorization of content by the users is called as ______________.
   (a) Tagging (b) Signalling
   (c) Authoring (d) Searching
2. Identify the website that is not an example of social media marketing.
   (a) Facebook (b) MySpace
   (c) Instagram (d) Office 365
3. Web 2.0 is not described by which of the following?
   (a) RIA (b) WOA
   (c) Social Curation (d) Social Web

4. Which of the following is an example of wiki-based site?
   (a) whatsapp
   (b) facebook
   (c) wikipedia
   (d) youtube
5. Mobile User can connect to internet by using ________________.
   (a) data connection
   (b) wi-fi
   (c) Both (a) and (b)
   (d) None of these

D Answer these questions briefly.

1. How is the flow of information in web 2.0 different from web 1.0?
2. Write a note on SLATES.
3. What are the advantages and disadvantages of Web 2.0?
4. How can a user overcome the disadvantages of social media marketing?
5. What is blogging? Explain with example.

E Application-based questions.

1. Write a brief note on Internet as marketplace.
2. What is your opinion on robots and integration of Artificial Intelligence?
3. Do you think AI will make life easier for human beings? Explain.
4. Compare Web 2.0 with that of Web 3.0.

Computer is my mentor!

Do a project work on the Evolution of Web 2.0 to Web 3.0.

11 Payment Gateways

Learning log

- Payment gateways
- Payment processors
- Online transactions and role of payment gateways
- Importance of payment gateways
- Securing online transactions

Introduction

We have studied about e-commerce in the previous classes. E-commerce is the purchase or sale of goods and services over electronic media. A lot of purchases that were done in retail stores are now being done online and every online purchase involves transaction of money. Just like in shops, we use credit and debits cards in e-commerce too and we can also use internet banking for online transactions.

Fig. 11.1: Elements of e-commerce

Do you know how these payments are made and how these transactions are processed and kept secured? In this chapter, we will study about services that execute and secure online transactions involving exchange of digital money.

Payment Gateways

A payment gateway is a service that secures payments for e-commerce websites. Payment gateways facilitate these transactions by communicating between websites and banks. The communication is always in the form of computer codes. Payment gateways play an important role in e-commerce transaction by authorizing the payment between the merchant (online store) and the customer.

Some of the popular payment gateways which operate worldwide are PayPal.com, SecurePay.com, Authorize.Net and Amazon Payments. In India, some of the popular payment gateways are CCAvenue, Citrus Pay, PayUBiz and PayUMoney.

Payment Processors

Payment processor is a service that relays transaction information between the merchant's payment gateway, the issuing bank (that is the bank that issues customer's card) and the acquiring bank (that is the merchant's bank). There are many payment processors to choose from, however, some of the popular payment processors are PayPal, Due, Stripe, Square and BitPay.

Word web

authorize: provide approval/permission

Payment processors and payment gateways are an important part of online transactions. The difference between a payment processor and a payment gateway is that a gateway authorizes the transfer of funds between the merchant and the customer and a processor analyzes and transmits transaction data between payment gateway and banks.

Online Transaction and Role of Payment Gateways

Payment gateways are a necessity to perform online transactions. Although payment gateways play different roles depending on the type of transaction (Net banking, Swiping Machines, etc.), we will study about the role of payment gateways in card (credit/debit) transactions. Following are the operations that take place in the background in a card transaction:

1. The customer clicks the Buy button after picking the product(s) on the online store/ merchant, on the browser.
2. The customer's browser encrypts the transaction data for security purpose and sends it to the merchant's server.
3. The merchant's server forwards the transaction details to their payment gateway.
4. The payment gateway authenticates the online store.

5. After authenticating, the payment gateway shows the available payment methods to the customer.
6. Once the customer picks a payment method, the payment gateway transmits the details to the payment processor employed by the merchant's bank.
7. The merchant's bank passes this information to the customer's bank that has issued the card.
8. The issuing bank goes over the customer's credit or debit limit and the payment method's validity and sends a response (approved or rejected) to the payment processor.
9. The payment processor then sends this response to the payment gateway. Finally, the payment gateway communicates the response to the website where a relevant message is displayed about the transaction and also to the merchant's server.

Hands-on practice

Do an online research to answer the following.

1. A service that securely authorizes payments.
2. An example of payment gateway service provider.
3. A service that relays transaction information between the merchant's payment gateway, the issuing bank and the acquiring bank.
4. Another name for a bank that a customer is associated with.
5. Another name for a bank that a merchant is associated with.

Importance of Payment Gateways

Payment gateways are very important in maintaining the confidentiality of sensitive information like card details, bank account number and transaction PINs. The importance of payment gateways lies in the fact that:

1. A payment gateway provider ensures that payment processing is secure and brings down the frequency as well as the severity of card frauds.
2. Payment gateway providers can be set up in a very short time and with low cost for maintenance.
3. Payment gateways are easy to use and support multiple currencies and offer multiple payment methods which improve the experience of online commerce.

Securing Online Transactions

Payment Gateways use several methods/protocols to secure online transactions. These protocols lay down the guidelines/architecture for security measures. Following are some of the security protocols that payment gateways use to secure transactions.

1. **Secure Socket Layer (SSL):** It is a protocol that encrypts payment and card data. It is mandatory for all online transactions to follow this protocol SSL keeps the data secured and private.

> **Word web**
>
> **protocol:** a set of rules that provide the framework on the exchange or transmission of data between devices.

2. **Payment Card Industry Data Security Standards (PCI DSS):** It lists the various rules/guidelines that need to be fulfilled to secure payment processing information. This standard was created to reduce the credit card fraud.
3. **3-D Secure:** This is an additional security protocol for card transactions, where the customer is required to authenticate using OTP (One time password) or secure PIN created by the customer for every online card transaction. 3-D Secure protocol is known by different names -Verified by Visa for Visa, MasterCard Secure Code for MasterCard and American Express Safe Key for American Express.
4. **Anti-fraud tools:** It is also known as fraud scrub technology, and is employed by payment gateways to scan and monitor every online transaction that the gateway executes and provide security from fraudulent transactions. Following are some of the commonly used anti-fraud tools.
   - **Address Verification System (AVS):** AVS Tool verifies whether the billing and IP address provided by the cardholder is correct.

> **You should know**
>
> In 1994, advancements such as online banking and the opening of an online pizza shop by Pizza Hut took place. In 1994, the German company Intershop introduced its first online shopping system. In 1995, Amazon launched its online shopping site and in 1996, eBay appeared on the World Wide Web.

- **Geolocation Check:** This involves checking the location from where the card is being used and the IP address of the user's device to identify fraudulent transactions.
- **Velocity Check:** Velocity check prohibits multiple transactions with the same card number or user details within a specific time. This can stop misuse of cards by fraudsters who try to make several successful transactions within a short period of time.

netsearch

For additional information, visit:
https://www.chargebee.com/blog/online-payment-gateway-service-provider/

Teacher's note

Provide instances of online frauds and help students relate on how security systems help in keeping transactions safe.

Concepts learnt

1. Payment gateway secures payments for e-commerce websites and facilitates transactions by communicating between websites and banks.
2. The payment processor relays transaction information between the merchant's payment gateway, the issuing bank and the acquiring bank.
3. During an online transaction, a payment gateway authenticates the online store, shows the available payment methods and transmits the details to the payment processor employed by the merchant's bank.
4. After the transaction is executed, the payment gateway communicates the response to the website.

5. Payment gateways provide security against fraudulent transactions. They're easy to set up and maintain. Payment gateways are very easy to use and flexible and offer multiple currencies and payment methods.
6. Payment gateways use several methods/protocols to secure online transactions. Some of the widely used protocols are SSL, PCI DSS, 3-D Secure and anti-fraud tools like AVS, Geolocation Check and Velocity Check.

Hands-on practice

1. Research the Internet and prepare a short report on Cryptocurrency. Give examples too. Use the space given below to write the same.

2. Discuss the various payment methods available for online shopping. Create a short presentation on same. Use the space given below to enumerate the main points.

Exercise

A Fill in the blanks.

1. CCAvenue and Citrus Pay are __________ (payment gateways/payment processors).
2. American Express Safe Key is a __________ (3-D Secure/AVS) protocol.
3. Anti-fraud tools are also known as __________ (fraud scrub/fraud rub) technology.
4. AVS Tool verifies billing and __________ (IP address/date) of the customer.
5. __________ (Geolocation/AVS) checks the location from where the card is being used.

B Write T for True or F for False.

1. Merchant's bank issues cards to the customer. ☐
2. BitPay is a payment processor. ☐
3. Payment processor communicates between the merchant and the customer. ☐
4. Customer's browser encrypts the transaction data. ☐
5. The issuing bank goes over the customer's credit or debit limit and the payment method's validity and sends a response. ☐

C Choose the correct option.

1. Which of the following is a payment processor?
   (a) Citrus Pay (b) CCAvenue
   (c) PayUMoney (d) Square
2. Which of the following is true with respect to payment gateway?
   (a) Supports multiple currencies
   (b) Communicates between issuing and acquiring bank
   (c) Displays the transaction status on the monitor
   (d) None of the above

3. Which of the following security protocols lists down the various rules/ guidelines that needs to be fulfilled to secure payment processing information?
   (a) SSL (b) AVS
   (c) PCI DSS (d) All of these
4. SSL stands for which of the following?
   (a) Security Safe Layout
   (b) Safe Security for Layout
   (c) Secure Socket Layer
   (d) Security and Safety Layer
5. 3-D Secure authenticates the transaction through which of the following methods?
   (a) OTP (b) Secure PIN
   (c) Phone call (d) Both (a) and (b)

D Answer these questions briefly.

1. Why is payment gateway used? What is its function?
2. What are payment processors?
3. Explain the process of an online transaction.
4. Name and briefly describe the security protocols used in payment gateways.
5. Briefly describe the anti-fraud tools that are used in payment gateways.

E Application-based question.

A person wants to establish an e-commerce company. Which service needs to be setup by the merchant to enable monetary transactions with the customer?

Computer is my mentor!

Find out the payment gateways used in at least 10 popular e-commerce websites in India and the most popular payment gateway among those. Also, search why is it so.

12 Computer as Career

Learning log

- Computers as a career
- Primary areas of career in computer science
- Academic programs for career in computer science
- Making a career in computer and technology

Introduction

A significant part of a person's life with progressive occupational opportunities is called a career. To secure a job opportunity in the field of computer science, one must have relevant knowledge and skill sets. The advancement of computer science and technology has led not only to mushrooming companies and prospects of commercial development but has also brought in its wake the development of computer languages, technology, etc. This has brought together people who are interested to build their career in computer science. We engage with the computer in various manner—hardware (Fig. 12.1), cloud computing services (Fig. 12.2), games and apps (Fig. 12.3), network security technologies (Fig. 12.4) whereby we can safeguard online data and information, etc.

Fig. 12.1: Computer hardware

Fig. 12.2: Cloud computing

Fig. 12.3: Playing games in Ipad

Fig. 12.4: Network security technology

The various career options that are associated with these are graphic game developer, network technician, multimedia programmer, computer hardware technician and software developer.

Computers as a Career

Marketing of computer devices and accessories, software development and testing, development of antivirus software, web development, digital marketing, search engine optimization, data analysis and database administration are some of the areas in computer and information technology for making a career.

There is a steady increase in computer related jobs annually. More than 10% of college students are graduating each year with a degree in computer science. These young graduates are becoming help desk specialists, computer operators, computer technicians, software engineers, system analysts, programmers, computer consultants, network administrators, desktop publishers, technical writers, corporate trainers and illustrators, etc.

You should know

Application software certification, also called end-user certification, is sponsored by Microsoft, Adobe systems, IBM and Macromedia.

Word web

computer consultant: a computer expert with expertise in an area of computers

computer scientist: a person who researches, invents and develops solutions to computer related problems

Primary Areas of Career in Computer Science

Some primary areas for building a career in computer science and information technology are listed below:

- **General business and government organizations:** Records or documentation and networking are the main areas of maintenance.
- **Computer equipment industry:** This includes design, manufacture, sales, service, maintenance and repair of computer and its accessories.
- **Computer software industry:** Developing, testing and problem-solving using programming language are the main areas of this industry. The professionals who work in this field are called software developers. Those whose specialization is building websites are called web designers.
- **Computer education and training industry:** The sector provides education and soft skill training to people aspiring to build a career in the field. Various schools, colleges and universities and private companies require education programs and training which are provided by this industry. People who are experts in such training are called corporate computer trainers.
- **Computer consulting industry:** This field provides customized software development, testing, support system, planning and hardware, and software integration to various companies or business set-ups. An individual who is a professional expert in an area of computer science and technology is called a computer consultant.

Hands-on practice

Name the following professions related to computer science.

1. One who develops and tests a computer program.
2. One who creates websites.
3. One who provides the customized software development, testing, support system, planning and hardware and software integration to the companies.

Academic Programs for Career in Computer Science and Technology

There are many academic and vocational training programs the completion of which entitles one to join the computer industry as an entry-level employee.

Part of the computer industry	Stream of learning	Academic programs available
Computer information systems	Design and implementation of information system	Associate of Science (A.S), Associate of Applied Science (A.A.S), Associate of Applied Business employment (A.A.B), Bachelor of Engineering (B.E), Master in technology (M. Tech), Bachelor of Science (B.Sc), Master of Science (M.S), Doctor of philosophy (PhD).
Computer science/ software	Computer hardware and software	Bachelor of Engineering (B.E), Master in technology (M. Tech), Bachelor of Computer Applications (BCA), Bachelor of Science (B.Sc), Master of Science (M.S), Master of Computer Applications (MCA), Doctor of philosophy (PhD)
Computer engineering	Computer hardware	Bachelor of Engineering (B.E), Master in technology (M. Tech), Bachelor of Science (B.Sc), Master of Science (M.S), Doctor of philosophy (PhD)
Computer information systems	Computing and its practical aspects, programming, networking, system analysis and design, database management, web development	Bachelor of Science (B.Sc), Bachelor of Computer Applications (BCA), Bachelor of Engineering (B.E), Master in technology (M. Tech), Master of Science (M.S), Master of Computer Applications (MCA), Doctor of philosophy (PhD)

Making a Career in Computer and Technology

After acquiring one or more of the academic qualifications listed above, one can seek job opportunities in his or her respective field of interest and expertise. Some companies post their job vacancies online. Naukri, Monster, Job.com are some of the websites that help people find jobs online.

There are some associations or organizations for computer professionals where specialists, researchers and learners come together for sharing their experience, discuss, applaud achievements and support each other. Some of them are listed below:

- Association of Computing Machinery (ACM)
- Association of Information Systems (AIS)
- Association of Information Technology Professionals (AITP)
- Associate of Internet Professionals (AIP)
- Information Systems Security Association (ISSA)
- Institute of Electrical and Electronics Engineers (IEEE)
- National Association of Programmers (NAP)

Fig. 12.5: An association at work

There are many user groups worldwide where people with common interest join for supporting, training, problem-solving, research and development, etc. Some such user groups are:

Fig. 12.6: Apple user group

Fig. 12.7: A java user group

Fig. 12.8: A java user group

- Apple User Group
- Association of Personal Computer User Group
- C/C++ Programming User Group
- Java User Group
- Linux User Group World Wide (LUGWW)
- Macromedia User Groups
- .NET User Group

Professional growth and continuing education in various streams is enhanced by attending workshops, seminars, conferences, convections and trade shows, most of which are organized by the associations or user groups exclusively. Some of such learning events are also conducted by educational and training institutes.

The mode of training could be in the form of printed materials, video-based, computer-based and web-based or instructor-based according to the choice of the aspirant. Proficiency in technical knowledge is acknowledged with certificates. Some vendors offer certificate as well as on-floor training that help the customer to be more productive. Some of the vendor certificates provide help in career placements.

Digital as well as printed newspaper, magazine and websites keep us updated about the openings in the computer industry.

netsearch

For additional information, visit:
https://www.computerscience.org/careers/
https://www.computerscienceonline.org/careers/

Teacher's note

Invite alumni of your school who are working in various fields of computer science and technology. Discuss their experience in seeking higher education, building career and future aspirations.

Concepts learnt

1. An occupation for which one is trained is called a career.
2. To get a job opportunity in the field of computer science and technology, academic qualification and skill set must be acquired.
3. A career in computer science and technology has numerous primary and secondary areas.
4. Many academic programs and training centres provide education and training that are suitable for building a career in computer science and technology.
5. Associations, organizations and user groups with professionals and experts help the members to share and enrich their skills.
6. The mode of training is chosen by the customer or job aspirant.
7. Digital and print newspapers, magazines and websites help people find a suitable job.

Hands-on practice

Create a database of at least 20 people you know from the field of computers. Now prepare a table of various professions you know in the field of computers. Write queries to find all the people from software industry and people from hardware industry.

Now write the field and the primary key used in the table structure. Also, write the queries in the space given.

____

____

____

____

____

Exercise

A Fill in the blanks.

1. A progressive occupation is called a ____________ (career/higher education).
2. A network technician will be equipped with a training in ____________ (networking/software) technology.
3. A computer hardware technician helps in assembly and maintenance of ____________ (software/hardware) components.
4. A ____________ (computer researcher/ computer consultant) invents and develops computer-related solutions.
5. People who provide computer education and training are ____________ (corporate job advertisers/corporate computer trainers).

B Write T for True or F for False.

1. A person with a Bachelor of Science (B.Sc) degree in computer science is called a computer graduate. ☐
2. A computer software expert is also known as a software consultant. ☐
3. The computer consultant industry provides customized services to business set-ups. ☐
4. Computer information systems include learning in design and information implementation. ☐
5. Apple user groups support Java developers. ☐

C Choose the correct option.

1. Which of the following is the abbreviation of B.E.?
   (a) Bachelor of Engineering (b) Bachelor of Education
   (c) Business of Engineering (d) Branch of Engineering
2. Which of the following is essential for a career in computer technology?
   (a) Recommendation (b) Academic qualification
   (c) A computer device (d) A computer network
3. Which of the following represents the 'Association of Internet Professionals'?
   (a) AIS (b) AUG
   (c) AIP (d) JUG

4. Which of the following enhances the professional growth of an individual?
   (a) Seminar (b) Workshop
   (c) Conference (d) All the above
5. Which of the following is the mode of computer training?
   (a) Video-based (b) Web-based
   (c) Instructor-based (d) All the above

D Answer these questions briefly.

1. What is the computer equipment industry composed of?
2. What is required to be certified as a software developer?
3. Which academic programs help to build a career in computer science and technology?
4. Name some websites that help in job placements.
5. What is a vendor certificate?

E Application-based questions.

1. Sanju is a businessman who wants to do digital marketing. Whom should he approach for the help?
2. Radhika was unable to solve Java problems. Do you think joining a Java user group can help her? If yes, how?
3. Geeta, a post-graduate student, received a participation certificate of the computer research conference she attended. How do you think this might help her?
4. Deepa is eager to receive updates on career openings in computer. What do you suggest?

Computer is my mentor!

Guide students to conduct a mock computer-science job fair in the classroom.

Worksheet-I

A Choose the correct option.

1. Which of the following number system is expressed with base 2?
   (a) Binary (b) Decimal
   (c) Octal (d) Hexadecimal
2. The octal equivalent of the decimal number $(8)_{10}$ is __________.
   (a) $(7)_{10}$ (b) $(10)_{10}$
   (c) $(8)_8$ (d) $(10)_8$
3. In which of the following views we can create and change the structure of the form?
   (a) Design (b) Datasheet
   (c) Layout (d) Form
4. Which of the following is NOT an option in the bottom panel of the query design grid?
   (a) Show (b) Field
   (c) Table (d) Record
5. Which of the following options shows ascending order of the pin codes given below?
   (i) 560015 (ii) 560179 (iii) 560009 (iv) 560027
   (a) (ii), (i), (iv), (iii) (b) (iv), (ii), (i), (iii)
   (c) (iii), (i), (ii), (iv) (d) (iii), (i), (iv), (ii)
6. The filter by 'selection' option helps to filter those records __________.
   (a) That satisfy the given criterion
   (b) That satisfy any of the given criteria among several criteria
   (c) That match an entity of the selected field
   (d) All the above

B Fill in the blanks.

1. The base __________ number system is also called decimal system.
2. The __________ number system uses 16 as its base.
3. The __________ button in the query design tab helps to apply the query and get the results.

4. The aggregate function that extracts the lowest value in a field is __________.
5. By default, Access sorts the records by __________.
6. Sorting and filtering options are available in ____________ group of __________ tab.

C Write T for True or F for False.

1. Binary number system contains digits 0 and 1 only. ☐
2. The binary expansion 1 x 2^0 is equal to decimal number 1. ☐
3. The aggregate function 'Count' calculates the total of the values in a field. ☐
4. The 'Make-table' action query creates a new table from the data in one or more tables. ☐
5. Access sorts the records in the field containing numbers differently depending on the data type of the field. ☐
6. The filtering options remain the same for all the fields irrespective of the data. ☐

Worksheet-II

A Choose the correct option.

1. Which of these is an empty tag in HTML5?
   (a) <img> (b) <src>
   (c) <url> (d) <head>
2. In HTML5, inside which of these tags can a user have a clickable area.
   (a) <img> (b) <url>
   (c) <href> (d) <map>
3. A numerical label assigned to each device connected to a computer network known as ____________.
   (a) FTP address (b) SMTP address
   (c) IP address (d) Machine Address
4. Which of the following is the data that is transported through datagrams?
   (a) Webpages (b) Encryption
   (c) Header (d) Payload
5. Which of the following is the method name of identifiers?
   (a) ActionListener (b) FirstName
   (c) ActionPerformed() (d) OrderNumber
6. Which of the following parameter in Java program is the return type of the method?
   (a) Static (b) Void
   (c) Class (d) Public

B Fill in the blanks.

1. __________ (<src>/<url>) is a necessary attribute that describes the source or path of the image in HTML5.
2. __________ (<imgsrc>/<href>) is an attribute to the anchor tag used to create a link to another web pagein HTML5.
3. __________ (Source/Departure) and __________ (Arrival/Destination) IP addresses is a part of the IP header.
4. __________ (FTP/TCP) and ____________ (HTTP/IP) protocols always work together.

5. ASCII value of alphabet 'A' in Java program is __________ (65/97).
6. In Java, __________ (Enterprise/Standalone) application is also known as desktop application.

C Write T for True or F for False.

1. In HTML5, alternate text appears when the image is missing from the given path. ☐
2. In HTML5, <url> indicates the location of the image where it is stored. ☐
3. Internet Protocol (IP) is the communication protocol which contains the formats of digital message and rules for exchanging messages between computers in a network. ☐
4. Simple Mail Transfer Protocol a protocol for sending e-mail messages on the internet. ☐
5. System.out.println () is used to print the values in console. ☐
6. Java supports multiple threads execution simultaneously. ☐

Worksheet-III

A Choose the correct option.

1. Which among the following is an advantage of cloud computing?
   (a) Increases the data storage ability (b) Online transaction
   (c) Communication (d) All the above.
2. Which of the following cloud is used for both B2B and B2C types of interactions?
   (a) Private (b) Hybrid
   (c) Community (d) Public
3. 1s 10f- represents a specific point on the timeline in Synfig Studio. 's' and 'f' in this stands for ___________.
   (a) Second and frame (b) Splits and frame
   (c) Second and first (d) Splits and first
4. Which of these is a technique of creating smooth transition between two images?
   (a) Cutout animation (b) Morphing
   (c) Animating (d) Rendering
5. Which of the following option from media files be used to cut the file into small portions in OpenShot?
   (a) Detail (b) Spilt Clip
   (c) Add to time line (d) Remove from project
6. What color does the keyframe change to if it supports the clip property in OpenShot?
   (a) Blue (b) Green
   (c) Black (d) Grey

B Fill in the blanks.

1. ___________ (Security and privacy/Data storage and accessibility) is an advantage of cloud computing.
2. Cloud computing improved business by ___________ (online transaction/ increase of privacy).

3. __________ (Alt + F/Ctrl + F) is a shortcut key to select Fill Tool.
4. A combination of Ctrl+ < keys, move the frame by __________ (two/one) second.
5. __________ (Transitions/Split clips) are represented by blue, rounded rectangles on the timeline.
6. The __________ (curve-based/straight line) animation framework of OpenShot handles most animation tasks with ease.

C Write T for True or F for False.

1. Cloud computing makes the business effective with reducing cost. ☐
2. Private computing is more useful for B2C than cloud computing. ☐
3. Animate Editing Mode should be switched off before saving the file in Synfig Studio. ☐
4. Spline Tool can be used to draw shapes. ☐
5. Interpolated values in animation of OpenShot is calculated only with linear values. ☐
6. Gradual fade between two clips can be imparted by transition option. ☐

Worksheet-IV

A Choose the correct option.

1. The second stage of development of the internet is ________.
   (a) Web 0.0 (b) Web 1.0
   (c) Web 2.0 (d) Web 3.0
2. Identify the website that does not use wiki model.
   (a) Wikiquote.com (b) Wikipedia.com
   (c) Youtube.com (d) AboutUS.com
3. Which of the following is a scrub technology?
   (a) 3-D Secure (b) PCI DSS
   (c) SSL (d) AVS
4. Which of the following technology checks the location from where the card is being used?
   (a) Velocity Check (b) Address Verification System
   (c) Geolocation Check (d) Payment Gateway
5. Which of the following professional creates a website?
   (a) Website designer (b) Website browser
   (c) Software developer (d) Technical writer
6. Media updates about the computer industry through ____________.
   (a) newspaper (b) websites
   (c) magazines (d) All of these

B Fill in the blanks.

1. Reddit is an example for ____________ (social networking/Social content curation) sites.
2. The 'S' in SLATES stand for ____________ (Social/Search).
3. A payment ____________ (processor/gateway) analyses and transmits transaction data.
4. SSL stands for ____________ (Secure Socket Layer/Secret Security Layer).
5. Naukri is one of the websites that help people find jobs ____________ (offline/online).
6. Proficiency in technical knowledge is acknowledged with ____________ (certificates/trophies).

C Write T for True or F for False.

1. Instant messaging is an example for UGC (User Generated Content). ☐
2. The latest robot Sophia is made without integrating Artificial Intelligence technology in it. ☐
3. The acquiring bank goes over the customer's credit or debit limit and the payment method's validity. ☐
4. Payment processor is a service that relays transaction information between the merchant's payment gateway, the issuing bank and the acquiring bank. ☐
5. Job opportunities can be explored only after acquiring relevant academic qualification. ☐
6. Web-based trainings are available to improve computer skills. ☐

Worksheet-V

1. What is meant by cloud computing? What are its benefits?

2. Explain the different types of cloud computing.

3. What is meant by morphing of images?

4. What is the function of loop spline tool?

5. What is the use of the tool 'Transform' in media files?

6. Write a note on different interpolation modes in animation.

7. What are the advantages of web 2.0 tools?

8. Write a note on content classification of web 2.0 tools.

9. What happens after the customer picks a payment method during an online transaction?

10. Explain the process of online transaction.

11. What is the role of a corporate computer trainer?

12. Write some of the academic programs for careers in computer science and technology.

Worksheet-VI

1. Convert the number 741 to a binary number.

2. Represent the number 23654 in its standard form.

3. Ramesh is maintaining an Access database of workers working in his factory. He wants to increase their wages by 10% from this year. He wants to know the updated wages of each worker. Help Ramesh to accomplish this task using his database.

4. Explain the different types of action Queries.

5. What are the different filtering options available in MS Access for fields containing dates?

6. Write the steps involved in Sorting by one field in MS Access.

7. Explain the steps for inserting an image on a web page.

8. What is alt attribute of the image? How can we set the height and width of an image?

9. What are IP and TCP? What is their functions?

10. What are the different network protocols? Explain each one in brief.

11. Write a note on data types and variables in java.

12. Write the steps to create simple Java program.

Revision Worksheet-1

Marks: 50

A Choose the correct option. (6 x 1 = 6)

1. Which one of the following uses 8 as its base?
   (a) Decimal number system (b) Octal number system
   (c) Hexadecimal number system (d) Binary number system
2. Which of the following options in query wizard creates a select query?
   (a) Cross tab (b) Simple
   (c) Find Duplicates (d) Find Unmatched
3. Arranging the records in a logical order based on the numeric or alphabetical value is known as __________.
   (a) Filtering (b) Sorting
   (c) Classifying (d) Sequencing
4. In HTML5, which of these is the proper way of using usemap attribute?
   (a) Usemap="#maping" (b) Usemap="maping"
   (c) Map="#maping" (d) Map="maping"
5. What do computers need in order to understand the electronic signals over the network?
   (a) Network Protocols (b) Network Hardware
   (c) Modems (d) Routers
6. Which of the following is non primitive data types?
   (a) int (b) long
   (c) string (d) char

B Fill in the blanks. (6 x 1 = 6)

1. The ______________ system is notation of numbers using digits and symbols.
2. In the query design grid, the ______________ row sets up alternate criteria.
3. Arranging text from A to Z or number from smallest to greatest is ______________.
4. In HTML5, ______________ syntax allows the user to use an image present in a subdirectory.

5. _____________ protocol specify the rules governing the transmission of information and communication between computers.
6. _____________ has a predefined meaning in the language and is reserved for a specific command action.

C Write T for True or F for False. (6 x 1 = 6)

1. In octal number system alphabets from A to F are used to denote digits form 10 to 15. ☐
2. To design a query manually we should click on query wizard button. ☐
3. Sorting helps us to view only the data that is required at that moment by hiding the unwanted data. ☐
4. <src> attribute searches the image in a path and informs the browser to display. ☐
5. File Transfer Protocol is a protocol for sending e-mail messages on the internet. ☐
6. In Java, a variable declared inside the class but outside the method is called local variable. ☐

D Answer these questions in detail. (6 x 2 = 12)

1. How are negative numbers represented in a binary number system?
2. Explain the steps to create a form using a wizard in Access 2013.
3. The following table shows the customers of 'ABC Company' at different regions. Write the expected output when the following records are sorted in Descending order first by region and then by city.

ID	Company	Mobile Phon	City	Region
1	Typre Pvt LTd	9456712583	Hyderabad	South India
2	Hexa Electronics Limited	9874125360	Delhi	North India
3	Noor Pvt. Ltd	8457136952	Kanpur	North India
4	Mangal stores	8214762548	Mumbai	West India
5	Kali Home Services	9236514781	Orissa	East India
6	Rama Printing Press	8283214576	Ahmedabad	West India
7	Lakshmi Narayana Pvt. Ltd	8963142154	Bangalore	South India
8	Jawar Goods and Services	7856491323	West Bengal	East India
9	Bags and Baggages Pvt Ltd	9548712365	Chandighar	North India
10	Anuroop Agencies	7845692145	Lucknow	North India
11	Kalikambal Enterprises	9457812361	Chennai	South India

4. What are the prerequisites to create an image map?
5. What are the functions of IP address?
6. What are the advantages and disadvantages of Java array?

E Answer these questions briefly. **(4 x 1=4)**

1. Write the hexadecimal expansion of the number $(165)_{10}$.
2. Convert the binary number 10101 into its decimal equivalent.
3. Pranav is the secretary for an association in an apartment. He has an Access database of all the families living in that apartment. He wants to know the list of members who are not using any of the club amenities. Explain how he can do it
4. Explain the steps to create a form using a wizard in Access 2013.

F Application-based questions. **(8 x 2=16)**

1. Mention the type of filter for each of the following filtering options. (Note: If they belong to more than one type of filter mention all of them.)

Filtering Option	Type of Filter
Greater Than	
Last Week	
Contains	
Today	

2. How to apply multiple filters to a table at a time? Explain with steps.
3. Write the steps to create an image map for a HTML5 web element.
4. Write the steps to add animated images in a webpage using HTML5.
5. Explain the function of IRC and SMTP.
6. Briefly explain TCP.
7. What are the different types of variable found in Java?
8. Write a short note on program internal.

Revision Worksheet-2

Marks: 50

A Choose the correct option. (6 x 1 = 6)

1. Which among the following is used for B2C?
   (a) Hybrid (b) Private
   (c) Public (d) Community
2. How many ways are there to render an animation created in Synfig Studio?
   (a) One (b) Two
   (c) Three (d) Four
3. Which of the following is the shortcut key to slice all the media files from both the sides in OpenShot Video Editor?
   (a) Ctrl + K (b) Ctrl + B
   (c) Ctrl + L (d) Ctrl + R
4. https://www.google.co.in In the link what does www stand for?
   (a) Web Wide (b) Wide Web
   (c) Wide world Web (d) World Wide Web
5. CC Avenue and Citrus Pay are
   (a) Payment Gateways (b) Payment Processors
   (c) 3-D Secure tools (d) Scrub Technology
6. Which of the following is a Java User Group?
   (a) Berlin Brandenburg JUG (b) Bangalore JUG
   (c) Apple User Group (d) Both (a) and (b)

B Fill in the blanks. (6 x 1 = 6)

1. ____________ (Security/Hardware) issue is a challenge in cloud computing.
2. In Synfig, by default, each second is divided into ____________ (24/12) frames.
3. The ____________ (slice/razor) tool cuts a transition wherever the user clicks.
4. The current stage of online technology is ____________ (Web 2.0/Web 3.0).
5. Payment gateway communicates between ____________(websites/computers) and ____________ (banks/users).
6. A computer ____________ (software/hardware) developer develops and tests a computer program.

Worksheet

C Write T for True or F for False. (6 x 1 = 6)

1. Cloud computing is better than private network for intra business interaction. ☐
2. A red outline is displayed on clicking switch to animate mode in Synfig Studio. ☐
3. It is difficult to add titles to the animation in OpenShot Video Editor. ☐
4. Mobile computing is used to connect from any location. ☐
5. Payment processors and payment gateways have the have function but differ in usage during transactions ☐
6. Participating in seminars improves an individual's professional abilities. ☐

D Answer these questions in deatil. (6 x 2 = 12)

1. Which are the different types of cloud computing? Briefly explain each.
2. What are the basic setting that needs to be set before animating shapes in Synfig Studio?
3. What is a profile in OpenShot?
4. Give any four examples for social networking sites.
5. Briefly describe the anti-fraud tools AVS and Velocity Check.
6. What are the uses of joining a user group?

E Answer these questions briefly. (4 x 1 =4)

1. What is cloud computing?
2. What are the challenges in cloud computing?
3. What are the different ways in which an animation can be rendered?
4. Define social curation.

F Application-based questions. (8 x 2 =16)

1. Write a note on the understanding of timeline.
2. What is the use of the option 'Add to time line'?
3. Write a note on 'File Properties'.
4. How is content in Web 2.0 classified?
5. What are payment processors?
6. Briefly describe a payment gateway.
7. What is application software certificate?
8. What does a computer scientist do?

CLASS 8

QUESTION PAPER SET A

KSHITIJ
IIT Kharagpur

NCO

SOF NATIONAL CYBER OLYMPIAD 2017-18

DO NOT OPEN THIS BOOKLET UNTIL ASKED TO DO SO

Total Questions: 50 | Time: 1 hr.

Guidelines for the Candidate

1. You will get additional ten minutes to fill up information about yourself on the OMR Sheet, before the start of the exam.
2. Write your **Name, School Code, Class, Section, Roll No.** and **Mobile Number** clearly on the **OMR Sheet** and do not forget to sign it. We will share with you your marks / result on your mobile number.
3. The Question Paper comprises three sections:

   Logical Reasoning (10 Questions), **Computers and Information Technology** (35 Questions) and **Achievers Section** (5 Questions).

   Each question in Achievers Section carries 3 marks, whereas all other questions carry one mark each.
4. All questions are compulsory. There is no negative marking. Use of calculator is not permitted.
5. There is only ONE correct answer. Choose only ONE option for an answer.
6. To mark your choice of answers by darkening the circles on the OMR Sheet, use **HB Pencil** or **Blue / Black ball point pen** only. E.g.

   Q.16: Which of the following is a type of printer?

   A. Cathode Ray Tube B. Light Emitting Diode

   C. Thermal Flatbed D. Liquid Crystal Display

   As the correct answer is option C, you must darken the circle corresponding to option C in the OMR Sheet. 16. Ⓐ Ⓑ ● Ⓓ
7. Rough work should be done in the blank space provided in this booklet.
8. Return the OMR Sheet to the invigilator at the end of the exam.
9. Please fill in your personal details in the space provided on this page before attempting the paper.
10. *For classes 8, 9, 10, 11 & 12 "TEENAGE PRODIGY" is being conducted by KSHITIJ IIT Kharagpur in association with SOF. For details, please turn to last page.*

SOF
SCIENCE OLYMPIAD FOUNDATION
Inspiring Young Minds Through Knowledge Olympiads

Name:..

Section:............. SOF Olympiad Roll No.:......................... Contact No.:..

1. There is a definite relationship between the terms on either side of : :. Establish the relation on the left side and find the missing term.

YTOJ : XSNI : : WRMH : ?

A. VQLG
B. TOJE
C. RMHC
D. UPKF

2. Which of the following Venn diagrams best represents the relationship amongst, "Females, Doctors, Patients"?

A. 
B. 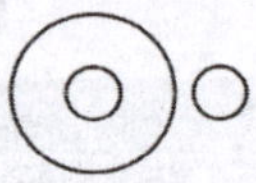
C. 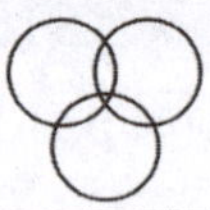
D. 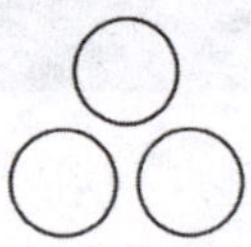

3. Select a figure from the options which will replace the question mark to complete the given series.

Problem Figures

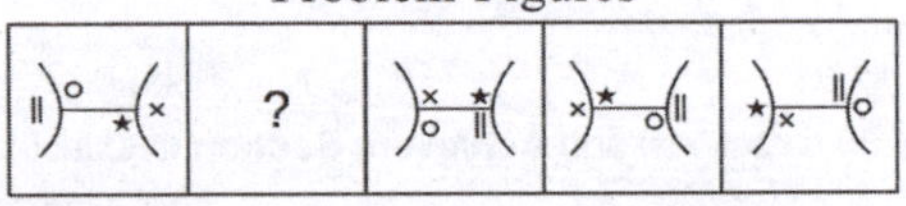

A. 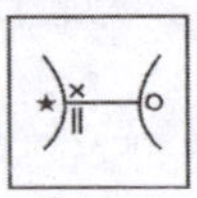
B. 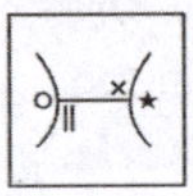
C. 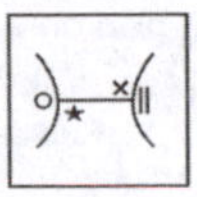
D. 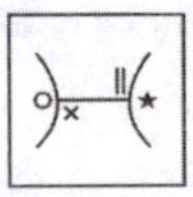

4. Study the given series and answer the question that follows:

N O P Q Y B Z A R S H I J K T M L U V G F E W X D C

If it is possible to make a meaningful word with 8th, 16th, 17th and 22nd letters of given series, then which will be the first letter of the word so formed? If no such word can be formed, then choose X as the answer and if more than one such words can be formed, then choose Y as the answer.

A. M
B. X
C. L
D. Y

5. In which of the following figures, Fig. (X) is exactly embedded as one of its parts?

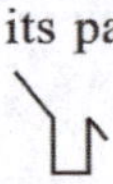

Fig. (X)

A. 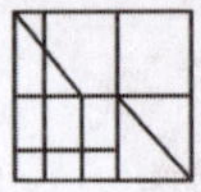
B. 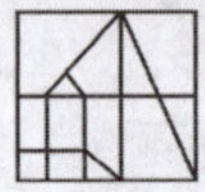
C. 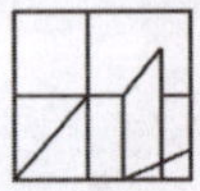
D. 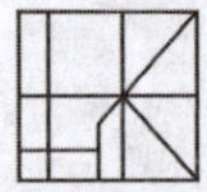

6. Five children are sitting in a row facing the North. S is sitting next to P but not T. K is sitting next to R, who is sitting on the extreme left and T is not sitting next to K. Who is/are sitting adjacent to S?

A. K and P
B. R and P
C. Only P
D. P and T

7. If 'P × Q' means 'P is to the South of Q'; 'P + Q' means 'P is to the North of Q'; 'P % Q' means 'P is to the East of Q' and 'P – Q' means 'P is to the West of Q', then in A% B + C – D; C is in which direction with respect to A?

A. South-East
B. South-West
C. South
D. West

8. The given question consists of a set of three figures X, Y and Z showing a sequence of folding of a piece of paper. Fig. (Z) shows the manner in which the folded paper has been cut. Select a figure from the options which would most closely resemble the unfolded form of Fig. (Z).

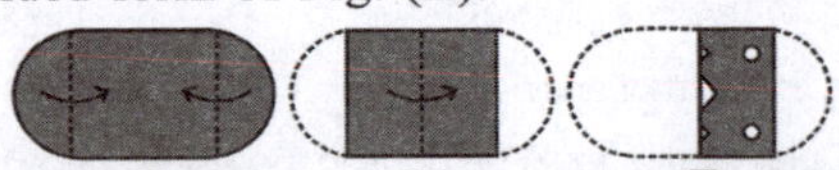

X Y Z

A. 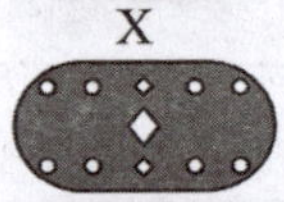
B. 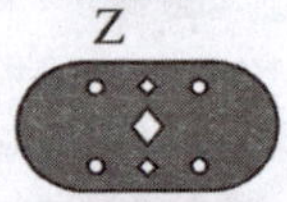
C. 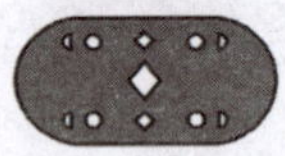
D. 

9. Count the number of cubes in the given figure.

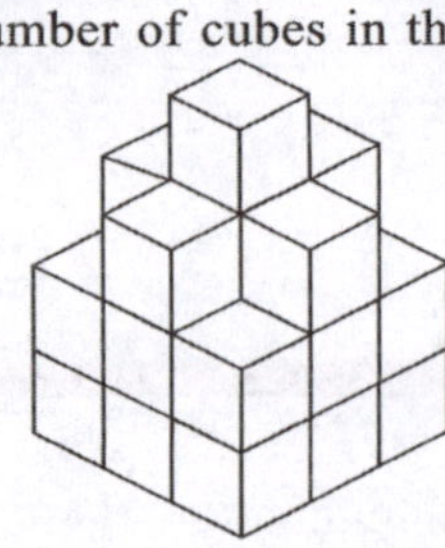

A. 18
B. 19
C. 21
D. None of these

10. Select a figure from the options which does not satisfy the same condition of placement of dots as in Fig. (X).

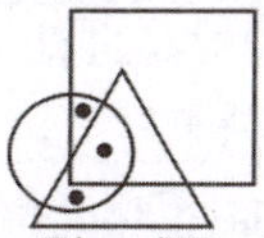

Fig. (X)

A. 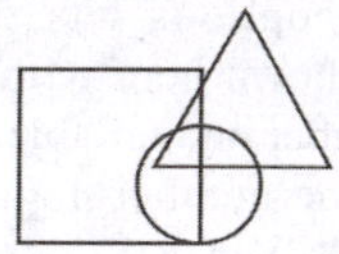

B. 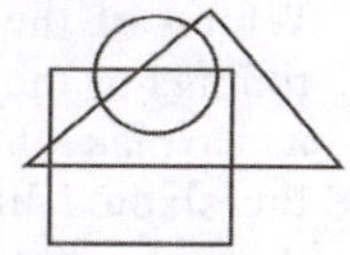

C. 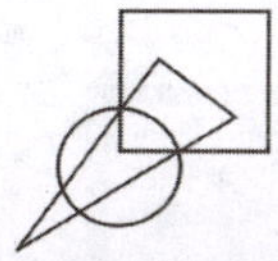

D. 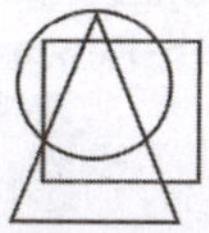

COMPUTERS AND INFORMATION TECHNOLOGY

11. Which of the following is the function of operating system as a memory management?
    (i) It manages the sharing of internal memory among multiple applications.
    (ii) It assigns memory to various programs whenever required.
    (iii) It provides security by means of passwords to prevent the misuse of computer.

    A. Only (i)
    B. Only (ii)
    C. Both (i) and (ii)
    D. Only (iii)

12. MS-Word 2010 is showing the hidden text in a dotted underline format (as shown here), instead of hiding/disappearing the text from the document. Which of the following Word options will allow you to display the hidden text in this format?

    abc

    A. Proofing
    B. Display
    C. Save
    D. Advanced

13. Complete the given steps to recover the unsaved documents in MS-Word 2010.
    File tab → ? → Click on 'Recover Unsaved documents' on the bottom right side of the screen.

    A. Info
    B. Recent
    C. Save & Send
    D. New

14. The cable shown in this image is called a _________ cable. It is an IDE (Integrated Drive Electronics) standard for connecting devices like optical drives and hard drives to the motherboard.

    A. SATA
    B. Ethernet
    C. EIDE
    D. PS/2

15. Which of the following steps is CORRECT to set the options displayed in the given snapshot of MS-Excel 2010?

    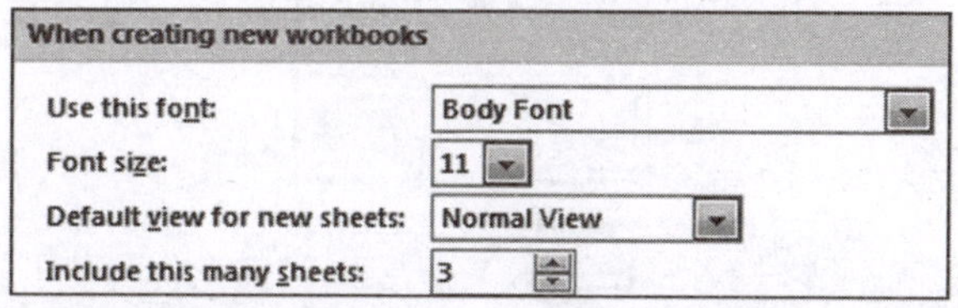

    A. File tab → Options → General
    B. File tab → Options → Proofing
    C. File tab → Options → Language
    D. File tab → Options → Advanced

16. Considering the given snapshot, where cells A1: A4 has been named as "NUMBER" with the help of Define Name feature of MS-Excel 2010, what would be the result of the given formula in MS-Excel 2010?

	A
1	"3"
2	a
3	3
4	0

    =COUNT(NUMBER)

    A. 1
    B. 2
    C. 3
    D. 4

17. What would be the result of the given formula in MS-Excel 2010, if cell A1=2016?
    =REPLACE(A1,3,2,"17")

    A. 20117
    B. 2017
    C. 17
    D. 2016-17

18. Which of the following PowerPoint Options allows you to end the slide show with a black slide in MS-PowerPoint 2010?

    A. Language
    B. General
    C. Advanced
    D. Proofing

19. Which of the following options lets you add the timings to the slide (as shown here with mark "X") and to make the slide number unavailable by showing the slanted line over slide number 1 (as shown in the image with mark "Y") in a Slide sorter view of MS-PowerPoint 2010?

A. X - , Y - 

B. X - , Y - 

C. X - , Y - 

D. X - , Y - 

20. Which of the following keyboard shortcuts will allow you to create a new blank Keyframe in Flash CS6?

A. F5 B. F7

C. F9 D. F8

21. What does the link attribute in given HTML represent?

```
<html>
<body link="blue">
<p><a href="https://www.sofworld.org">sofworld</a>
</p>
</body>
</html>
```

A. The link attribute specifies the default color of unvisited links in a document.

B. The link attribute specifies the default color of active links in a document.

C. The link attribute specifies the default color of visited links in a document.

D. All of these

22. Which of the following statements is CORRECT about the given utility program?

A. It is a compression technique which helps to reduce the consumption of storage space and ensures faster data transfer.

B. Using this tool, we can compress multiple files or folders into a single file, which is stored in a different format.

C. It is also used to recover data in case of damage or accidental loss in computer system.

D. Both A and B

23. What would be the output of the given HTML code?

```
<ol>
  <li>Soy</li>
  <li>Wheat</li>
  <li>Peas</li>
</ol>
<ol start="50">
  <li>Soy</li>
  <li>Wheat</li>
  <li>Peas</li>
</ol>
```

A. 1. Soy
2. Wheat
3. Peas

50. Soy
51. Wheat
52. Peas

B. • Soy
• Peas
• Wheat

50. Peas
51. Wheat
52. Soy

C. I. Soy
II. Wheat
III. Peas

50. Soy
51. Wheat
52. Peas

D. a. Soy
b. Wheat
c. Peas

50. Soy
51. Wheat
52. Peas

24. Match the Adobe Flash CS6 term names given in Column-I with their descriptions given in Column-II.

	Column-I		Column-II
(a)	Movie	(i)	Transparent sheets containing various objects, can be placed on top of each other.
(b)	Scene	(ii)	The first file that opens when you open a flash document
(c)	Timeline	(iii)	Area where you add every piece of content to be added in a movie
(d)	Layer	(iv)	It consists of animated objects.
(e)	Stage	(v)	The area on screen to work with layers and frames

A. (a) – (iv), (b) – (v), (c) – (i), (d) – (ii), (e) – (iii)

B. (a) – (ii), (b) – (v), (c) – (i), (d) – (iii), (e) – (iv)

C. (a) – (ii), (b) – (iv), (c) – (v), (d) – (i), (e) – (iii)

D. (a) – (ii), (b) – (v), (c) – (iii), (d) – (iv), (e) – (i)

25. Which of the following is/are the multi-user operating system?

A. Linux B. Unix

C. Mac OS X D. All of these

26. Which of the following statements hold(s) true regarding DDR (Double Data Rate Memory)?

Statement 1 : It is a type of RAM, used in microprocessors.

Statement 2 : It requires less power and has a speed which is double than that of SDRAM.

A. Only Statement 1
B. Only Statement 2
C. Both Statement 1 and Statement 2
D. Neither Statement 1 nor Statement 2

---

27. Match the following terms with their descriptions.

	Column I		Column II
(a)	Interpreter	(i)	Special programs which control the execution of a hardware device.
(b)	Compiler	(ii)	It converts an entire program written in High level language into Machine language program line by line.
(c)	Device drivers	(iii)	It converts an entire program written in a High level language into Machine Language Program.

A. (a)-(ii), (b)-(iii), (c)-(i)
B. (a)-(i), (b)-(ii), (c)-(iii)
C. (a)-(ii), (b)-(i), (c)-(iii)
D. (a)-(iii), (b)-(ii), (c)-(i)

---

28. Which of the following is a technology that is primarily used in defence services to facilitate secret communication and privacy of data?

A. Encryption
B. Flex
C. Authentication
D. Repudation

---

29. Which of the following HTML codes is CORRECT to display the unordered list with filled circles?

A. <ul type="disc">
<li>Coffee</li>
<li>Tea</li>
<li>Milk</li>
</ul>

B. <ol type="circle">
<li>Coffee</li>
<li>Tea</li>
<li>Milk</li>
</ol>

C. <uo type="none">
<li>Coffee</li>
<li>Tea</li>
<li>Milk</li>
</uo>

D. All of these

30. Identify the following:

– It is a type of ROM memory that is manufactured with its contents. This chip contains a software that is burned on the chip during phase of semiconductor manufacturing process.
– It is used in the computer systems that required long term sustainability.

A. Marked Flash
B. Masked ROM
C. DROM
D. SROM

---

31. Identify the following terms marked as X and Y.

X – It refers to unorganized raw facts and figures given to a computer.
E.g. Name – Kabir, Marks – 85%, Year – 2011.

Y – It refers to the meaningful processed data.
E.g. "Kabir, who passed in the year 2011, secured 85% marks."

A. X – Information, Y – Data
B. X – Data, Y – Information
C. X – Result, Y – Data
D. X – Process, Y – Data

Directions (32-33): Answer the questions that follow:

32. Why Linux is considered a very safe operating system?

A. A powerful firewall and encryption technology makes Linux almost virus free.
B. You don't need to shut down this operating system, hence it won't lead to any accidental loss of data.
C. It is not a multi-user system, which makes it more secure.
D. All of these

33. Linux operating system possess the capability of "Multiple Workspaces". What does that mean?

A. It has multiple desktop screen, and you can switch from one workspace/screen to another and customize them as per your need.
B. It works only on multiple processors.
C. It supports multi-user and has only one desktop, as in Windows.
D. All of these

---

34. In Windows 7, in the search box of Start menu, type __________ to verify that every installed device is working as it should.

A. Install Manager
B. Device Manager
C. Install Device
D. Check Device

35. Which of the following is the hardware requirement of Windows 7?
(i) 1-Ghz or faster Processor (CPU).
(ii) 1 GB RAM (32-bit version), 2GB RAM (64-bit version).
A. Only (i)
B. Only (ii)
C. Both (i) and (ii)
D. None of these

36. Which of the following statements hold(s) true about Windows 7 Aero feature?
Statement 1: Aero Peek feature is only available when you are using an Aero theme, if you are not using an Aero theme, then hovering the mouse pointer over a taskbar button displays each windows full title.
Statement 2: You do not get thumbnail previews, if you are not using an Aero.
A. Only Statement 1
B. Only Statement 2
C. Both Statement 1 and Statement 2
D. Neither Statement 1 nor Statement 2

37. ________ is a videotelephony and VOIP software application, developed by Apple Inc.
A. FaceTime
B. Facebook
C. Safari
D. Skype

38. In the given networking diagram, the client initializes the transactions by sending a request message. The server replies by sending a response message. It illustrates the __________ transaction between the client and server.

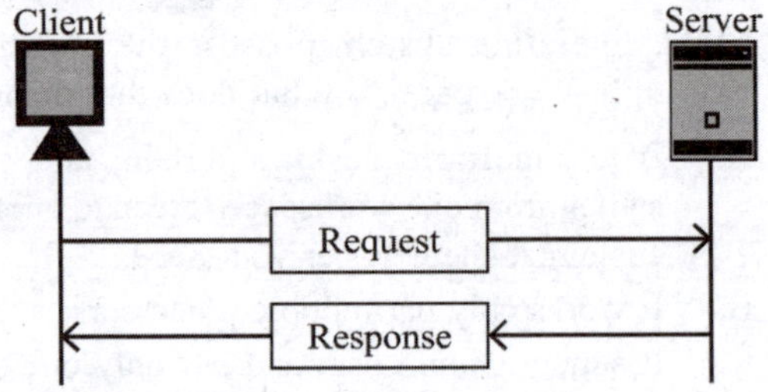

A. Peer-To-Peer
B. HTTP
C. NAP
D. NIC

39. A ________ is a standard for creating and handling dynamic web documents.
A. Common Gateway Interface
B. Command Gateway Interface
C. Transaction Gateway Interface
D. Server Mail Interface

40. FTP (File Transfer Protocol) is used to transfer the file from one system to another. Which of the following problems is/are dealt by FTP while copying a file from one host to another?
A. Two systems that may use different file name conventions
B. Two systems that have different ways to represent data
C. Two systems that have different directory structures
D. All of these

41. Select the INCORRECT match regarding the viruses with their examples.
A. Boot Sector Virus – Stoned
B. File Virus – Sunday
C. Multipartite Virus – Cascade
D. Macro Virus – Melissa

42. Which of the following statements hold(s) true regarding stealth virus?
Statement 1 : It uses various methods for hiding themselves to avoid detection.
Statement 2 : It infects only Microsoft Word application/programs.
A. Only Statement 1
B. Only Statement 2
C. Both Statement 1 and Statement 2
D. Neither Statement 1 nor Statement 2

43. Which of the following steps is CORRECT to clear browsing data in Google Chrome web browser?
A. Customize and control Google Chrome → More tools → Clear browsing data
B. Bookmark → More tools → Clear browsing history
C. Bookmark → Settings → Clear browsing history
D. Bookmark → Tools → Delete history

44. Select the odd one out.
A. OneDrive B. BACKBLAZE
C. CARBONITE D. UCBrowser

45. A backbone network allows several LANs to be connected. The given diagram represents a bridge-based backbone with four LANs.

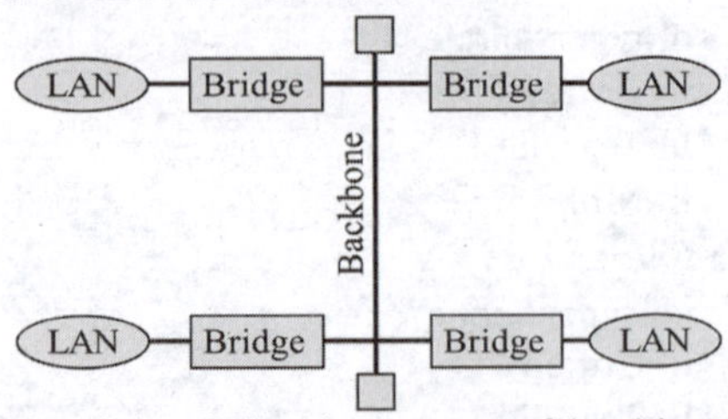

Which of the following types of backbone network is formed here?
A. Mesh backbone B. Bus backbone
C. Ring backbone D. Tree backbone

46. Which of the following features of Control Panel of Windows 7 will allow you to view the basic network information in your computer system (as shown here)?

A.  B. 

C.  D. 

---

47. What would be the output of the given HTML code?

```
<html>
<body>
<h3>HTML</h3>
<p>HTML is a web language</p>
<hr>
<h3>html</h3>
<p>HTML is used for web designing</p>
</body>
</html>
```

A. **HTML**
HTML is a web language

---

html
HTML is used for web designing

B. HTML is a web language
HTML

---

html
HTML is used for web designing

C. **HTML**
HTML is a web language

HTML is used for web designing
html

D. HTML is a web language
HTML

HTML is used for web designing
html

48. When does the given snapshot of Revisions pane in MS-PowerPoint 2010 become active?

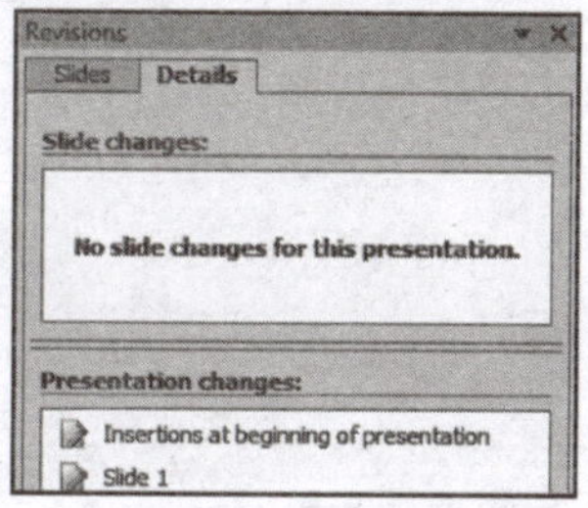

A. When you compare and combine another presentation with your current presentation
B. When you add comments from another presentation with your current presentation
C. When you end reviewing the presentation
D. Both A and B

---

49. Considering the given snapshot, what would be the result of the given formula in MS-Excel 2010?

=IF(AND(B2>30,B3>50),"Good, keep it up!", "Work hard")

	A	B
1	Name	Marks
2	Anu	50
3	Bhanu	60
4	Amit	70

A. Work hard
B. Good, keep it up!
C. #Name
D. #Error

---

50. Observe the given snapshot of MS-Word 2010. It is showing the inspection results as a warning message. Which of the following steps is CORRECT if you want to apply the Accessibility Checker feature in the document to make sure that the people with disabilities should not have difficulty reading the document?

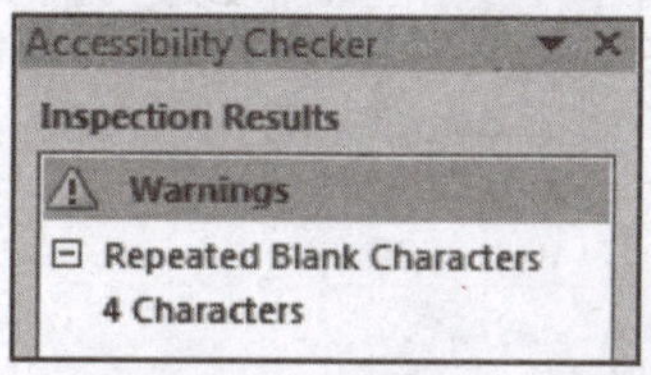

A. File tab → Info →  → 

B. File tab → Info →  → 

C. File tab → Info →  → 

D. Home tab → Editing group → 

SPACE FOR ROUGH WORK

SPACE FOR ROUGH WORK

ANSWER KEYS

1.	(A)	**2.**	(C)	**3.**	(B)	**4.**	(D)	**5.**	(A)	**6.**	(A)	**7.**	(B)
8.	(A)	**9.**	(D)	**10.**	(C)	**11.**	(C)	**12.**	(B)	**13.**	(B)	**14.**	(A)
15.	(A)	**16.**	(B)	**17.**	(B)	**18.**	(C)	**19.**	(A)	**20.**	(B)	**21.**	(A)
22.	(D)	**23.**	(A)	**24.**	(C)	**25.**	(D)	**26.**	(C)	**27.**	(A)	**28.**	(A)
29.	(A)	**30.**	(B)	**31.**	(B)	**32.**	(A)	**33.**	(A)	**34.**	(B)	**35.**	(C)
36.	(C)	**37.**	(A)	**38.**	(B)	**39.**	(A)	**40.**	(D)	**41.**	(C)	**42.**	(A)
43.	(A)	**44.**	(D)	**45.**	(B)	**46.**	(B)	**47.**	(A)	**48.**	(A)	**49.**	(B)
50.	(A)												

SOF SCIENCE OLYMPIAD FOUNDATION

National Office: Plot 99, First Floor, Sector 44 Institutional area, Gurgaon -122 003 (HR) India
Email: info@sofworld.org | Website: www.sofworld.org
Regd. Office: 406, Taj Apt., Ring Road, New Delhi-110 029
Note: Please address all communication to the National Office only.

Updates on Open Office

You have studied the computer applications like MS Word, MS PowerPoint, MS Excel and MS Access which comes as the package called MS Office. There are many free open source software available in the market using which we can perform the same tasks that we do in MS Word, MS PowerPoint, MS Excel and MS Access. LibreOffice is one such package which allows you to create documents similar to that of MS Word, presentations similar to that of MS PowerPoint, data entry and calculations as in MS Excel and databases as in MS Access.

LibreOffice Base Database

LibreOffice Base Database document allows you to create a document similar to that of MS Access. It can be opened by clicking on the **Base Database** button on the LibreOffice window as shown below.

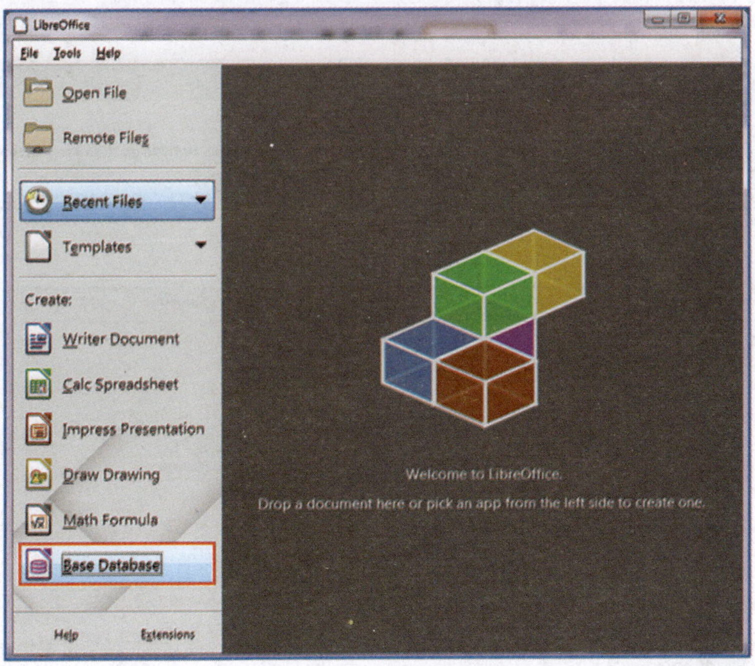

We can create **Tables**, **Queries**, **Forms** and **Reports** by clicking on their respective buttons as shown below.

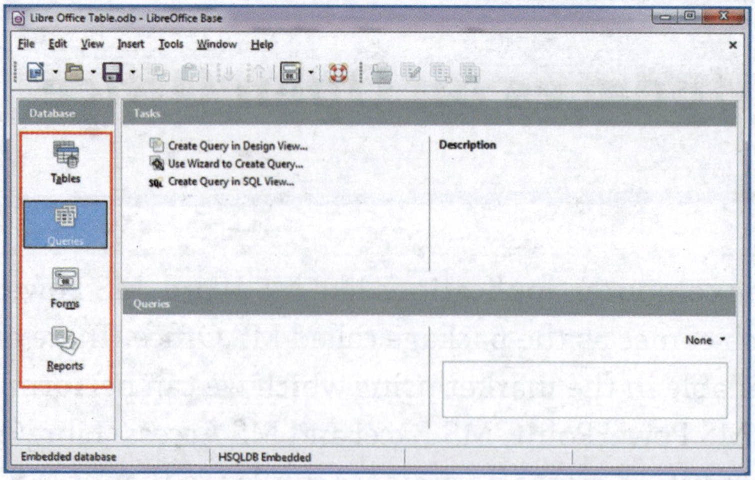

Queries in LibreOffice Base Database

To create a query, click on **Query** button as shown in the above figure. We can create the query in two ways: In **Design View** or **Using Wizard**.

Queries Using Wizard

- Click on **Use Wizard to Create Query**. It will guide you through the process of creating a query.

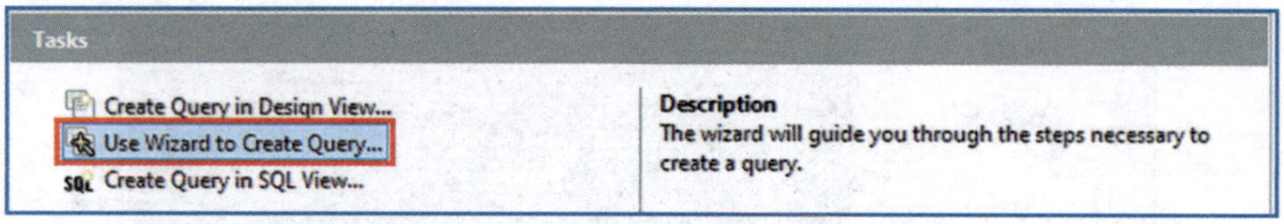

- Follow the steps as shown below and create a query.

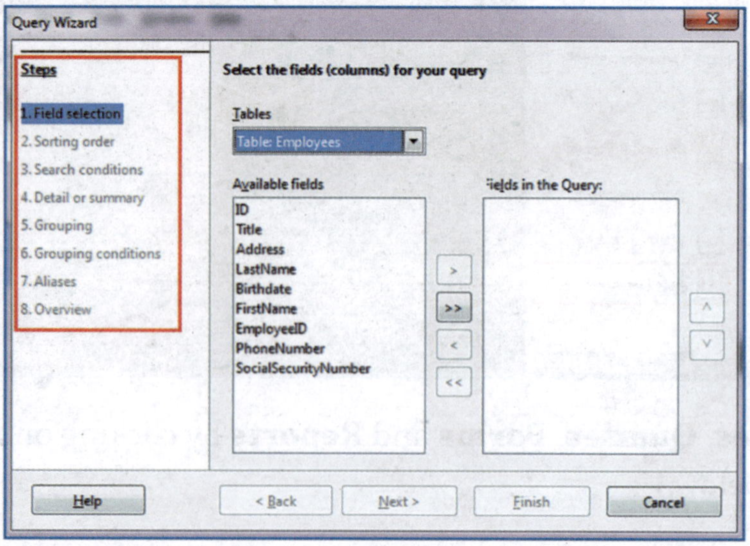

Queries Using Wizard

- Click on **Create Query in Design View**.

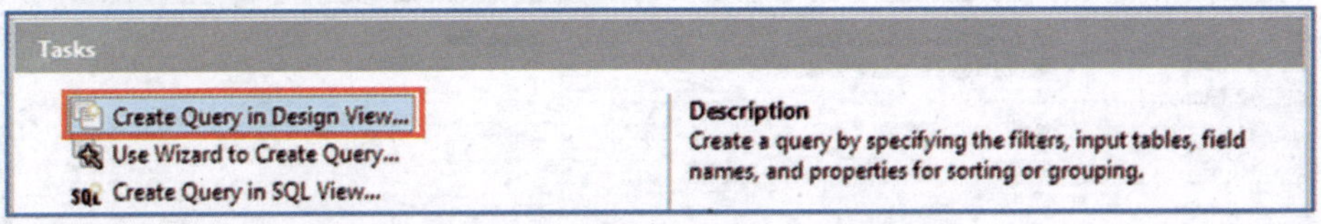

- Add the table on which query should be created and specify the criteria.

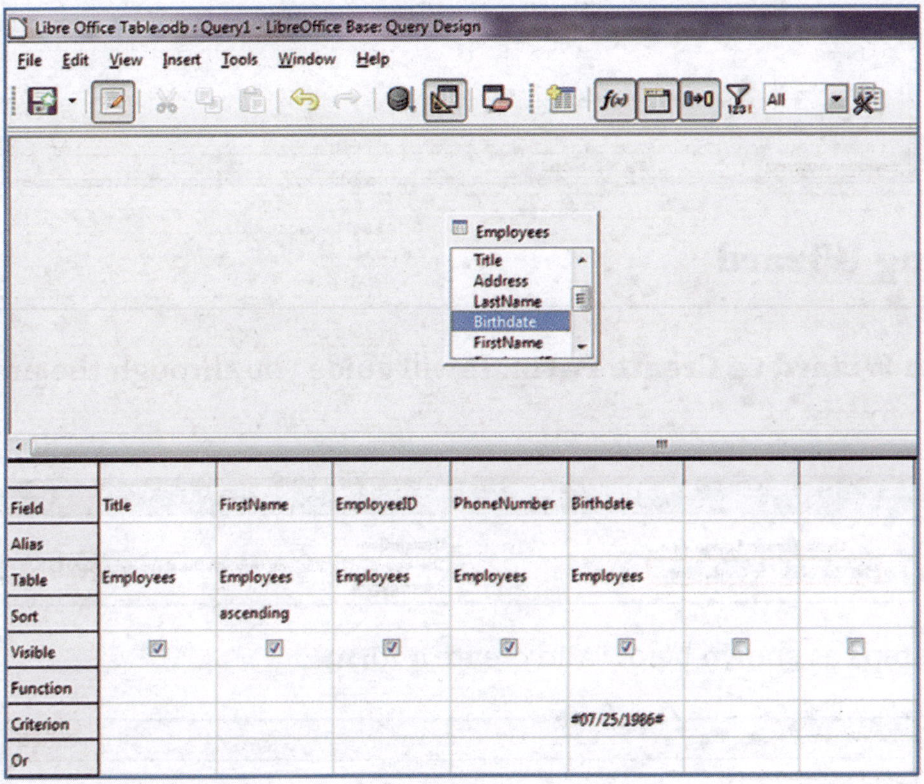

Forms in LibreOffice Base Database

To create a form, click on **Form** button as shown below. We can create the form in two ways: In **Design View** or **Using Wizard**.

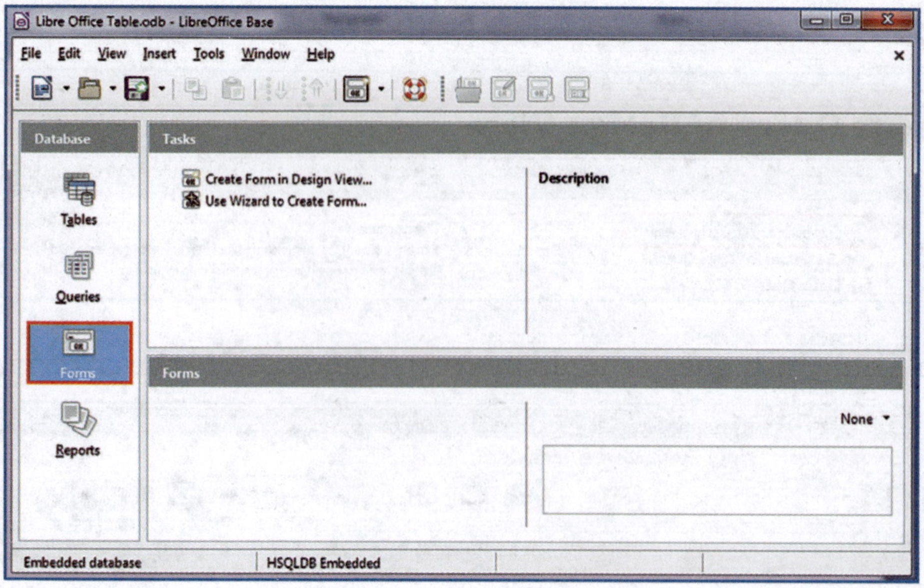

Forms Using Wizard

- Click on **Use Wizard to Create Form**. It will guide you through the process of creating a form.

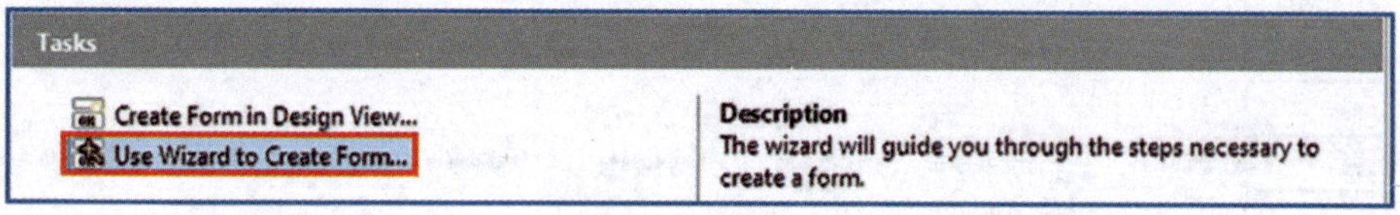

- Follow the steps as shown below and create a form.

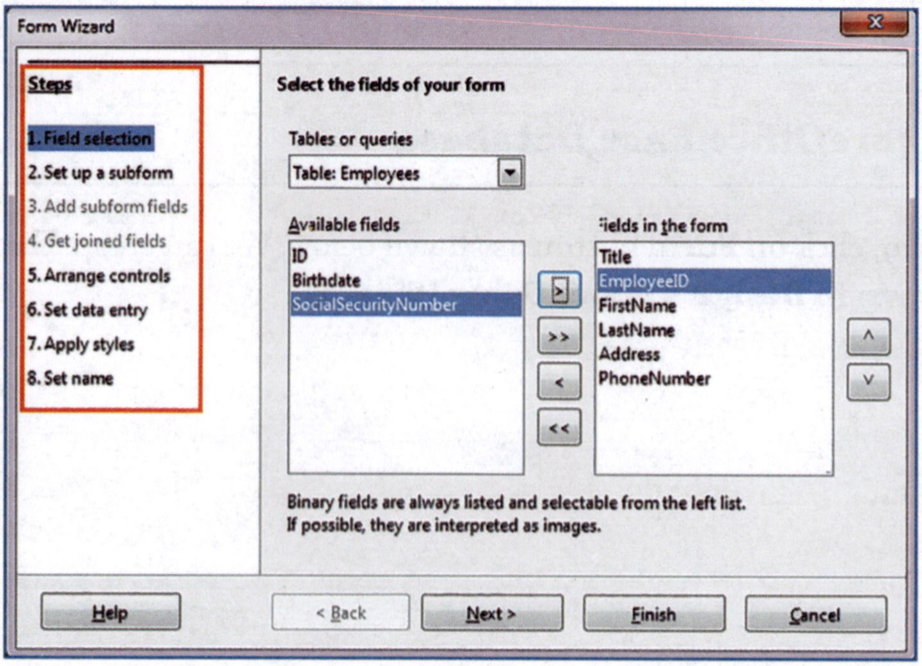

Forms in Design View

- Click on **Create Form in Design View**.

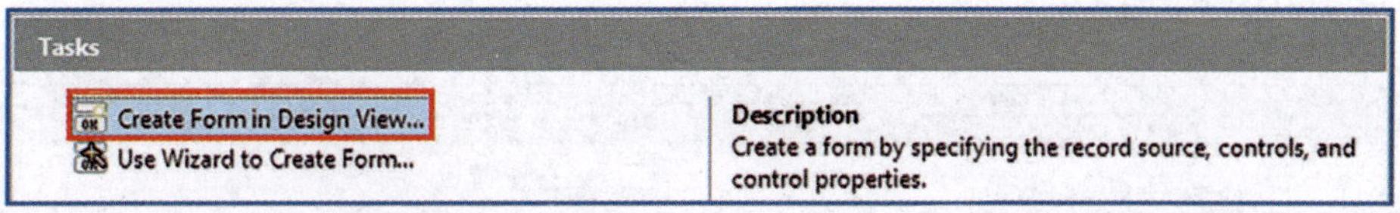

- A blank form design window appears. Use various controls available and design the form. A sample form is shown below.

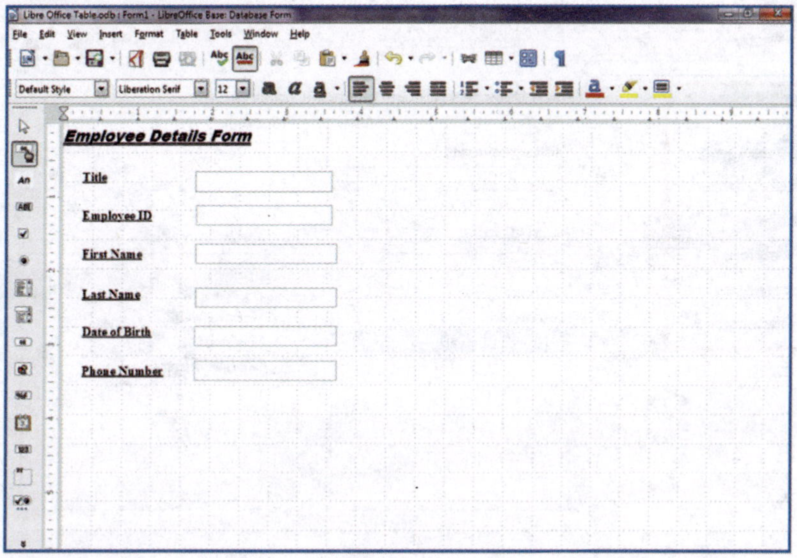

Reports in LibreOffice Base Database

To create a report, click on **Report** button as shown below. We can create the report in two ways: In **Design View** or **Using Wizard**.

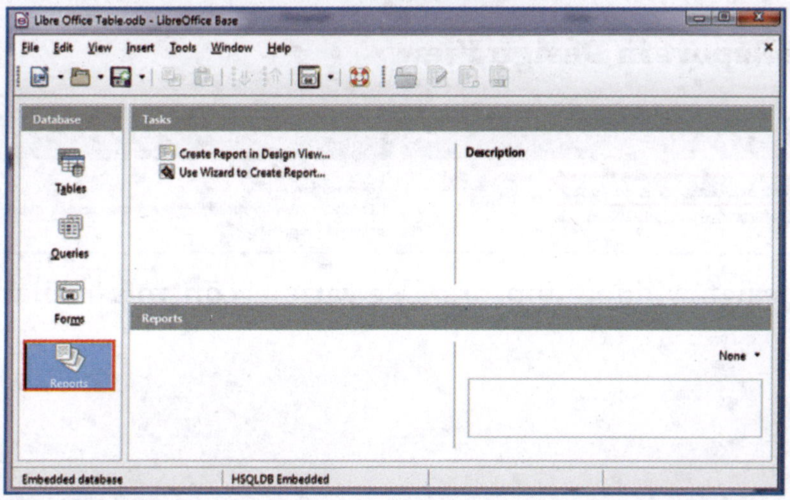

Reports Using Wizard

- Click on **Use Wizard to Create Report**. It will guide you through the process of creating a report.

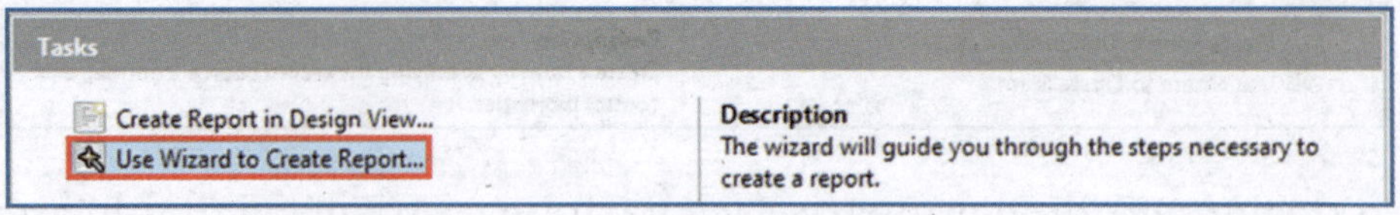

- Follow the steps as shown below and create a report.

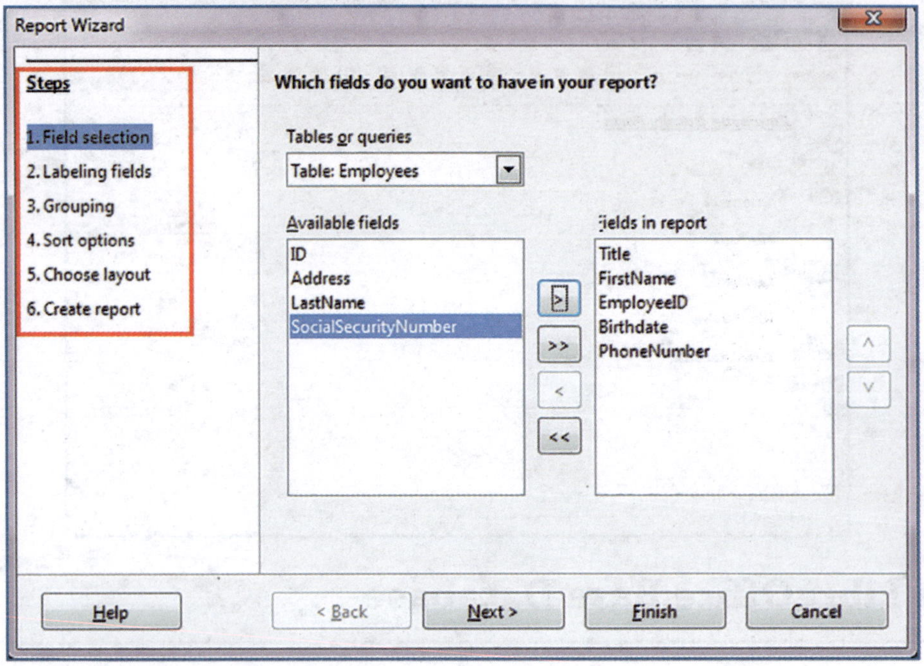

Reports in Design View

- Click on **Create Report in Design View**.

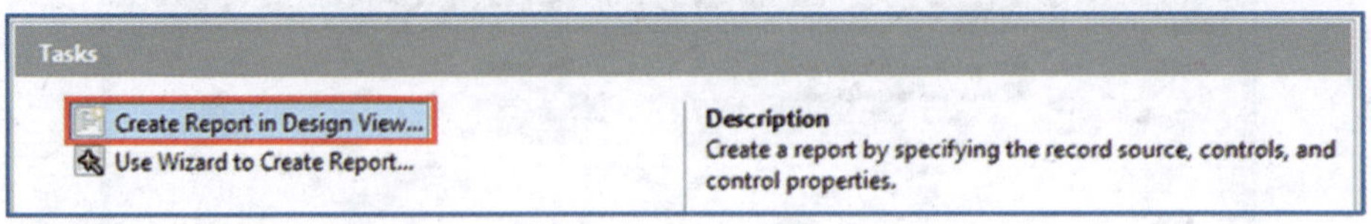

- A blank report design window appears. Use various controls available and design the report.

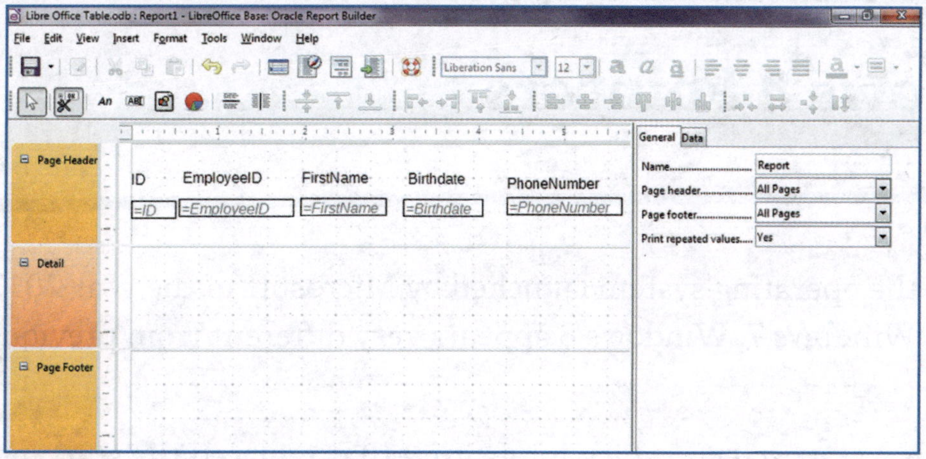

- A sample report is shown below.

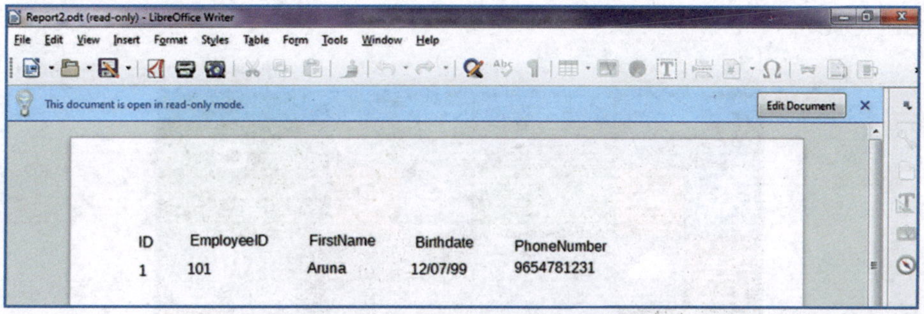

Windows 8 Pointers

Windows 8 is the operating system launched by Microsoft in the year 2012 which was released after Windows 7. Windows 8 appears very different from previous versions of Windows.

Windows 8 has a start screen, which is a feature that replaced the start menu. It displays all the applications as tiles. The start screen also has live tiles, which provide information and show notifications. It requires staying connected to the internet for live tiles to function.

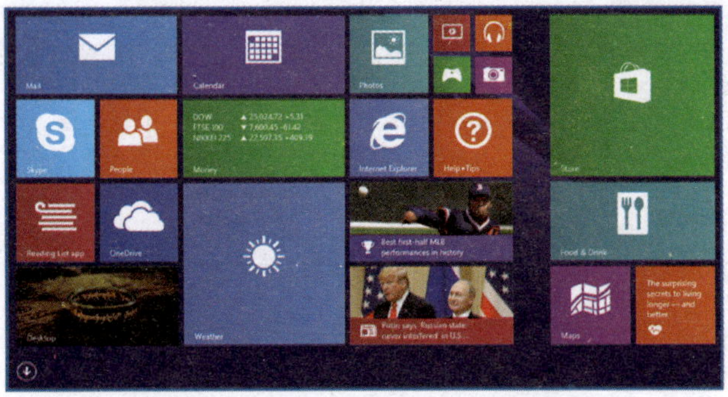

Fig. 1: Windows Start screen

SkyDrive integration

SkyDrive is a Microsoft's cloud storage and file synchronization platform.
It allows users to upload files that could then be accessed over the internet and automatically stores the files and settings on the computer on the cloud.

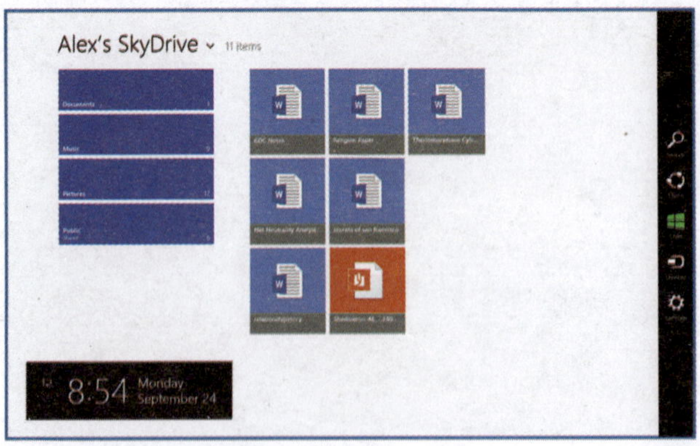

Fig. 2: Sky Drive

Snap View

Microsoft has included a new feature in Windows 8 to enable multitasking that allowing users to run apps side-by-side on a single screen. With snap views the user can see more than two apps on your screen and resize those apps. Users can have the same app running on multiple windows as well.

Fig. 3: Snap View

NOTES

NOTES

NOTES